CHILDREN'S THEATRE AND CREATIVE DRAMATICS

Three Little Kittens. Seattle Creative Activities Center
(Photograph by Yuki)

CHILDREN'S THEATRE AND CREATIVE DRAMATICS

*Edited by Geraldine Brain Siks
and Hazel Brain Dunnington*

UNIVERSITY OF WASHINGTON PRESS

Seattle and London

Copyright © 1961 by the University of Washington Press
Second printing, 1966
Third printing, 1967
Fourth printing, 1974
Washington Paperback edition, 1967
Second printing, 1971
Third printing, 1974
Library of Congress Catalog Card Number 61-11578
ISBN (cloth) 0-295-73741-7
ISBN (paper) 0-295-97875-9
Printed in the United States of America

To
CHILDREN *and* YOUTH

A child, more than all other gifts
That earth can offer to declining man,
Brings hope with it, and forward-looking thoughts.

- William Wordsworth

Foreword

To apply the rigors of scholarship to the volatile spontaneity of children's theatre in all its delightful and fearful evanescence is no mean trick, but Geraldine Siks and her contributors have gone a long way in bringing it off—and just in time.

Our world today is not as simple and beautifully direct as a child might wish to see it—in fact *must* see it to be a healthy, growing child instead of a miniature adult. The arts—as Aldous Huxley has suggested—may serve to bring complicated ideas and feelings to the youngster for his exploration, in ways which are direct and meaningful to him. And, being the art closest to life itself, the theatre often has a comprehensible immediacy in expressing ideas and feelings about human beings.

No longer, however, can the arts, any more than the sciences, meet the realities of our world simply through anthropomorphic insight and a brilliant style. Scholarship, experiment (*true* experiment), and new techniques revealing hitherto unavailable aspects of human beings and their relationships to themselves as well as their world must be used to give us and our children deeper insights and new opportunities to grow in ways that will match an open-end universe. The Rousseauian nature boy has no place in our world. Like Albert Camus we must seek to express our primitive feelings and beautiful as well as dreadful experiences through the disciplines of rational thought and a developed consciousness of feelings.

By examining the field of children's theatre systematically and with demands for reportage and careful scholarship, the editor and her sister (Hazel Dunnington, the associate editor, who obviously defies sibling rivalry!) have brought forth this book. It seeks not only to bring a field into focus but also to give a comprehensive description of the condition of children's theatre which may lead to a breakthrough into an even more meaningful artistic experience for children. Insight and style, as they have before, will bring a simple excitement and delight but with new and beautiful ideas and experiences equal to children's demands.

Such a breakthrough depends upon many efforts in many areas and the introduction defines a multiple approach to the field. Writers, directors, producers, designers, educators, community workers, and laymen have available for the first time a comprehensive statement of what makes up the varied field of children's theatre.

The response to my original inquiry about producing such a monograph was, in itself, descriptive of interest in the field. Individuals, the governing board of the Children's Theatre Conference, the board of the American Educational Theatre Association—all went to work with a speed that is unparalleled. Former AETA President Edward C. Cole and his administration put the project into editorial operation and, with the help of the Dean of the Graduate School at the University of Washington, funded the publication.

Those using this volume are welcomed to its pages and challenged to make them look outdated in a hurry.

Jack Morrison
University of California
Los Angeles, California

Preface

Starting with a few isolated experiments at the beginning of the century, children's drama—both children's theatre and creative dramatics—has become a major activity in the United States. In 1941 there were 150 members of the Children's Theatre Conference; in 1960 there were ten times that many. A number of pioneers have written their personal insights and philosophies. Now that many of the programs have had years of experience and new programs are being developed throughout the country, we need the kind of stocktaking that will pool the experience and judgment of leaders. It seems wise to make a survey, to take stock of basic concepts. This has been our chief purpose in this study.

The book is divided into three parts: Part I considers backgrounds. Part II considers children's theatre. Part III considers creative dramatics. An introduction begins the study, and appendices, bibliography, and index conclude it. The book may be read from beginning to end to gain concepts of development and philosophy, or it may serve as a handbook for detailed study of principles and practices. It may also be used as a reference, and it may serve to stimulate further research in specific areas of children's drama.

The study was developed at the request of the American Educational Theatre Association. In January, 1957, Jack Morrison, president of the association, appointed a committee to investigate the feasibility of producing a volume on the principles and practices of children's theatre in the United States. Committee members included Winifred Ward, Eleanor York,

Barnard Hewitt, Paul Kozelka, and Geraldine Siks, chairman.
Working over a seven months' period the committee recognized a need for such a study and developed a tentative outline
of procedure. The committee selected theatre leaders to contribute to the study. In December, 1957, a report was submitted to the advisory council and to Edward Cole, newly elected
president of the association.

On February 17, 1958, President Cole informed the committee that the editorial board had approved the study's outline
and appointed Geraldine Siks as editor. Hazel Dunnington was
appointed associate editor, and contributors were invited to
begin their research. In view of the comprehensive nature of
the study and the need for time in which to guide its development, the editor applied to the Graduate School of the University of Washington for a summer research grant. The grant
was approved in an arrangement between the Graduate School
and the association.

Early in 1959 most contributors completed their final drafts
of chapters. Although contributions were edited, each individual
author remains responsible for his authorship. In a few instances chapters were referred to the committee for evaluation. The committee members originally appointed indirectly
guided the study; however, in February, 1959, Lillian Voorhees
and James Popovich were appointed to replace Barnard Hewitt
and Paul Kozelka. During the summer and fall of 1959, Hazel
Dunnington worked closely with the editor to unify the publication.

Though their specific forms of assistance remain unstated,
the association wishes to thank the following individuals: Jack
Morrison, Edward Cole, John Wray Young, Samuel Selden,
Kenneth L. Graham, John A. Walker, Gary Gaiser, George
R. Kernodle, and monograph committee members; Eleanor
York, Director of the Children's Theatre Conference (1957-59),
regional chairmen, and individual members of this division;
Glenn Hughes, Henry A. Burd, Joseph L. McCarthy, Lloyd
S. Woodburne, Agnes Haaga, Kenneth Carr, James Crider, and
Barbara Likens of the University of Washington; Lyman Par-
tridge of Central Washington College of Education; and Eric
Nordholm of Pacific Lutheran College.

The association thanks the respective staffs of the following

University of Washington libraries: reference room of Henry
Suzzallo Library, Padelford Memorial Library, and the School
of Drama Library. Acknowledgment is also aue the National
Recreation Association; the research department of the Na-
tional Broadcasting Company; the research department of the
Columbia Broadcasting System; Grace Johnsen of the American
Broadcasting Company; and Madge Tucker, Milton Cross, and
Vera Eikel. We wish to express our especial appreciation to
Ruth Ann Bodwell for her painstaking efforts in behalf of this
volume. Appreciation to other writers and organizations is
indicated in the notes and bibliography.

The editors thank each one who assisted directly and indirectly with the study.

January, 1961   G.B.S.

Contents

Part I: Backgrounds

1. Introduction   3
   Geraldine Brain Siks

2. Clarification of Terms   8
   Ann Viola

3. Development of the Children's Theatre
   Conference   13
   Dorothy Thames Schwartz

4. History of Children's Theatre in the United
   States   21
   Nellie McCaslin

5. Values to Children from Good Theatre   27
   Kenneth L. Graham

Part II: Children's Theatre

6. Children's Theatre Produced by Adult Groups   33
   Albert O. Mitchell

7. Children as Theatre Producers   45
   Dorothy Kester

8. Children's Theatre in Radio and Television   54
   Gloria Chandler

9. Films as a Medium for Children's Theatre   71
   Burdette Fitzgerald and Ernest Rose

10. Children's Theatre in Puppetry   75
    George Latshaw

11. Producing Theatre for Child Audiences   82
    Jed H. Davis

12. Writing Plays for Children   98
    Sara Spencer

13. Recommended Training for Children's
    Theatre Director   104
    Frank M. Whiting

Part III: Creative Dramatics

14. Development of Creative Dramatics in the
    United States   115
    James E. Popovich

15. Values to Children from Creative Dramatics   124
    Eleanor Chase York

16. Creative Dramatics in Elementary and
    Junior High Schools   132
    Winifred Ward

17. Creative Dramatics in Programs for
    Exceptional Children   152
    Barbara M. McIntyre

18. Creative Dramatics in Religious Education   159
    Emily Gillies

19. Survey of Creative Dramatics in
    Correctional Institutions   168
    Werdna Finley

20. Creative Dramatics in Community Programs   176
    Margaret S. Woods

21. Creative Dramatics: An Approach to
    Children's Theatre   185
    Isabel B. Burger

22. Creative Dramatics in Recreation Programs   192
    Virginia Musselman

Contents

23. Recommended Training for Creative   198
     Dramatics Leader
     Agnes Haaga

Appendix A: A Directory of Children's Theatre
            and Creative Dramatics   209
            Hazel Brain Dunnington

Appendix B: Composite Course Outlines for
            Children's Theatre and Creative
            Dramatics at the College Level   229
            Richard G. Adams

Appendix C: Twenty-Five Recommended Three-
            Act Plays for Children's Theatre   235
            Rita Criste

Notes   241

Bibliography   257
Paul Kozelka

Index   269

PART I

I hear America singing, the varied
carols I hear.
                    - Walt Whitman

Jack and the Beanstalk. Palo Alto Children's Theatre
(Photograph by Anita Fowler)

1 Introduction

Geraldine Brain Siks ✦

Once the moon asked a question. This occurred in a poem, but the question is one that man asks man often these days.

"Where are you going and what do you want?" the old moon inquired of three young adventurers.

Today the whole world seems to be asking, and answering by saying we are searching for creativity in men's minds. It is a mysterious search, closely akin to the search for life. The seeking and finding hold an unknown future. It is imperative that creative thinking be constructive—motivated by men who care for fellow men.

When we ask what a creative person is like, we think at once of great artists, great scientists, great statesmen, great leaders in philosophy, religion, and education. We know that creativity occurs in science, in the arts, and in all human endeavors. We know that there is potential creativity in every human being. We recognize it in child's play when a handful of blocks suddenly becomes a skyscraper, in a mother's touch when burlap potato sacks become bright kitchen curtains, in a theatre when men become roused by the power of a *Hamlet*.

Adults look hopefully to youth, for they hold the promise of the future. It is natural that scientists who have achieved heights of creativity in scientific endeavors should advocate scientific pursuits for youth. But it is natural too that artists would want youth to experience and appreciate arts—not alone for the stimulation of creativity but for the development of sensibilities.

Every morning forty million boys and girls wake up in the continental United States. [1] (This is the number of children from five through seventeen years of age.) Each child's life is influenced by daily experiences in his home, school, community, nation, world, and each child's life likewise influences these. On the whole our children and youth are, we hope, happy, but educators look constantly for ways in which youth may be guided toward richer, fuller lives.

Educators who know and understand the art of drama have posed these pertinent questions: How may drama which has expressed fundamental human needs since the dawn of civilization become vital for children and youth? How may drama be woven into children's lives in such a way that cultural values become rooted in society? How may drama become an integral part of education so children's creativity and sensibilities are developed?

The "International Report on Theatre for Youth in Twenty-Seven Countries," published in 1955, revealed that children's drama in the United States is part of an international theatre movement. [2] Several of the twenty-seven countries have professionally trained theatre artists who serve both in children's theatre and creative dramatics. A close liaison is evident between theatre and schools, with no apparent problem of educating the public to the importance of dramatic arts. This is due to a long-established cultural heritage in theatre in countries of European influence.

Children's drama in the United States is a twentieth-century educational endeavor. The term children's drama encompasses both children's theatre and creative dramatics. Children's theatre is based on the traditional theatre concept and is concerned with producing plays for children. Creative dramatics is concerned with the process of encouraging children to create informal drama through effective leadership.

In the United States, the rapid growth of children's drama resulted in a national movement characterized by breadth, but with the rapid expansion a divergence of standards developed. Evidence of the strict disciplines necessary in all creative expression was not always present in children's theatre plays and in creative dramatics guidance.

Educators were concerned. In 1957 the American Educational Theatre Association launched a definitive study to appraise standards. Twenty-five children's drama leaders examined and evaluated basic principles and practices. Their investigations resulted in the development of this monograph. Its conclusions focus attention on the following exigencies:

1. A need to introduce children's drama training programs at college and university levels and to improve those programs that already exist.

2. A need to strengthen the standards of present children's drama programs by examining and improving basic principles and practices.

3. A need to increase opportunities in school and community programs so that drama becomes accessible to every child.

4. A need to educate the public to the philosophy of children's drama to insure school, community, and national support.

What is the philosophy of children's drama? If it were possible to define the word *child* in such a way that the vast mysteries of a child's unique nature were understood, a basic step would be taken in childhood education. To paraphrase Gertrude Stein, a child is a child is a child is a child. He is not just another number in a population count. A child is more wonderful than a bird, a beast, or a fish because he is a young human being.

To observe almost any girl or boy in any country in any century is to recognize that a child's mind is thinking, a child's body is rhythmic, a child's spirit is sensitive. For a child to exist is mystery in itself, but it is his ability to consciously create that mysteriously sets him apart from all other living creatures. In order to realize himself, an individual must develop his trinity of self.

Tolstoi, endeavoring to explain the need for art in living, recognized that "art is human activity having for its purpose the transmission to others of the highest and best feelings to which men have risen."[3] He further observed that through the arts people in all centuries have experienced heights and depths of living. He explained that "if art has been able to convey the sentiment of reverence for images . . . and for the king's person; of shame at betraying a comrade, devotion to a flag,

the necessity of revenge for an insult . . . the duty of de-
fending one's honor or the glory of one's native land—then that
same art can evoke reverence for the dignity of every man . . .
can compel people freely, gladly, and without noticing it to
sacrifice themselves in the service of man. "[4] He further emphasized that if the basic laws of human nature were respected,
art and only art could cause violence to be set aside.

Following World War II, Leon Chancerel spoke similarly in
respect to the need for theatre arts for children. He said:
"There is in children a thirst for the marvelous and even more,
a need for laughter and emotion. *It must be fulfilled*. The impressions of childhood always remain. It is necessary that they
be worthwhile. Children who do not laugh become disillusioned
men. Those whose hearts are not touched become men with
hearts of stone. It is not to men that it is necessary to teach
love, but to children. "[5]

More recently, Sir Herbert Read explained the need for arts
by stating that the "cultivation of the arts is an education of the
sensibilities, and if we are not given an education of this kind,
if our hands remain empty and our perception of form is un-
exercised, then in idleness and vacancy we revert to violence
and crime. When there is no will to creation the death instinct
takes over and wills endless, gratuitous destruction. "[6]

Drama is an art which nurtures creativity and sensibilities.
A good play is always a story about what happens within the
heart and mind of a person. And in a good play the person or
protagonist is always in some kind of trouble. He becomes
involved in a situation which motivates inner conflicts between
forces of good and evil. Good theatre pinpoints attention and
causes an audience to identify, to "feel-with" the protagonist
as he struggles with conflicting forces and eventually triumphs
or yields to defeat; but in the end, because of his moral convictions and actions, becomes always a more admirable person. Whenever people in a theatre audience identify, they
participate in the struggles. They meditate on the thoughts,
feelings, and actions of mankind. Maxwell Anderson believes
that the "theatre is the central artistic symbol of the struggle
of good and evil within men. "[7]

A good play always entertains while it instructs, for by its
artistic nature it portrays but does not preach. Children in a

theatre audience will laugh heartily at a pompous, vain emperor parading proudly in an undergarment while at the same moment they will be alerted to the necessity of honest living. Children will always squeal with delight as they watch Cinderella's self-ish stepsisters preen themselves for the castle ball; yet, at the same moment, love tugs at children's hearts. Empathy arouses universal truths and creates moments of belief which cause theatre to mediate between reality and eternity.

Good drama feeds a child's heart and mind and causes him to dwell in realms of wonder. Whether a child experiences theatre vicariously as he sits in an audience or actively as a participant in creative dramatics, each time he grows. He becomes a little more understanding of the glory of creative living.

Will our society with its present values system recognize in drama the unique contributions that this art offers for children and youth? The 1960 report of Dwight D. Eisenhower's Commission on National Goals is encouraging. [8] In regard to the arts it recognizes that within the present decade "our society must . . . stimulate and support richer cultural fulfillment. "[9] It states that as a means of achievement "our theatre must be revitalized; it must have the kind of support in universities, colleges and communities that will give it greater strength at the roots. . . . We should raise our critical standards and widen the area and depth of public appreciation. "[10]

Will there be leaders trained and inspired with a desire to bring vital theatre arts into the lives of children and youth? Will our universities and colleges take action which will strengthen the cultural and creative life of our nation?

2 Clarification of Terms*

Ann Viola ✒

Voltaire said, "If you wish to converse with me, define your terms."[1] Let us then make clear the meaning of basic theatre terms to be used. Let us distinguish between "Children's Theatre," and "Creative Dramatics," and note the relations between dramatic play, creative play, and the formal play. The Committee on Basic Concepts of the Children's Theatre Conference has agreed on the following definitions:

I. Two different concepts are included in the term "Children's Drama."[2]

A. Children's Theatre, in which plays, written by playwrights, are presented by living actors for child audiences. The players may be adults, children, or a combination of the two. Lines are memorized, action is directed, scenery and costumes are used. In the formal play the director, bending every effort toward the primary purpose of offering a finished product for public entertainment, engages the best actors available and subjects them to the strict discipline required of any creative artist recognizing his obligation to the spectator.

B. Creative Dramatics, in which children with the guidance of an imaginative teacher or leader create scenes or plays and perform them with improvised dialogue and action. Personal development of players

---

*Monograph drawn from Children's Theatre Conference Study on Definitions: Ann Viola, "Drama with and for Children: An Interpretation of Terms," Educational Theatre Journal, VIII (May, 1956), 139-42.

is the goal, rather than the satisfaction of a child audience. Scenery and costumes are rarely used. If this informal drama is presented before an audience, it is usually in the nature of a demonstration.

II. What activities are included in "Creative Dramatics"?

A. Dramatic Play

    1. Of little children. The imaginative play in which a child relives familiar experiences and explores new ones. In so doing he "tries on life" and begins to understand people and social relations. Examples of various phases of dramatic play: imitative sound and actions; acting out nursery rhyme bits and familiar home experiences; play with imaginary companions; make-believe play with toys; dramatic use of rhythms; imaginative play after hearing poems, songs, and stories. (Little attempt at pattern or plot.)

    2. Of older children. Interpretation of musical moods; characterizations suggested by rhythms; original pantomimes; charades; improvised parts from literature, social studies.

B. Story Dramatization. The creating of an improvised play based upon a story, whether original, or from literature, history, or other sources. Guided by a leader who tells the story and helps the children realize its dramatic possibilities, they plan the play and act it with spontaneous dialogue and action. Only a small unit of the story is played at one time. The group evaluates the work after each playing and gradually develops a complete play.

C. Creative Plays Developed to the Point Where They Approach Formal Plays. This may be an integrated project with the play at the center. In school it is often the culmination of a country, a movement, a period, etc. Research done in social studies or background materials enriches a book or story chosen as the basis of the play. As the play is developed over a period of several months, the children are designing and making simple scenery and properties in arts and crafts classes. Songs and dances are learned in music and gymnasium periods. No lines are learned; but the children know the story and characters so thoroughly and have played the various scenes so often as they developed the play that when they play it for the school, as they usually do in such cases, it moves almost as smoothly as a formal play.

D. The Use of Creative Dramatics in a Formal Play.

1. In tryouts mood may be set with music; for trying out royal personages, witches, dwarfs, etc. Short scenes may be played with spontaneous dialogue after the children hear the script read.

2. Formal scenes may be turned temporarily into improvisations in order to achieve naturalness in players who tend to recite lines.

3. Improvised dialogue may be developed in crowd scenes.

III. Is there any conflict between the use of formal and informal drama with children? There should be none at all, as long as the objectives of each are understood. The two should actually complement each other. For example:

A. Children's Theatre provides standards for the children's work in Creative Dramatics by helping the children to visualize, to be objective, to play parts in such a way that they will be interesting to others.

B. Creative Dramatics experiences build appreciation for formal plays, because children learn much about play construction as they work out their own plays, guided by an adult who understands formal drama. They come to know the essentials of playmaking: characterization, action, dialogue, plot structure, climax, tempo, and teamwork. Furthermore, experience in Creative Dramatics is most valuable for those children who may act in Children's Theatre productions.

C. *Young children up to the age of approximately eleven or twelve years should participate in informal drama exclusively,* for they tend to recite memorized lines unless they are well grounded in the ability to think them out as they say them. If children have had plenty of experience in the creation of dialogue, however, by the time they are older they have formed the habit of thinking through their speeches and can be counted on for a much greater degree of naturalness in Children's Theatre roles than if they had not had a background in Creative Dramatics.

The clarification in sections I, II, and III represents an agreement of the Children's Theatre Conference Committee on

Basic Concepts. Although individual members may differ in some degree as to method, philosophy, or technique, each is willing to subscribe to the opinion that children's drama exists as an art form. Whether it be informal playmaking *with* children or formal theatre *for* children, if given the proper guidance or direction, children's drama becomes art.

IV. As the many organizations concerned with children's theatre will be referred to by their initials, here is a check list giving the full name and a phrase or two to indicate the purpose and scope of each organization.

AAUW - (American Association of University Women) Organization carrying on "projects and studies in the field of international education, child development and parent education, educational standards and trends, the arts, economic and legal status of women. "[3]

ACEI - (American Childhood Educational Association, International). "Individuals interested in and promoting the education and well-being of children two to twelve. "[4]

AETA - (American Educational Theatre Association) A nonprofit, professional organization established to encourage the development of theatre in education. "Teachers of speech, playwriting, acting, directing, design, etc. , " devoting major energies to these fields. [5]

AJLA - (Association of Junior Leagues of America) "Volunteers rendering service in local, social, cultural and civic agencies. "[6]

ANTA - (American National Theatre and Academy) "Organization stimulating and advancing public interest in the theatre. "[7]

CTC - (The Children's Theatre Conference) "A division of the American Educational Theatre Association dedicated to enriching the lives of all children through drama (professional, education, community). "[8]

PTA - (National Congress of Parents and Teachers)

Organized groups promoting "the welfare of children and youth in home, school and community."[9]

UNESCO - (United Nations Educational, Scientific, and Cultural Organization)

An organization of member states of the United Nations "contributing to peace and security by promoting collaboration among the nations through education, science and culture."[10]

YMCA   - (Young Men's Christian Association)

YWCA   - (Young Women's Christian Association)

Organizations sponsoring "greater opportunities for self-development."[11]

YMHA   - (Young Men's Hebrew Association)

A division of the National Jewish Welfare Board.[12]

3 Development of the Children's Theatre Conference*

Dorothy Thames Schwartz

Between the years 1941 and 1959 the Children's Theatre Conference (CTC), a Division of the American Educational Theatre Association (AETA), has been a meaningful part of the American theatre scene. In these years it has developed, within the framework of AETA, from a small committee of dedicated leaders to a well-organized division conducting educational theatre projects of national and international scope. It has grown from a membership of 150 to one numbering over 1,500. It has attracted to its program child psychologists, educators, community volunteers, and leaders in religious education. It has won a place of respect in theatre councils, both national and international. Today CTC conducts an annual meeting, independent of the AETA Convention; it has fifteen regions whose chairmen comprise a Regional Council. More than eighteen committees, concerned with the development of children through the medium of the drama, carry out the program and projects of the organization.

The purpose of this study is to trace the chronological development of CTC from its inception through May, 1959. This development will be delineated in terms of programs, projects, and organization.

---

*Monograph drawn from Master's thesis: Dorothy Thames Schwartz, A History of the Children's Theatre Conference, 1944-55, University of Alabama, 1956; minutes of CTC Board meetings; reports of annual meetings; and personal files.

Northwestern Meeting, 1944

In the years leading to the formation of CTC there was considerable uncoordinated children's theatre activity. In 1937 AETA, organized the previous year, designated children's theatre as one of its work projects. A chairman was appointed and programs on children's theatre were made a regular feature of the AETA Conventions. In 1941 a survey of children's theatre activities was conducted. This was followed in 1943 by a questionnaire directed at colleges and universities. This activity culminated in 1944 in a national meeting of children's theatre workers called by Winifred Ward of Northwestern University. This meeting had far-reaching results. It provided a nucleus for the discussion of problems and the exchange of ideas relating to children's theatre; it directed attention to immediate problems in the field; and it served to stimulate an interest on the part of AETA in the program of children's theatre.

Children's Theatre Committee, 1944 to 1952

Organizational Development

The term "Children's Theatre Committee" had a dual meaning in the years 1944-50. It was used to specify, first of all, the large group which attended the Annual Conference. It was also used to specify the small group which, together with the chairman appointed by the AETA Advisory Council, formed the policies and administered the program of the organization. The committee had no budget of its own. As a work committee of AETA its plans were subject to the approval of AETA and were financed by funds which the AETA Advisory Board approved.

Problems of organization were given much attention from 1947 through 1952. At the December 1950 meeting of the Children's Theatre Committee and the AETA Advisory Council, the name of the organization was changed from Children's Theatre Committee to Children's Theatre Conference, though it remained a working committee of AETA. The Annual Conferences were renumbered and the Northwestern Meeting of 1944 was designated as the first Annual Conference; a nine-member board with considerable autonomy was recognized;

and a newsletter to be issued quarterly by the Children's Theatre Conference was approved. This framework of organization was formally adopted by the conference in August, 1951. During the ensuing year an operating code was drawn up by Conference Chairman Kenneth L. Graham. The code clarified certain nomenclature. The chief executive of CTC was termed director; the summer meetings were officially called *annual meetings*. This operating code was approved by the CTC Board in August, 1952, and by the AETA Advisory Council in December of that year. At that meeting the council officially accepted CTC as a division of AETA.

Annual Conferences

The first of the Children's Theatre summer conferences, held annually since 1946, convened in Seattle in August of that year. These conferences have been a major project of CTC. They provide an opportunity for children's theatre workers to share ideas, observe demonstrations of informal and formal drama, and learn new technical skills. These meetings represent five days of discussion, lectures, demonstrations, and productions.

The 1946 conference established certain procedures: several local organizations served as hosts for the meetings; a conference planning session was held at the preceding AETA Convention; and the meeting was evaluated at a postconference session. Innovations which have been introduced at succeeding conferences have become established features of the meetings. The program of the 1949 conference included a panel of psychologists with national and international reputations. Since that time, many acknowledged authorities on child psychology, sociology, and education have participated in the annual conferences.

Delegates to these annual meetings represent a marked diversity in training and experience. They share, however, a singleness of purpose. The director of the School of Communication Arts at the host university of 1948 had this to say:

At this conference professionals exchanged ideas with non-professionals; college directors and community directors discussed their common problems; Junior League representatives made valuable contributions from a rich background of experience, and delegates from city sponsored projects and private schools pooled their problems and solutions in a common hopper. All through the five-day conference, one was impressed not only by the drive and enthusiasm of the leaders in the field, but also by their imagination and vision and especially by their determination to make children's theatre a significant segment of the American Theatre scene, filling a need which it alone can satisfy.[1]

Annual Workshops

In keeping with one of the expressed purposes of CTC, namely, to raise standards of children's theatre programs, it was decided to conduct a workshop in various aspects of children's theatre activity in conjunction with the annual meeting. Three days prior to the annual meeting in 1950, the University of Minnesota offered the first workshop. This consisted of classes in creative dramatics, costuming, make-up, directing, and playwriting. Since that time, annual children's theatre summer workshops of from two to five weeks have been held by the host institution, guest lecturers and directors often supplementing the regular university staff.

Regional Organization

The impetus for greater local development in children's theatre was provided by a session of the annual meeting in 1952. At that time the United States, Canada, and Hawaii were divided into fifteen regions and regional chairmen were elected. Since that time, regional meetings and newsletters have served to interpret the program and extend the influence of CTC. They provide an opportunity for wider participation in the children's theatre program, enriching the experiences of many who may never attend an annual meeting.

Theatre Projects

Five projects have been a part of the Children's Theatre Committee program since its early years: play standards, directory, college survey, bibliography, and international children's theatre.

The play standards committee was originally charged with establishing criteria for play standards. It has consistently implemented its findings by evaluations of productions at annual meetings. In 1952 the committee created a significant innovation, instituting a "New Script" room where directors may discover potential productions, where new and experienced playwrights may discuss mutual problems.

Directories issued in 1948, 1950, and 1952 have provided information as to the form and locale of children's theatre activity throughout the nation. Three college surveys have been conducted, two of which have been published.[2] These surveys and publications have served to keep students informed on institutions offering children's theatre training and to direct the attention of departments of theatre to the need for the addition and revision of courses.

The bibliography committee was established to locate publications in the field and to encourage further publication of studies. A bibliography was published which includes publications in children's theatre, creative dramatics, puppetry, and a selected list of children's theatre plays.[3]

International Children's Theatre was one of the earliest concerns of the Children's Theatre Committee. Delegates to the 1947 conference adopted a resolution supporting the aims and program of UNESCO, and in 1951 an International Children's Theatre Committee was formed. In 1952 an entire issue of *World Theatre* was devoted to children's theatre. In April, 1952, Children's Theatre Committee delegates attended the Paris Conference on Children and Youth. In 1950 the public relations of the Children's Theatre Committee were furthered by its participation in the Mid-Century White House Conference on Children and Youth and by its representation in regional theatre meetings of AETA.

Children's Theatre Newsletter

In 1951 the first *Children's Theatre Newsletter* was published.[4] It served to keep members informed of children's theatre activities throughout the country and provided opportunity for exchange of ideas between annual meetings. With the rapid development of CTC since 1954, both in membership and in program, the editorship of the *Newsletter* became a full-time responsibility. The cost of publication was assumed by three publishers of children's plays: the Children's Theatre Press, the Coach House Press, and Samuel French.

Children's Theatre Conference 1952 to 1959

Organizational Development

A tone of self-evaluation has characterized the Children's Theatre Conference. This self-appraisal was emphasized by the keynote address of Clarence T. Simon at the annual meeting in 1956. "New ideas and developments seem to go through two stages. An early stage . . . during which each new movement pushes out its borders, enlarges its concepts, develops enthusiasms . . . and secondly a more seasoned maturity marked by self-appraisal and criticism . . . without any loss of enthusiasm."

The organizational structure of CTC has undergone little change since the adoption of the operating code. The weighty problem of finance has been accentuated by an expanding program and a membership which in one year, 1955, grew from 152 members to 829. In the years since 1954 the administration of CTC with its ways and means committee has worked to build up a financial reserve, carried as the Ways and Means Fund of CTC.

Projects Development

The CTC projects reflect both an evaluative tone and a broadening circle of influence. In 1953 mimeographed committee reports distributed to the membership included: "The College Curriculum Survey"; "Preliminary Selected Bibliography"; a recommended list of children's plays. A yearbook, the first to be prepared, was distributed at the annual meeting in 1954. It contained reports of the director, regional council, and fourteen committees. During 1955 the definition committee, originated in 1953, submitted the report, "Children's Drama: An Interpretation of Terms," prepared for distribution through educational channels. Ever increasing emphasis on new scripts and consequent concern with standards of production has motivated playwriting contests. These contests offer cash awards and, often, production for the winning plays.

Committees Development

The committees listed as of August, 1958, give some indication of the widening scope of the CTC program at the present time.[5] The committees included are Creative Dramatics in Elementary Education; Creative Dramatics in Religious Education; New Plays; Bibliography; Research; International CT Committee; CTC-ANTA Liaison; Awards; Arena Handbook; Legislation; Contact Placement; Public Relations; Ways and Means; Recreation; Radio and Television; Puppetry; and workshops and conferences.

Annual Meeting Progress

A number of features of annual meetings point up progress of the past several years. Development in the quality and extent of exhibits during the past five years is significant. These exhibits represent programs in formal children's theatre, creative dramatics, or programs encompassing both the formal and informal approach to child drama. In 1956 the Charlotte Chorpenning Award was created and is now presented annually to the exhibit adjudged most outstanding for the quality of its presentation as well as the initiative of the program depicted. The Zeta Phi Eta Award, named in honor of Winifred Ward, was established in 1957. This award will be made annually to a newly organized theatre—institutional, community or professional—making the greatest contribution to its own children, to the community, to CTC, or to theatre in general.

Careful studies have been completed for two awards soon to be initiated: the Monte Meacham Award to be given annually to a national figure who during the year has made the most valuable contribution to the field of children's theatre; and a playwriting award to be made for superior scripts only: not necessarily an annual award. An important new development in the children's theatre program is the incorporation in 1958 of a Children's Theatre Foundation. The purpose of the foundation is to promote children's theatre nationally and internationally through scholarships, grants-in-aid, workshops, lectureships, and the stimulation of more activity by professional theatre writers, directors, and producers.

Regional Growth

The regional organization, which in 1953 was designated Regional Council, has assumed increasing responsibility for promoting the program of CTC. Joint sessions of council and board were established in 1953, and since 1954 there has been particularly close coordination between the council and the *CTC Newsletter,* membership, and publicity committees.

Children's Theatre Conference in Future

The Children's Theatre Conference has made marked progress in its brief history. It has had more than 100 per cent increase in membership each year for each of its fifteen years. It has developed an organization whose administration combines vision and competence. Through its program and projects it has tried to promote artistic theatre experiences for children and youth.

From a background of rapid but sound development CTC faces the present and looks to the future in a world of tensions and opportunity. A basic CTC tenet states that the values of child drama are the prerogative of all children. The realization of this tenet might well be furthered by closer coordination of CTC and other educational organizations including the regional organizations of AETA, the Congress of Parents and Teachers (both state and national), the National Education Association, state education associations, and religious education groups. Cooperation with these organizations can work toward the aim of increasing children's theatre productions of quality, improving drama courses, motivating a broad program of public education on the values of child drama, and establishing a place for child drama in the school curriculum. It is with the stimulus of great belief in the inherent worth of its program that CTC looks to the future.

4 History of Children's Theatre in the United States*

Nellie McCaslin 🙠

Children's theatre, as we conceive of the term today, is a twentieth century movement. The lingering prejudice against the theatre in America as late as the turn of the century and the general prevalence of the traditional school curriculum, which placed its emphasis on academic subjects, contributed to the cultural climate in which theatre for children was not yet an established part. The concept of entertainment planned, organized, and executed for the express purpose of giving children wholesome pleasure was shared by few. First to recognize the need for such entertainment were the social settlements in the late nineteenth century, but the first significant children's theatre was not founded until 1903.

Children's Educational Theatre

This enterprise was the Children's Educational Theatre in New York City, the founding date of which therefore became the birth date of the movement. Directed by Alice Minnie Herts, this pioneering organization had a definite educational policy governing production, and it established a budget and maintained a high standard in the selection of plays, acting, and staging. While it lasted only six years, it was, from

---

*Monograph drawn from Ph. D. dissertation: Nellie McCaslin, A History of Children's Theatre in the United States (New York: New York University, 1957). MS available from University Microfilms, Ann Arbor, Michigan, Microfilm 57-377.

all reports, an excellent and influential undertaking. Aside from the Children's Educational Theatre, however, very little activity took place anywhere in the country before 1910.

1910 to 1920

The years 1910 to 1920, by comparison with the preceding decade, were important ones in children's theatre, even though relatively few individual programs were established. The Drama League of America, the first national organization dedicated to the promulgation of community theatre and improvement of professional offerings, was founded in 1910. Through this organization dramatic activities in community centers and schools received an unexpected stimulus. Another national organization which was to achieve remarkable results in the ensuing years was the Association of Junior Leagues of America, a women's service organization with branches throughout the United States. While its dramatic program was not yet clearly defined, leagues in New York, Chicago, and Boston reported activity in connection with community centers and settlement classes.

The interest of the social settlements in children's dramatics, however, was being continued with some significant results. Among these were Karamu House in Cleveland and, in New York, the Neighborhood Playhouse of the Henry Street Settlement and Christadora House. Other types of community projects established during these years were the Chicago Civic Theatre and the Children's Theatre of San Francisco, both of which were set up under the auspices of municipal recreation departments.

1920 to 1930

The ten years following the First World War were years of expansion for community theatres, including theatre for children. The Drama League, now in its second decade, had assumed leadership and reported at its annual conventions work being done by hundreds of groups in schools, colleges, social settlements, churches, and civic theatres throughout the country. The Junior League of America, which in 1921 formally established a program of dramatic activities, embarked upon the production of plays by members in a number of American cities. Among the most significant programs under the auspices of educational institutions during this period were those established at Emerson College in Boston, Northwestern University in Evanston, Illinois, the Goodman Theatre in Chicago, the University of Tulsa in Oklahoma, and the King-Coit School of Acting and Design in New York. While these programs followed different patterns, each was founded according to specified objectives and conditions and has served as a model for many groups.

Meanwhile, in the professional theatre, one company which was to last for nearly thirty years was founded. This was the Clare Tree Major Children's Theatre in New York, which survived the vicissitudes of depression and war to become one of America's principal touring companies.

1930 to 1940

The decade of the thirties, despite the disastrous effects the economic depression had on the professional stage, was a period of accelerated growth for the children's theatre movement. The Federal Theatre established within three years' time live entertainment for children in a large number of cities scattered throughout the forty-eight states. Beyond the scope of the program, however, were the creative approach to problems involved and the contribution of new scripts and production techniques. Among educational institutions increased interest and expansion took place. *Players Magazine* was the principal source of information regarding activity on college campuses, while *Recreation* carried news of children's theatre in playgrounds and community centers. Four civic organizations located in Maplewood, New Jersey; Binghamton, New York; Milwaukee, Wisconsin; and Seattle, Washington, were established for the purpose of sponsoring worthwhile entertainment for children.

A professional enterprise which has been described as a miracle was also founded during the thirties. This was Junior Programs, Inc., which, under the guidance of Dorothy McFadden, within a very few years included three companies offer-

ing ballet, opera, and drama for children. Through schools
and community organizations its programs were toured to hundreds of cities and towns. While other professional offerings
were available during the thirties, Junior Programs, Inc.,
conducted the most extensive campaign to bring entertainment
of quality to boys and girls at a moderate cost. According to
its records, during the seven years of its existence 1,300 performances were given by this company, 700 performances were
given by other companies which it booked, and over 4,000,000
children made up a total audience in forty-three states. [1]

In the area of publication perhaps the most important event
which took place was the founding of the Children's Theatre
Press by Sara Spencer in 1935. Starting with only four titles,
this company has remained a publishing house devoted exclusively to the printing of children's plays and related materials.
At the present time over one hundred titles are listed in its
catalogue.

1940 to 1950

The years 1940 to 1950 may be more accurately described as
years of expansion than experimentation. While the Federal
Theatre was no longer in existence, the American National
Theatre and Academy, a federally chartered organization,
was established to serve the interests of both professional
and nonprofessional groups. Probably the most important organization, however, was the Children's Theatre Committee,
founded in 1944. Later to become CTC, a division of AETA, it
has concerned itself exclusively with children's theatre activities including those of educational, community, and professional origin.

The Fifties

The work of the past decade is marked less by change than
by the stabilizing of programs already established. CTC, which
by 1950 had begun the publication of its own newsletter, by 1955
was reaching a mailing list of over one thousand, quarterly,
with issues of ten pages. In addition to summer conferences,
workshops were established, and a regional type of organiza-

tion made possible the activity of many members who had pre-
viously had no opportunity for participation. And finally, the
survey of college curricula completed in 1953 produced evidence that both plays for children and courses of study were
being included in 127 institutions.[2] The trend toward university
and community cooperation has continued to the point where today it is the usual rather than the exceptional pattern.

According to publicity of professional companies and commercial agencies in New York, a greater amount of entertainment is available today than in any preceding period. The de-
centralization of cities and the prevalence of sponsoring organizations are said to be contributing factors in the phenome-
nal increase in touring engagements.

The publication of books and articles pertinent to children's
theatre is rapidly increasing. Many master's theses and at
least eight doctoral studies have been written in the children's
drama area. Through the *Educational Theatre Journal, Players
Magazine,* and the *Children's Theatre Newsletter* material is
disseminated, and through the ANTA office information regarding national and international ventures is released.

Analysis of Trends and Developments

In analyzing the more than fifty years of children's theatre
history in the United States, three factors must be considered:
rate and extent of growth, organizations and institutions responsible for this growth, and objectives which have guided
them. While systematic surveys were not conducted until recent years, there is sufficient evidence in records and accounts
to indicate extraordinary and continued growth. When the Children's Educational Theatre was founded in 1903, it was hailed
as a unique experiment. Subsequent ventures multiplied rapidly
until by 1944 eighty groups were represented among the delegates to the first meeting of the Children's Theatre Committee.
Within a decade this number was close to 500. It is furthermore acknowledged that this does not constitute a complete
count, since not every leader is a member of this national organization, and many plays are produced sporadically each
year as individual entertainments.

Professional progress has been somewhat slower. The

Broadway stage has contributed relatively little, with five different presentations of *Peter Pan* and one of *The Blue Bird,
Snow White,* and *Treasure Island,* respectively, comprising
the offerings. With the founding of Children's World Theatre
in the late forties, probably the third most important professional company began activity. The death in 1955 of its
director, Monte Meacham, halted the progress just as the
company was becoming nationally known.

The children's theatre movement has been guided by certain
specific objectives, two of which have been repeatedly stated.
These are (1) to provide worthwhile and appropriate entertainment for young audiences, and (2) to promote individual and
social growth through experience in the dramatic arts. A recent survey conducted by CTC has disclosed that these purposes have not changed but that a greater emphasis is being
placed upon the entertainment value today than formerly. This
emphasis may be the result of the distinction now made between children's theatre and creative dramatics. This clarification, for which Winifred Ward must be given credit, seems
important since it has led to the distinction between product
and process. In view of the early growth and vitality of children's theatre in America, child drama seems to be emerging
as a cultural force. Major obstacles continue to be the lack of
qualified leaders, good dramatic literature for production, and
funds. It is apparent that a new period in the history of children's theatre has arrived.

5 Values to Children from Good Theatre

Kenneth L. Graham ✍

On stage a Tartan chieftain, Okkadai, has the little
Princess Kogatin in his captivity in a remote mountain
area. "You are my captive. You shall stay here forever," he proclaims fiercely. In the audience a six-
year-old steps into an aisle, and as he strides toward
the stage he declares in a clear, firm voice, "I'll save
you." Fortunately before he actually reaches the stage
he is retrieved by an alert adult.

Such an occurrence at a recent production of *Marco
Polo*[1] is evidence of the strong empathy which children
experience in viewing a living stage performance. Of
course children are fascinated with films and in front
of picture tubes, but in these there is less identification than with the living actor. The aesthetic experience of *mutual communication* between audience and
actor, available only in the living theatre, is the
underlying fundamental value which must never be
overlooked.

Entertainment

Specifically, the most obvious value to children in
good theatre is entertainment, a value often taken for
granted and sometimes ignored. Often entertainment
is misconstrued to mean merely amusement, which is,
indeed, only an ingredient of entertainment. Good
theatre should be delightful but not just a passing delight. If a play is to be considered fully entertaining,
delight must linger on after the final curtain call,
must have lasting effects. The word *entertain* is derived from the Latin *tenere,* meaning "to hold."

27

A good children's play will "hold" an audience by presenting opportunities for children to identify themselves with personalities in situations they can comprehend—interesting, worthwhile, absorbing. Charlotte Chorpenning lists example after example of these lasting effects upon youngsters who have experienced a truly entertaining play.[2]

Psychological Needs

Entertainment is foremost in children's theatre, but of itself is not enough. An engrossingly entertaining play will also incorporate another specific value of good theatre, namely that of fulfilling certain psychological and developmental needs of young growing personalities. These needs have been expressed in various ways such as: (1) "the desire to see the abstract pictures of the imagination realized in concrete form";[3] (2) "the craving for a conception of life higher than the actual world offers them";[4] (3) "the propensity to express the larger life of the race in the individual";[5] (4) "an outlet for the natural drives for adventure and excitement";[6] (5) "the need to enter worlds larger than their own and there encounter people different from themselves";[7] (6) "the need to experience emotions that might not be evoked in everyday living";[8] (7) "the imaginative satisfaction of the 'ego' and mutuality needs of the growing child";[9] (8) "the need to escape from inferiority, rid themselves of handicaps, compensate for weaknesses, fulfill thwarted desires, and enjoy vicarious pleasures and adventures."[10]

A realization of these desires, cravings, propensities, and needs by way of make-believe or imagination appears to be vital to the development of a healthy personality. Since living drama furnishes a most impressive means of such vicarious realizations, we may conclude that the fulfillment of these psychological needs is one of the important values of good theatre for children.

Learning Opportunities

A third specific value is that the child is given an opportunity to learn. Such an opportunity involves the identification of the

child with the protagonist, the antagonist, and other characters
in the play by which the child's sympathies are worthily aroused
because of the situations involved. As Mark Twain once wrote:

> It is my conviction that the children's theatre is one of the very,
> very great inventions of the twentieth century, and that its vast edu-
> cational value—now but dimly perceived and but vaguely understood—
> will presently come to be recognized. . . .
>
> It is much the most effective teacher of morals and promoter of
> good conduct that the ingenuity of man has yet devised, for the reason
> that its lessons are not taught wearily by book and dreary homily,
> but by visible and enthusing action; and they go straight to the heart,
> which is the rightest of right places for them. Book-morals often get
> no further than the intellect, if they even get that far on their spectral
> and shadowy pilgrimage; but when they travel from a children's theatre
> they do not stop permanently at that halfway house, but go on home. [11]

A play need not, however, obviously instruct in order to
provide these opportunities. Unfortunately, this value of children's theatre is sometimes simply stated as the "educational
value," and thereby often gives rise to the misconception that
a children's play must instruct in some direct way. The result-
ant plays often then utilize dramatic appeal as a means of instruction, but from the standpoint of drama, they are perver-
sions of the art. For example, one character may *explain*
many times how brave another character is (sometimes even
directly stating that bravery is a virtue which all in the audience should acquire), but if the second character can be *involved* in a dramatic situation whereby his actions evidence his
bravery the children will have *an opportunity to learn* as they
live through the situation vicariously with the character, and
"bravery" as such need never be mentioned.

As Yasha Frank once said, "Children love to learn but they
hate to be taught—so all we have to do is frame our plays in
such a way that we never tell them anything but just evolve,
with as much participation as we can get from them, the behavior patterns we want them to follow."[12] Good theatre for
children should provide a wide variety of experiences wherein
children can identify themselves with characters in situations
which make concrete the vital phases of life. Children should
have many opportunities to learn sympathetic understanding of
people and the *reasons* for commonly accepted moral ideals.

Aesthetic Appreciation

Good theatre will allow children to experience the aesthetic satisfactions of good dramaturgy well produced. Such qualities will be found in all good theatre, but they *must* be in children's theatre if the child is to be introduced to the true value of drama as an art. In a well-written play the basic compositional principles—unity, balance, variety—will be evidenced in a plot with a clear, forward-moving, unbroken story line; fully developed yet not overly complex characterizations, delineated primarily by their own words and actions and capable of logical and consistent growth; and dialogue which is inspired, imaginative, and refreshing. In a well-produced play, these same aesthetic principles will be evidenced in the direction, the acting, the design, and the other arts synthesized by individuals skilled in the theatre who know and understand child audiences.

Future Adult Audiences

A final value to children of good children's theatre is a vitally important long-range one. It is hoped that a generation which has experienced the values suggested above will comprise the intelligent, critical, and appreciative adult theatre audience of the future.

PART II

. . . The purpose of the theatre is to find, and to hold up to our regard, what is admirable in the human race.

- Maxwell Anderson

Arthur and the Magic Sword. Honolulu Theatre for Youth
(Photograph by John Bonsey)

6 Children's Theatre Produced by Adult Groups

Albert O. Mitchell ᴣᴇ

Adults who produce children's plays employ many of the same practices they use in producing plays for grownups and, indeed, many practices that children employ in producing their own plays. This investigation does not compare producers, however, but examines such general practices as organization and operation, program selection, and audience control. It is not a statistical study, but a statement of general rules and habits. The approach to the present study was through published accounts of adult producing groups in dramatic and general periodicals, in pamphlets, newsletters, books; through text descriptions of principles and practices; through extensive correspondence and interviews with leaders about their own conditions and procedures.

Types of Adult Groups

In the United States more than 1,200 units, largely amateur, produce from one to four plays annually for children. [1] More and more community groups, 200 high schools, [2] and at least 220 colleges are producing. [3] The last figure is significant when contrasted with the lone university, Northwestern, producing for children three decades ago. Of the 220 institutions offering training in children's theatre, ninety-three offer graduate courses. And although in 1952-53 only 5 per cent of major college productions were for children, by 1956-57 more than 8 per cent were. [4] Numerous organizations of adults producing for children may be classified into three main types: com-

munity-service, educational, professional-commercial. [5] While
these categories are not mutually exclusive—groups often associate in action—they may include all units.

Principles of Adult Producers

General motives given by adult producers include the following: to offer as much and as excellent theatre to as many children as possible—eventually to "all the children of all the
people"; to offer not only entertainment but education and training for appreciation of theatre, of art, and of life. In order
to attain these goals, adults try to perfect their organizations and to gain active cooperation of the whole community.
Their aim is to give vocational training to some few but avo-
cational outlet to many. Few producers for children evince
much concern for gain or glamour.[6] Professionals, no less
than educators, assure us of their dedication to the child and
to humanity.

Organization and Operation Methods

Community-Service Groups

This type of group is more often a sponsor than producer.
Since their principles include providing the best theatre for
the most children, as well as enlisting the support of the whole
community, their boards are made up from many units. While
they follow no ready-made pattern, some general rules may be
observed. For example, the Omaha Junior Theatre has a board
of thirty.[7] Its members represent almost that many units from
schools, museums, libraries, radio and television stations,
community playhouse, university, recreation department, the
Council of Jewish Women, service leagues, and other groups
concerned with youth. Each representative has a definite function.

In the Raleigh, North Carolina, Children's Theatre, the
Junior League supplies costumes and make-up; the Junior
Women's Club, publicity and tickets; Little Theatre, technical and construction assistance; PTA, hostesses; Girl Scouts,
ushers; city schools, rehearsal facilities; city library, play
reading and meeting space; Recreation Department, drayage,

working budget, and part of the director's salary. [8] Governing
boards seem to have executive officers plus chairmen of membership, budget and finance, program, theatre facilities, tickets, promotion, education. Constitution and by-laws seem
traditional.

In the service type of group, a director is frequently the
only paid member, and many plays are produced entirely by
volunteers. Directors are often invited from educational and
civic theatres. If the group acts merely as sponsor, the producing unit furnishes the play, including the director. Service
groups operating in conjunction with adult civic theatre may
utilize the same professionally trained director. Some groups,
however, use temporary directors recruited to fill in for a
play or season. Most groups try to avoid this, and authorities
strongly advocate a paid permanent director. [9] As representing
the actual process of organization, take the case of one community-service type of theatre. [10] There, initiative was taken
by the Junior League. A representative arranged with the civic
theatre board for use of the theatre. Then the schools, through
superintendents, were enlisted. Soon the entire community co-
operated in a permanent organization. Two boards were formed.
An advisory board from PTA, community theatre, school systems, art supervisors, and the Junior League selected the
plays and decided on dates. A technical board, made up of
Junior League president, production manager, publicity manager, and others produced the shows.

Junior Leagues, a good example of how important volunteers
are in community children's theatre, often start by producing
plays themselves. Eventually they join with others to sponsor
other producers, educational, professional, or volunteer. They
often act, direct, stage, promote, and manage. They often
troupe their plays widely to public and parochial schools and
community audiences. They emphasize good plays and productions. They sponsor well-rounded programs utilizing theatre
arts and the related fields of ballet, concert, cinema, puppetry.
That their audiences have responded is evident from increasing attendance. [11]

Among volunteer units is the Junior Programs, Inc. These
groups may actually be made up from such pioneers as AJLA,
AAUW, and PTA. Seattle Junior Programs, Inc., serves more

than a million people. Enlisting almost every child-interested
organization in the greater Seattle area, it earns its budget
annually. It maintains a central office and a paid secretary.
Operating entirely as a sponsoring group, it has reached annually over fifteen thousand children. Most of its productions
have been produced by the University of Washington, with bal-
lets from local studios and schools. To stimulate improvement of children's plays, an annual, nationwide playwriting
competition is held and thus many plays are made generally
available for production. The group has offered demonstrations in creative dramatics, international fellowships to the
university, a radio program of children's classics, and has
sponsored a weekly newspaper column, "Playtime," listing
good current entertainment for children. Seattle Junior Programs, Inc., compiled a manual describing its operations
in response to requests from other communities desiring to
organize according to its pattern. These communities sponsor productions from educational, professional, and service
units.

Junior Entertainment, Inc., of Denver, functions similarly,
in cooperation with the University of Denver. It has invited
other educational groups like the University of Utah and professionals like Strawbridge. Beginning with the 1958-59 season
it plans to spread responsibility for programming to suburbs
and adjacent communities, so that each may furnish part of
its own plays, either by local or by outside producers, depending on the central committee for only two productions a
year. [12]

In municipal recreation departments, community-service
theatres find that only occasionally are public funds as available to adult producers who produce *for* children as they are
for producers who produce *with* children. With centralized
performances, box-office receipts become the chief source of
revenue. Prices are usually fixed with due consideration for
size of auditorium, movie prices, and the child's ability to
pay. [13] In some cities, the Junior League or another service
group will underwrite a play or project to make free admission
possible. Some groups charge adults more than children, partly
to save seats for children. [14] These groups desire homogeneous
audiences, feeling that children enjoy plays more by them-

selves, that their theatre is really "a kingdom of the child, where the adult, like Gulliver in the land of the Lilliputians, is entirely out of place. "[15] Other groups welcome adults and schedule performances for "family night" or matinee showings. In an effort for security most sponsors sell season books. Many conduct block ticket sales to service clubs for free distribution through schools and welfare agencies. Some, since income from patron donations or benefit performances is uncertain, are fortunate enough to secure outright subsidy. Most of the fund raising for children's theatre is done by the volunteer groups, by means of ticket sales. Campaigns are usually handled through cooperation of the schools.

Where do community-service groups present their plays? Most commonly in a municipal auditorium connected with a museum in the park. Omaha Junior Programs presents plays mostly at Technical High School, but also at the art museum; Cincinnati, at the civic theatre; Seattle, in commercial theatres. When service groups troupe their plays it is usually to schools during school hours. The producer has to decide whether to bring the children to the play or the play to the children. When a central auditorium is available, the children are usually taken there. This often means more performances—possibly on Saturday, or even Sunday. In some cities it seems better to use several auditoriums in different parts of the city since, by touring, they can favor larger audiences with fewer productions, and by fewer centralized programs offer more productions to more children. Some cities combine the two systems. [16] The Children's Theatre of Portland, Maine, offering central productions during the winter, maintained a trailer theatre during the summer to take its plays to the parks. The Community Children's Theatre of Kansas City, Missouri, depends on colleges for centralized productions, with trouping units from the Junior League and the historical museum.

Educational Institutions

Many colleges and universities, public and private, following the lead of Northwestern University have become producers for children. The University of California at Los Angeles may be taken as an example. Its Department of Theatre Arts gives two plays a year with often a third as a thesis project. Each

play is performed fourteen times to audiences of from 500 to
750. Plays are toured also under the auspices of Junior Programs. They are directed and supervised by two full-time
faculty members. They are financed from the department's
budget, which also provides for upper division and graduate
courses in children's theatre and creative dramatics. Representative of both higher and secondary schools, Vallejo,
California, Junior College and Senior High School, under a
common director, produce two plays each, during school time.
These plays run for as many as fifteen performances, financed
by small donations from the schools to which they troupe their
plays.

High schools, through their national organizations, give increasing emphasis to children's theatre. Both *Dramatics* and
Players Magazine feature it regularly. More than two hundred
troupes, as noted, now produce for children. A recent report
stating that many thespian troupes received impetus from service groups and CTC shows that while theatre in most high
schools is extracurricular, in a "significant minority" it is
curricular. [17] Some schools produce three or four children's
plays a year. Some produce independently, others as one unit
in a community association. In Racine, Wisconsin, two public
schools and one parochial school cooperate with seven volunteer organizations to give children six plays a year. Performances are scheduled round-robin fashion. [18]

Children's theatre, in most schools, is a function of the department of dramatic arts, speech, or English. In a university,
as part of the theatre program, a children's theatre may be
staffed from the regular faculty. The director may or may
not direct adult theatre, but he is usually a salaried teacher.
He has usually completed his master's degree or Ph. D. He
often has wide experience in teaching and producing. He may
have other faculty associated with him in children's theatre.
Designers, costumers, technicians are usually paid faculty
or staff. Sometimes they are graduate assistants on a stipend.
In smaller colleges, the teacher-director usually produces
alone, or with volunteer student assistance. In larger schools,
course work and laboratories insure volunteer assistance in
production. In high schools the director is likely to have the
entire burden. The director usually operates on an extra-

curricular basis with little backing or budget. His theatre training may be meager, his major being English or history rather than drama.

School theatres, as many of them are virtually subsidized, often have their overhead already covered. They have only to collect their immediate expenses. Facilities are free, or only nominal charges are made for them. Directors' and often technicians' salaries are assured from their teaching functions. Many of the costs of production are absorbed by instruction and laboratory budgets. College and university theatres usually conduct season ticket campaigns. If this is not done for them by the community group with which they are sometimes affiliated, it is apt to be done directly through the schools. Some sell tickets at the door; others ask a small flat fee of the participating schools. When educational troupes tour, whether in town or out, it is usually under sponsorship either of individual schools or of community groups. Sponsors commonly guarantee their expenses.

Publicity for most colleges and universities is a function of the public relations department although many theatres have their own managers who handle children's theatre as part of their regular promotion. In high schools the drama club does most of the publicity and promotion. Some clubs even sponsor outside productions. School theatres, as functions of nonprofit, community projects, often receive free publicity from mass media.

Educational producers present their plays in their own theatres.[19] As already noted, the high school theatre is much utilized, not only by its own actors but by colleges and other producers for elementary schools and junior high schools. Most children's plays by college producers are given in the main college theatres, which have quite adequate stages and facilities. Many educational theatres are modern and excellent. Educational producers are expanding to meet the convenience of audiences, thus maintaining both centralized and trouping systems. Approximately one fourth of high schools reporting troupe their plays during school hours; the rest bring the schools to their theatres, more than half of them during school hours. Others perform late afternoons, early evenings, and Saturdays. School producers open first on their own stages, then often accept limited engagements in their own and nearby communities. Even more of them schedule short annual or semiannual tours, even into neighboring states.[20] A few keep one or more units on the road for long periods.[21] Some tours are on an extracurricular basis; some gain academic credit for cast and crew. Most depend on local arrangements by sponsors who guarantee expenses. They do not try to make a profit.

Professional-Commercial Producers

These include private studios and touring companies, of which there are at least a half-dozen currently offering productions of a consistently good standard. Touring companies commonly offer from one to three productions a year, often fielding several companies at once, either with the same play or alternating different plays in territories. A pioneer in this category was Clare Tree Major who, beginning in 1921 with young professionals in New York City, spread her repertories over the United States during three decades. Mrs. Major, manager and director, also wrote most of her plays. They were usually presented Saturdays and late afternoons, in school auditoriums and small theatres. They reached vast audiences of small children who otherwise would not have seen good plays.[22] Edwin Strawbridge performed a similar service, trouping ballet for children.

Children's World Theatre, National Children's Theatre, and Merry Wanderers Theatre—all have moved outward from New York. The latter, currently operating cross-country tours, tries to provide two plays a year, with enough companies to fill demands. Grace Price Productions, originating in Pittsburgh, serves presently forty-two communities in Pennsylvania, West Virginia, Maryland, and Ohio. Rockefeller Productions, operating outward from the Young Hebrew Associations in New York[23] where the director is in charge of drama, offers seven plays—in Ohio, Indiana, Illinois, Iowa, New York. Professional groups organize around professional leaders like Clare Tree Major and Edwin Strawbridge, with staffs of paid professionals, often young apprentices. Opening in home theatres, they depend on touring for their main income. For promotion, they depend considerably on local sponsors who, often connected with professional booking agencies, furnish publicity material. They may require a flat guarantee from sponsors or a minimum guarantee plus a per cent of gate receipts.

Selection of Programs

"Children's theatre exists solely for the benefit of the audience, and its aims naturally differ from those established for creative dramatics."[24] Considering audience appeal, producers list *entertainment* as the first criterion. To be entertaining, a play must have a "strong story line," building to strong climax. Action must dominate dialogue. But true entertainment comes from strong characters with whom children can identify. It also comes from humor and beauty. Adult producers look for fun and fantasy, music and dance.

Producers look for plays that appeal to audiences of mixed ages. Selecting plays for a given age span is also widely practiced; producers then consider the realistic period, the imaginative period, and the heroic period. Another principle of selection is intrinsic worth. Educational producers insist, however, that truths and information be woven into the dramatic action. Entertainment and artistry demand this integration.

"Balancing the season" is another consideration: thus fantasy, a historical play, a modern realistic play are frequently selected. However, to the concern of some, producers lean too heavily on fantasy. Producers cling to the "name play," because of prestige and box office. Some children's theatres balance not only the season but, since they may have the same child audience for several years, try to introduce many types of plays and productions. That producers are relying on past successes is evident from offerings of the past five seasons. Of nearly four hundred productions listed, only twenty-eight new titles appeared.[25] A list circulated at the 1950 CTC meeting, under the heading "Most Popular Plays, in Order of Preference," gives mostly fantasies. Of twenty "most-used" children's plays in 1957-58 listed by a publisher, fourteen are fantasies.[26] Of thirty plays produced repeatedly, classical and fairy tale plays are definitely in the majority. These facts may explain the fear expressed by a publisher that we are reactionary, leaning on foreign cultures.[27]

Practical considerations in play selection include finance,

staging, trouping, and casting. Budget-conscious groups often choose nonroyalty plays, or make their own dramatizations. Although they are being converted to royalty plays, too few are producing plays of *Peter Pan* quality, because of royalty. Of those questioned, the only groups who mentioned royalties averaging lower than $15.00 were professional touring companies. These, because they play many performances to earn their entire budget, often make their own versions of "name" plays. Many groups, nonetheless, encourage new plays by offering substantial fees or prizes. Technical considerations frequently lead to choosing plays that can be adapted to a few cut-down sets and to practical costume budgets. Elaborate costumes for two dozen characters would strain most budgets. Advanced producers are finding ways, however, to stage more complex plays.

From what sources do producers obtain plays? Most frequently from *Children's Theatre Press, Samuel French, Inc.*, and *Coach House Press*. These three houses are actively promoting children's theatre. Association of Junior Leagues of America is a good source. The "New Scripts" room, now traditional at CTC annual meetings, is one of many indications that producers are determined to have more and better plays. Playwriting competitions support this effort. At colleges, standard royalties for acceptable new plays, along with free experimental production, encourage playwrights. Consideration for children's fare, in playwriting courses as well as in workshops in playwriting under service group sponsorship, is beginning to become established.

Audience Comfort and Control

Most producers enforce no age segregation. Northwestern University, however, offers two series, one for elementary and intermediate, one for preschool and kindergarten. Age segregation is used by some producers to insure better reception. A producer soon discovers that no matter how good his show, it may fail if he cannot control his audience. The problem is to control without repressing. Some producers employ ushers to forestall confusion in finding reserved seats; they use reserved seats to break up the gang at the door. Others, feeling that children like to be put on their own, omit ushers in favor of guides for the guests. And adult producers, conditioned to adult behavior, soon discover that a completely quiet child audience is not only impossible but undesirable; that there is a "difference between a rowdy, discourteous audience and one that is having a good time. . . ."[28] To aid in control without repression, producers sometimes provide a mascot or character to fill in for scene changes or give announcements. This strategy helps to eliminate waits and to integrate the entire show smoothly. The director also looks for and develops "exercise spots" and other opportunities for children to stand up and cheer or otherwise participate. Others warn against this practice. Few sponsors, no matter how earnest about manners, would forego the overwhelming audience response to Peter Pan's plea: "Do you believe in fairies?"

Summary

Starting with a few pioneers of a quarter century ago, children's theatre now boasts several hundred producers. These are better trained, have better plays and facilities. But they know there are still only 4,000,000 children privileged to see productions. More adult producers are needed. Only a third of our colleges and universities produce for children, and fewer than 35 per cent of these have consistent programs.[29] More and better plays about life and times today are needed. More and better-trained directors and actors are needed. Too few are now ideally trained, in theatre departments with courses in child psychology and children's literature and with practical producing for children.

If children's theatre is to grow, this movement has an immediate need for the following: technicians trained in children's theatre; textbooks on theatre crafts slanted toward staging for children; authors to write children's theatre plays; directors with imagination; artists with a child's sense of beauty; actors who respect the child; musicians, philosophers, and psychologists to interpret child's dreams. And "the only way we can enlist the talents of such people . . . is to improve . . . the

calibre of our plays and productions, until we can make the
children's theatre a truly exciting medium for the artists of
the world to work in. "[30]

7 Children as Theatre Producers

Dorothy Kester ✺

Theatre by children—according to the plan of this study—consists of formal plays produced by children of elementary or junior high school age, performed for audiences of children, usually younger than the players. Casting of children in children's roles in adult plays may occur in any type of theatre organization including high school, university, and community theatres. Such practice is not strictly within the scope of this section of the study, and it is enough to note that this does occur. First let it be understood that this study cannot be definitive. A comprehensive survey of all public schools, church schools, recreation programs, and all community and private theatres in the United States has not been possible. Hence, a selective survey has been the basis for this study.[1]

Appeal and Challenge

For generations, teachers have been producing plays with children in all the roles. The familiar "school play" has been a part of the academic rationale for longer than any living person can remember. As early as 1784 Madam de Genlis was presenting French children in miniature performances for the delight of the nobles and the education of her young charges.[2] Through succeeding years teachers have discovered values in live theatre. In the hands of an enthusiastic and inspired teacher, when that teacher is also knowledgeable and skillful, the play becomes a vital force. Because of the receptiveness of a child and the peculiar endowment of drama, which is a mixture of intellect

45

and emotion, impressions made upon the participants and upon the audience may have lifetime implications. What these may be can only be guessed at until there is time and persistence to make vertical studies following children into their adult years and somehow estimating the effects of their exposure to theatre. A teacher using drama sets a fuse on a time bomb which will not detonate for twenty years.

Traditional Principles and Practices

Granted that there is an innate fascination in drama, especially for children, what are the uses to which it is currently put? This section will describe traditional practices in theatre at the elementary and junior high levels. Unfortunately, an objective view of dramatic productions by children is not encouraging.

Elementary School

A fourth-grade teacher wants to increase the flexibility of her teaching. She chooses a docile and earnest girl to be the director of a children's play. The child takes an educational magazine the teacher provides, which contains what might be called a script. The child recruits a cast from among the other docile and earnest members of the class. The children rehearse at recesses and noons and report a week later that they are ready to show their teacher and their classmates what they have been doing. With much *sub rosa* exhorting by the director and much self-conscious giggling by the cast, the exercise is completed. The cast retires, flushed with enthusiasm. The elated teacher reports to her colleagues in the cafeteria how exhilarating the experience was, and she adds that she "didn't have to do a *thing*." The tragedy is not so much that not anyone connected with the enterprise knows what is wrong, but that none of them even suspects.

Junior High School

It is certain that there are similar poor practices in dramatics for the junior high school youngster. A social-studies teacher with a free period is persuaded by administrative pressure to form a drama club of eighth graders. He sends for play

catalogues and combs them for a nonroyalty, one-act play with
the expedient number of characters and sets about to produce
the play for the November PTA meeting. The fact his class
wins a prize for having the most parents in attendance more
than offsets the traumatic experience to himself and the children of struggling through unanticipated difficulties in bringing
a script to life. The next fall the teacher volunteers early to
sponsor the Stamp Club.

These examples are duplicated throughout the organizations
included in this study. The examples are an indictment of theatre with young children and seem to give support to the theo-
retical convictions of many concerned leaders in the field of
children's drama. In 1953, members of CTC subscribed to a
set of principles called "An Interpretation of Terms." In part,
these state: "Young children up to the age of approximately
eleven or twelve years should participate in informal drama
exclusively."[3]

Reasons for Inadequacies

Instances of good work in formal plays by elementary school
children are so few that they may be classed as isolated experiments, and not at all typical of the nationwide situation.
This may be explained by the lack of trained personnel, both
among classroom teachers and among their supervisors. Relatively few cities and almost no towns have directors of speech
education. Most of those directors are in charge of speech and
hearing therapy and are not qualified to supervise children's
theatre. This means that there is no trained person available
to carry on experiments or to help classroom teachers, if
there happen to be qualified ones. It takes in-service training
and supervision of a high order for such an activity to grow.
This does not mean that formal plays are not being attempted
constantly, but the process of production and the results are
so far from acceptable as to be disturbing to observe and report.

A director of plays with children is primarily a teacher,
whether he works in a school, a community theatre, a recreation program, or a church school. Because his students have
had time to acquire little knowledge of theatre, he must instruct as he directs. Suppose he is a knowledgeable, skillful,

and inspired teacher. Then he has at least an adequate understanding of the theatre. This implies that he requires his script
to be good drama. It also implies that he knows his students
well enough to select a script that will give them maximum
chances for growth. Since his responsibility as a director of a
formal play is for a good production for an audience, he must
know the backstage and managerial aspects of theatre. He must
also know how to achieve good acting on the part of his cast
members, so that credit is done to the script and to the production as a whole.

The teacher's dilemma becomes critical when he realizes
that he must reconcile the responsibility to his audience which
he has as a director and the responsibility to his class which
he has as a teacher. However, to be well meaning is not to be
well qualified. In public schools, elementary teachers rarely
bring to their jobs even rudimentary training in the theatre. [4]
Teachers may understand children, they may appreciate drama,
but they do not know theatre. If theatre has been their chief
interest as undergraduates, they probably seek positions in
higher grades where opportunities are provided and therefore
these persons do not appear in elementary classrooms. In
church schools, where parents are recruited to teach classes,
the problem is compounded. Not only are they not trained in
theatre, but also in most instances they are not trained in educational techniques. Therefore, when teachers contemplate
producing a formal play they become discouraged because of
the difficulties of managing both children and a new medium.

In recreation programs, the great majority of workers are
enlisted from among coaches of athletics and from classroom
teachers. Again there is a shortage of personnel trained in
theatre. With masses of children to handle and little or no
theatre training, formal productions of high caliber are indeed
rare. Community and private theatres may be presumed to
have directors who know the techniques of theatre. Unfortunately, however, most often the person assigned to work
with children is a director of adult shows. In most instances
this director does not know how to get the best from children
and he becomes troubled when their abilities are different from
those of adults.

Scripts are unworthy. In most instances scripts are under-

developed in concept and structure. A didactic quality charac-
terizes most scripts which are used in classrooms. If a script
serves to teach facts it is generally approved.

Casting is on the basis of "his mother will make his costume" or "best reader." A teacher fails frequently to plan and
prepare for rehearsals. Dress rehearsals reflect the teacher's
reliance for comfort on the old theatre adage "a bad dress
rehearsal means a good performance." The performance itself
is consistently inadequate in technical details, acting, and
audience impact. To complicate the picture, stages are crowded
and poorly equipped. From sheer expediency, setting aside
philosophical and psychological considerations, the observer is
inclined to recommend that formal plays never be produced in
elementary grades.

Effective Principles and Practices

There is a reverse side to the theatre picture coin. Here and
there, over the country, instances of informal experimentation
in good theatre experiences involving casts and crews of children are found. Two areas stand out as possible proving grounds
for the effective use of formal theatre with children. One is
with gifted children, even as young as third grade, who have
had creative activities which have taught them how to recognize, release, channel, and communicate thoughts and emotions, and who have a skilled director-teacher to guide them.
The other is with those children at the upper edge of the age
bracket of "children" as defined by theatre leaders. [5] These
are the junior high school students, again with the stipulation
that they have wise direction.

Elementary School

In an advanced third grade in a public school a teacher and
principal were eager to challenge the abilities of the children
with a formal, disciplined theatre experience. The undertaking
was experimental. It was agreed that it would be given up at
any point at which unwholesome stresses were evident in the
players. The outcome was gratifying. The bright children had
no trouble learning lines. They invented business within the
framework of the directed movement. They learned to project

their voices without strain, and they were able to sustain characterization without self-consciousness. An added value was that older children, attracted by the activity, volunteered to be designers, builders, and shift crews. It must be stressed that the director was a person trained in theatre who was able to give professional guidance to teachers, volunteer mothers, and the children involved.

Junior High School

In junior high schools evidence of progress is more heartening. With the reinstatement of the three-year school as a buffer between grades and high school, opportunity is provided for activities within the interests and abilities of the early adolescent. With his striving for maturity, his attraction toward glamour, and his aspiration to "try on" life in the safe concealment of a character other than his own, good theatre experience gives him a much-needed opportunity for expression. Even so, only rarely in the United States can a junior high school theatre that comes near to meeting the requirements for good theatre of any age be found. However, three junior high schools may be mentioned where progress is being made. Waco, Texas, has had one of the pioneer producing groups of junior high students. Columbia, South Carolina, has another. Junior Jesters of Akron, Ohio, has produced good theatre despite encountering most of the hazards that stand in the way of easy production: lack of enough trained help and of construction space, inexperienced casts and crews, and the necessity for training willing volunteers. As these conditions are duplicated over the country, so are they being faced and overcome gradually by trained theatre leaders. There are still many inadequacies, but the number of trained teachers is increasing every year, and the quality of productions is continuously showing improvement.

Enlightened leadership is gradually emerging to make it possible for plays to be well produced by children. There is no pattern for this. What is done is fabricated on local facilities and personnel. Community theatres and private studios, for instance, may have children's workshops if there are hours and directors available at times which are not in conflict with adult play schedules. A notable exception to this is the Palo

Alto, California, Children's Theatre. Part of a civic development for children, the project includes a museum, a library, Boy and Girl Scout buildings, and a theatre designed
especially to provide dramatic experiences for children. A
permanent director and a technical crew work with volunteer
help from the community in training children in formal theatre.[6] In Seattle, Washington, there is an active community
emphasis upon participation by children of all ages in suitable
drama, some of it formal and some informal. Evanston, Illinois, has a theatre season presented by junior high school
students for preschool and primary grade children. Madison,
Wisconsin, has a director of dramatics in the summer recreation program who produces plays with junior and senior
high school casts. Their plays are trouped to the parks of the
city. Milwaukee, Wisconsin, has a well-developed program
of theatre for children, using actors of all ages in the plays.
Chicago and Evanston, Illinois, have had children's summer
play festivals during which plays that are produced in various
park programs are performed in a central location at the end
of the season.

In recreation programs, either municipally organized or a
part of the training of Boy and Girl Scouts and YMCA and YWCA
youth groups, dramatics is emphasized wherever trained personnel is available. Portland, Maine, has supported a Trailer
Theatre in which plays are taken to city and county parks with
casts of junior and senior high students. In·some areas, workshops and short courses are held by city-wide councils of
leaders. Sessions of national conventions are given over to
lectures and demonstrations of theatre techniques. However,
the emphasis locally is determined by the training of the leaders
and the availability of facilities. With a few exceptions such
as those mentioned above, actual productions of formal drama
are of a low order and the tendency is toward informal drama
to an increasing extent.

Several instances of outstanding accomplishment in the field
of theatre by children are a hopeful sign of a realization of the
importance of this kind of experience. The citing of three will
suffice: (1) Before 1950 Raleigh, North Carolina, drew up plans
for a children's theatre building in conjunction with the community theatre plant. (2) Community cooperation made possible

the establishment of the Youngstown, Ohio, Civic Children's Theatre, under the direction of a trained leader. Their group was the first recipient of the Winifred Ward Prize for the best new children's theatre in 1957. Their plays are produced with casts chosen from the children of Youngstown who wish to try out for parts in the casts and crews. (3) Most recently Nashville, Tennessee, has announced plans for a children's theatre designed to be used by a trained staff of workers. These examples build hope in professional children's theatre persons that general public awareness of the value of theatre for children is growing. Bombarded as children of today are by the current emphasis on science, theatre and other art experiences are increasingly important.

There is one type of formal theatre which has not been mentioned and which appears frequently: the formalizing of a creative dramatics play. This occurs when a class has completed a story creatively and wishes to show parents or another class what they have learned, not only about doing a play but also about a unit of work they have been studying. It is possible to construct simple scenery, make or collect properties and costumes that are suitable to the subject matter, and perform the play as a formal theatre experience. When this is done carefully and with taste, it can enrich children's understanding of regular class work.

Summary

There are both encouraging and discouraging aspects to the producing of plays by children. To look at the activity as it is generally carried on is to see it as less than successful for a variety of reasons: lack of good scripts for children to produce; evidence of poor facilities for production in most elementary schools and community theatres; inadequacy of training and experience for teachers, directors, and child actors; and lack of research and study in this area.

1. Universities must offer and require for graduation for elementary and junior high school teachers adequate courses in children's drama. A graduate who expects to direct children in plays should have as much preparation in theatre as a music teacher has in music or an art teacher in art. For

teachers already working in schools, churches, or theatres, there should be conferences, workshops, and demonstrations. Summer sessions should offer courses in children's drama which carry both graduate and undergraduate credit. Universities should assist by setting up problems in the areas of children's theatre for theses and dissertations. Research on a large scale should be financed through grants.

2. Schools and organizations need to give thought to a training program for child actors if these are to be used in producing plays for child audiences.

3. Theatre facilities need to be strengthened. Progress should be made in utilizing to advantage what is already available. This may imply that experimentation could be attempted with arena staging in large empty spaces such as gymnasiums or large classrooms.

4. Playwrights should be encouraged to write plays for production by children if the practice of using child actors is continued. Playwrights should be paid substantial royalties for writing plays of artistic worth.

5. Further study needs to be carried on to prove or disprove the statement in "Interpretation of Terms" which says that children of these ages profit most from engaging in creative dramatics and not in formal theatre.

8 Children's Theatre in Radio and Television

Gloria Chandler ᴔ

Defining the Area

Since the early thirties, when radio really became an integral part of everyday living, children's programming has been the subject of great controversy among parents, teachers, and psychologists, and also script writers, artists, and program managers in the broadcasting industry. In discussing the basic principles and problems of radio and television as they relate to children's theatre in the mass media, we will be concerned with only those programs that are planned specifically for children's leisure-time listening and viewing.

Although surveys have shown that since the beginning children have not limited their listening and viewing to those programs specifically designed for them, we will confine our consideration to these programs. Furthermore, let us also narrow our field to a discussion of those programs designed for children up to fourteen years of age.

Story Programs

Children's radio programs were developed in the early stages of the medium without any special thought or special planning as to the needs of the child. When radio was still a publicity medium, when chain broadcasting was only in the making, story programs appeared. These were told by The Story Lady or an Uncle Bob or Auntie Kate. No thought was given to age levels—the stories were supposed to satisfy all children from five to fourteen years. Out of the early days of the story-telling programs, however, comes Irene Wicker, The Singing Lady, who held sway from 1932 to 1938. Irene Wicker's name was synonymous with high artistic quality. Her program consisted of nursery rhymes and stories, with musical background interspersed with simple songs.

Child Talent Programs

A second type of programming that grew out of the early days of radio was the program in which children themselves participated. One of the first of these was N.B.C.'s *Children's Hour* which originated about 1922 on WJZ in New York. This program gave opportunity to musically talented children; there was no script, and the music used on the program was largely drawn from opera. Milton Cross was associated with this program in its early stages, and from him we learned that among those who were heard on the program was Rïse Stevens, then about eleven years old. When the N.B.C. network was formed in 1926, "The Children's Hour" was taken over by Madge Tucker and was called "Coast to Coast on a Bus." It ran Saturday mornings until November, 1948, presenting hundreds of children in songs and dramatic sketches and, in fact, acted as a junior training school for children who were looking to motion pictures and the stage for a career.

From the early days of radio on the Columbia Broadcasting System came another child-participation program which gave children and young adults a chance to take part in dramatizations of fairy tales and favorite stories of childhood loved by children and adults. This was known as "Adventures of Helen and Mary," and later as "Let's Pretend." It was written and directed by Nila Mack and was enjoyed from coast to coast from 1929 to 1952. "Let's Pretend" was carried as a sustaining program until 1943. The format remained the same during the life of the program. Although it was a springboard to fame for many young actors and actresses, the fact that its performers were young people was not the reason for its great popularity. The group was a small one, and under Nila Mack's direction brought a sincerity and understanding to the performance that stimulated the imagination of the listening audience.

"Thrillers"

It is not strange that advertisers seeking the home market saw, at a very early date, the possibility of using children to appeal to parents. Radio was the perfect means, and the era of the box top and the "thriller" with its cliff-hanging endings was upon the listening audience before it realized what had happened. In seeking material that would catch the attention of the largest number of children, the advertiser turned naturally to the comic strip, which had long been popular with adults and children. Immediate success followed the dramatization of these familiar characters, and this stimulated the imagination of script writers. They realized that boys and girls loved adventure, conflict, suspense, secrets and mysteries, villains, and brave heroes. These programs were put on five days a week, Monday through Friday. As far as the advertiser was concerned they were highly successful—box tops flooded the stations. However, a great outcry was raised against this type of program. Many of the daily episodes dealt with suspense, danger, kidnaping, and situations that built up real fear in the minds of the listeners. Many parents reported frightened reactions of children while they listened; other parents reported nightmares. Parents and professional groups became more and more concerned with children's program fare; surveys of children's listening were made in various parts of the country; newspapers and magazines published editorials. Now the broadcasters were genuinely concerned as they realized that there had been no criteria set up for children's programs.

Committees were formed to bring the criticisms to the broadcasting industry; notable among them was the Women's National Radio Committee. [1] The networks came forward with statements of policy toward children's programming. This development was followed by the introduction of several new programs such as "Wilderness Road," a dramatic serial of American frontier life which won an award from the Women's National Radio Committee for the best children's program for 1936.

Code and Criteria

In 1939 the Radio Council on Children's Programs was organized.[2] This group was made up of representatives of the radio industry, national sponsors, advertising agencies, organized women's groups, educators, librarians, and other organizations interested in children's welfare such as the Girl Scouts and the Association of Junior Leagues of America. The purpose of the council was to work closely with the industry and advertisers to help evaluate and promote programs and to act as an advisory group. From the beginning the council worked closely with the National Association of Broadcasters, made up of the networks and representatives of local stations. The NAB was at this time working on a self-regulating code to bring to the public the best service in every phase of radio. The council acted as an advisory group for the section on children's programs. The code reads:

> Programs designed specifically for children reach impressionable minds and influence social attitudes, aptitudes, and approaches and, therefore, they require the closest supervision of broadcasters in the selection and control of material, characterizations, and plot.
>
> This does not mean that the vigor and vitality common to a child's imagination and love of adventure should be removed; it does mean that programs should be based upon sound social concepts and presented with a superior degree of craftsmanship; that these programs should reflect respect for parents, adult authority, law and order, clean living, high morals, fair play, and honorable behavior. Such programs must not contain sequences involving horror or torture or use of the supernatural or superstitious or any other material which might reasonably be regarded as likely to overstimulate the child listener, or be prejudicial to sound character development. No advertising appeal which would encourage activities of a dangerous social nature will be permitted.[3]

The Federal Radio Education Committee of the United States Department of Education published a pamphlet in 1942, with an introduction by John Studebaker, United States Commissioner of Education and chairman of the Federal Radio Education Committee, containing a set of criteria for what constitutes a good program for children. In the opinion of the writer, it still contains the best set of criteria available for children's programs. In his introduction Dr. Studebaker says,

> It has not been difficult to get agreement that children's radio programs should enrich childhood experience, but just how the purpose

should be achieved and in what specific directions radio should attempt
the enrichment process, are questions that continue to challenge the
broadcaster, the script writer, the parent, and the teacher. [4]

One of the sources for these criteria was a document prepared
by Herta Herzog, *Children and Their Leisure Time Listening
to Radio,* which summarizes the published research on children's programs and their listening habits. [5] This was done at
the request of the Radio Council on Children's Programs. The
third contribution of the Radio Council was to authorize a survey of children's programs which was being aired by local
stations and community groups throughout the country. [6]

A. B. C. Network Programs

In 1942 when the Red and the Blue Networks were separated
the Blue Network became the American Broadcasting Company,
making a special effort in the children's program field. In 1943,
at the meeting on children's programs at the Institute for Education by Radio, Grace Johnsen, director of women's and children's programs for A. B. C. , described the new Saturday programs:

> *Little Blue Playhouse,* a series of weekly plays based on American
> history, into which are woven stories of persons who, through their
> courage and initiative, contributed something really fine or heroic
> to the growth of our country; *Land of the Lost,* a magical kingdom
> under the sea to which everything that has ever been lost on earth
> eventually finds its way; *The Sea Hound,* produced in cooperation with
> the Office of the Coordinator of Inter-American Affairs, for the pur-
> pose of creating desirable attitudes toward our Latin American neigh-
> bors. [7]

Grace Johnsen then pointed out the new approach to the emphasis on the adventure serials:

> *Hop Harrigan,* designed to stimulate air-mindedness; *Terry and the
> Pirates,* locale in China, and centered around favorite characters
> of comic strip, pointed to increase our knowledge and understanding
> of Chinese life and to deepen our sympathy for China's great strug-
> gle; *Dick Tracy,* best known detective of comic strips, used to give
> young listeners an understanding of the menace of black markets in
> our war effort; *The Lone Ranger,* the modern Robin Hood. [8]

Local Programs

From 1937 on it was increasingly evident that new and fresh ideas in children's programming were coming from local groups—in the field of children's programs—working with the local station management, particularly the management that was sensitive to and interested in community needs. These groups represented children's theatre personnel that began to see radio as an extension of their work with and for children; librarians who saw radio as a possible bridge to a greater interest in children's books; civic theatres; and high school, college, and university drama departments with special interest in children's theatre.

Local radio planning for children was an extension of community planning and usually needed the combination of several groups in order to attain the best results. It was evident from the first that any local attempt had to compete with network programming. One of the earliest programs (1933) coming out of a children's theatre group was "Christopher and His Friends," which ran for a year on a local station in San Francisco and was part of the activities of the Children's Theatre of the San Francisco Junior League. This program was a far cry from one which appeared some ten years later—again the project of the San Francisco Junior League, but professionally written and produced—called "California Stepping Stones." The dramatized material in this program had special significance for the schools of the state so that recordings were made available for audio-visual libraries.

Probably the local program most frequently developed was the weekly dramatization of children's stories. Since 1937 AJLA has maintained a radio script library from which scripts can be obtained for local use on payment of a small royalty. [9] "Reading Is Fun," from Portland, Oregon, began in 1935 and remained on the air until 1953, jointly produced by station KGW, the Multnomah County Library, and the Portland Junior League. The prime objective of the program was to stimulate an interest in reading, and the over-all proof of its success was that over the years the Multnomah County Library was to order forty extra copies of each book presented on the series. [10] Another field of local programming has been music—dramatization of the lives of great musicians such as *Up and Down the Scales*, a series from Salt Lake City which also won recognition at the Institute for Education by Radio and Television in 1948. [11] This series has been recorded for use by groups throughout the country.

Children's Theatre groups gradually introduced classes in radio writing and techniques and presented radio series over local stations. The Palo Alto Children's Theatre presented "Pudge," the adventures of its mascot, "the liveliest cocker spaniel that ever wagged a stubby tail—and who has more friends than any dog you know because he's part of the Children's Theatre in the Palo Alto Community Center." This was an interesting combination—a children's theatre, a sponsor, and a radio program—and the revenue from the program bought the theatre new equipment which it needed. In 1948-50 the Junior Theatre of the University of Washington also presented weekly dramatized stories over a commercial station. Each program was recorded and made available to sixteen other stations throughout the state, sponsored by Seattle Junior Programs, the School of Drama of the University, and the Communications Department.

In 1940 Dorothy Lewis visited 372 stations in 168 key cities in thirty-nine states for her survey of children's programming over the country. She found that 12 per cent of children's programs were transcribed, 48 per cent were national, and 40 per cent produced by local organizations. [12] Of that 40 per cent, comparatively few were of high artistic quality but at least there was a field for experimentation. The problem that met the local groups was to find adequate talent and production help. The members of the station staff in many instances were doubling in several jobs and the groups were expected to bring in a show all ready for the air. The station was willing to give the local production a chance but was not in a position to work with it and help it develop. Those groups that came from theatre backgrounds of universities and colleges giving training in radio writing and techniques found themselves better equipped to face the problem of fitting into the tempo and situation of the commercial station. In both the educational and commercial station, excellence of performance was largely dependent on the director's interest in the production.

The forties saw the steady decline of the local dramatic show and the development of new program patterns. The pattern of the children's disc jockey show began to develop with the increase in the number of children's records. In 1950 an hour's show from Seattle called "King's Three Ring Circus" won a first award at the Fourteenth American Exhibit of Educational Radio Programs at the Institute for Education by Radio in Columbus, with the citation:

> For a program which embraces all the desirable elements of sensitive planning and production to insure the best in listening experience and motivation for children in a wide age span. Ingredients include delightful music, drama, suspense, news for children, with an appropriate moral interwoven throughout the script—skilled use of available records must have kept the costs relatively modest. Here is a program which reflects an understanding and a sympathy for the needs of children and an ability to meet those needs with sophisticated entertainment at its best.

On the heels of this program came, from Cincinnati, an hour program which ABC carried first as "No School Today" and later as "Big Jon and Sparky." Through the use of Sparky, many ways of listener participation were devised. There was excellent selection of recordings, and the whole program reflected the respect with which the author and principal character, Big Jon, regarded his child audience. About the time of the development of the children's disc jockey show, a number of transcribed dramatized series were made available by national organizations. One of the first moves in this direction was the release of six of the Dupont Cavalcade of America programs to the Girl Scouts for local broadcasting over the country. Not only were these programs released for airing but all the Dupont advertising message was removed and a Girl Scout message dubbed in.

In 1944 the first thirteen of the "Books Bring Adventure" series were released by AJLA to any group over the country for use on a local station.[13] In 1947 the "Books Bring Adventure" series received a special George Foster Peabody citation, the first time that award had recognized a recorded series. About the same time, the Joint Religious Radio Committee of the National Council of Churches of Christ put out the "All Aboard for

Adventure" series which won the citation in 1949 "For a religious program tailored to the needs and interests of children
and presented with the skill necessary to win their enthusiastic
attention. "[14] This series was particularly well received because there had been a dearth of children's programs in the
religious field.

The Future

With the advent of television, the responsibility for children's radio programs reverts to the local station (which means
the local group or organization), or to the transcribed series,
or to student planning in the educational stations. Present-day
patterns of broadcasting have to be studied. The tendency to
have as little talking as possible on the local station should be
taken into consideration. There is always room for ideas and
imagination. A thorough knowledge of music in general and
children's records in particular, as well as of children's literature, offers an excellent background for this field. Radio
is very much alive, but willingness to experiment and change
patterns is needed by anyone who is trying to get a chance to
develop an idea. There are still many untapped fields in children's interests—and to try out an idea on radio is not as costly
as on television. Radio has come a long way and has seen many
changes—and the future looks promising.

Television Enters the Living Room

Television was more readily recognized as a new medium,
with attributes of its own, than was radio. Television was
accepted almost immediately as a guest in the living room,
and thereby its intimate quality and its social responsibility
also early accepted—the cost first of all to the family, which
meant that some time would elapse before there was more
than one set per family. Unlike radio programs, therefore,
television programs had to be shared. The cost of production
was known to the industry from the start, with the need for
greatly increased technical crews. This was to be true for
local as well as network stations, unless the station ran solely

on network and film. These high costs were bound to be reflected in programming, where the sponsor was interested in the number reached for dollar spent. Television also opened a door to new writers, artists, and producers. The fact that this was a new industry has continued to exert influence from the top executives on down. Although some of its patterns are remade from radio most program planners have not come from radio to television.

It is hard to realize the overlapping of the radio and television fields. In August of 1939 the first children's program, "Madge Tucker's Children," was telecast on the New York station of the National Broadcasting Company. At this same time, on radio, Madge Tucker was producing "Coast to Coast on a Bus" and "Our Barn"—all three programs performed by children. After the war, in 1947, the first contributions to the children's field by network stations were "Howdy Doody" (N. B. C.)—now in its twelfth year—and "Scrapbook: Junior Edition" (C. B. S.). By 1949 these, plus "Kukla, Fran and Ollie" (N. B. C.) and "Lucky Pup" were carried on the New York-to-Chicago cable.

Television Code and Criteria

By 1952 the television industry had drawn up and adopted a Television Code—which in 1959 is in its fifth edition. The responsibility of programming for children is stressed in the preamble of the code as well as in the section detailed to children themselves.

Television and all who participate in it are jointly accountable to the American people for the special needs of children. . . . It is not enough that only those programs which are intended for viewing by children shall be suitable to the young and immature. Television is responsible for insuring that programs of all sorts which occur during the times of day when children may normally be expected to be viewing shall exercise care.

The code then lists and defines six areas. [15]

In 1956 a set of criteria and program suggestions, "Television for Children," was published by the Foundation for

Character Education, Boston.[16] It was the outgrowth of a three-day planning conference of thirty-four participants chosen—for their experience, present work, and interest in the project—from commercial and educational television personnel, school personnel, national organization members interested in child development and education, social scientists, and professional educators experienced in research and educational planning. The booklet is concerned with the 10 to 15 per cent of all television program broadcasts that are especially produced for, or selected to meet the interests of, children from two to twelve, ". . . a disturbingly wide range but an inevitable one if television must reach always for the largest possible audience with all of its programming." *Television for Children* endeavors to give some insight into the child's actual world and provide television producers, managers, and parents with a more realistic map against which they may check present children's programs; suggest fresh opportunities for program material and creative techniques; and perhaps alleviate for parents and educators some fears about television by summarizing what is known of its effects.

New Fields in Television

One of the first things that became evident with the coming of television into the home was the fact that children were attracted to it at a much earlier age than they had been to radio. Radio people, network and local, had been reluctant to plan programs for the preschool primary group, feeling they were not a large enough audience. Luckily, the success of "Ding Dong School," with Miss Frances, occurred comparatively early in television programming. Because of its success in the Chicago area it became available on the network in almost record time. The greatest benefit from its success was its demonstration of the need for programming for this age group, a success which in turn gave courage and incentive to the local station to develop other formats in this area. The five-day-a-week, half-hour program "Wunda Wunda" created and performed by Ruth Prins on KING-TV in Seattle is one example. This program, now in its sixth year, won the coveted George Foster Peabody award for the outstanding local children's program for 1957 with the citation, "Wunda Wunda features well chosen world-wide story material, songs, and action games integrated with highly imaginative musical background. All segments of this delightful and wholesome series lend themselves to indirect teaching of manners, attitudes, speech and better human relations."

Television has also opened wide a door to the puppetry program. "Kukla, Fran and Ollie" which originated in Chicago set high standards of subtle manipulation as well as program content. The warm, human relationship within the puppet group won a place in the hearts of adults as well as children. Puppetry programs have been added to local programming both by film and live production. "Bible Stories," told for children, and distributed by the National Council of Churches of Christ in the U.S.A., [17] was created by Mabel and Leslie Beaton, with David Pritchard as puppet master. Not only is this one of the fine examples of artistic performance, but it is one of the very few available programs for children in the religious field.

Network Dramatic Programs for Children

On April 24, 1949, "Mr. I. Magination," planned and produced by the Columbia Broadcasting System and featuring Paul Tripp, went on the air as a sustaining program. In 1950 this program won a first award and the following citation at the Institute for Education by Radio and Television, "For the skillful blending of education and entertainment; for a lack of condescension in dramatizing literary classics and original stories for young viewers." "Mr. I. Magination" was an expensive program but it was on the air for three years, during nine months of which time it was sponsored. It was also made available—by the network and by kinescopes—to other parts of the country. There was some effort on the part of the viewing audience to keep it on the air but this was not enough. Then, too, the audience rating did not justify its continuance in the eyes of the network's program department. This cancellation points up the vital role which groups interested in children's programs can and must play. A case in point is "Captain Kangaroo," the

C. B. S. 's program for the preschool and primary child. Strong public opinion kept the program going just as it was about to be taken from the air for seeming lack of support.

A second dramatic series that should be remembered in the comparatively early days of television was the Children's Theatre Series, written and directed by Charlotte Chorpenning and carried by N. B. C. as a summer replacement in 1951. It was sponsored and came out of Chicago on the then existing cable. This series opened with "Tom Sawyer" and included "Midas," "Jack-and-the-Beanstalk," "Aladdin," and others. It is regrettable that there are no kinescopes of these experimental productions for they showed one of our great writers and directors struggling with the limitations and opportunities of a new medium. The series also showed the medium's demand from the performers in character portrayal.

Since these two series we have had to look to special productions geared to family viewing for a television children's theatre experience. One of the first of these was the production of "Sara Crewe: The Little Princess," on Studio One, in 1952. It was one of the first network programs which pointed up to libraries and book stores the demand which the television performance engenders for the book. Omnibus has given us "Johnny Tremaine," one of the comparatively few uses of recently written material. N. B. C. in 1955 gave us "Peter Pan," which still holds the record for commanding the largest percentage of the television sets of the country, 66. 1 per cent— a viewing audience of 67, 300, 000. The Rogers and Hammerstein "Cinderella," televised by C. B. S. in 1957, actually played to 72, 246, 000, the largest audience ever to view a single television performance. This latter, however, was only 60. 6 per cent of all the sets. [18] These two figures, of course, mean family viewing.

It is sobering to think of these figures in comparison with the probable audience reached throughout the country by our combined effort in children's theatre during, say, the last twenty years. On the other hand, it is heartwarming when we think of the children reached for the first time in remote areas with the magic of the theatre, for these same statistics tell us that every area in the United States is now covered by television and that 84 per cent of the homes of the country have television sets. In the last two years these children's classics have been offered: *The Pied Piper, Ali Baba and the Forty Thieves, Hansel and Gretel, Pinocchio, The Prince and the Pauper, Huck Finn, Aladdin, Beauty and the Beast, Rumpelstiltskin, The Chinese Nightingale, The Legend of Sleepy Hollow, Dick Whittington, The Land of Green Ginger, Hans Brinker, The Nutcracker Ballet, Little Women, The Emperor's New Clothes, Swiss Family Robinson, Amahl and the Night Visitors.* We may not always agree with the manner of presentation, such as the turning of *Little Women* into a musical, or with the changes that have been introduced into the story, but no one can deny that this is basically good material. Reports from around the country show that children have not just enjoyed programs passively—they have been challenged by them. In an article in a recent TV Guide, Alice Norton of the Denver Public Library says, "We at the Denver Public Library feel that television stimulates rather than competes with reading. As a result of the television presentation of *Little Women* all our copies of the book have been borrowed. The Shirley Temple series has sparked new interest in fairy tales. *The Legend of Sleepy Hollow* sat on our shelves unread until it appeared on television, and our *Johnny Tremaines* and *Robin Hoods* are now threadbare."[19]

It can, of course, be pointed out that these special performances are sprinkled in a sea of daily programs of violence and mediocrity. This is partly true, but I firmly believe that the constructive approach is best in the long run. I agree with Josette Frank, of the Child Study Association, who says, "Neither censorship nor codes will suffice to give us fine children's programs on the air and the television screen. What is needed is the development of a young audience educated in appreciation and the enlistment and encouragement of the best creative efforts of fresh and imaginative producers in the interests of children."[20] Here is where the home and the school both need to play a part. The teaching of an appreciation of radio and television is just beginning. We have for years taught regard for literature. We have made a start in awakening the critical perception of young people toward motion pictures, but there is much to be done in helping them to develop keener evaluation

which will lead to greater selectivity. The teacher who is
familiar with the child's favorite listening and viewing can
develop discussion in the classroom which in turn leads to
more critical viewing and listening.

Local Programming for Children

Local programming falls into two main categories: film and
live studio. Of these the simplest, production-wise, is film,
with a local personality as master of ceremonies. This type
of program is to be found on station after station. The master
of ceremonies may be a singing cowboy, a sea captain, a clown,
a space pilot—and the setting may be the clubhouse, the shack,
the circus tent. Certain activities may be developed around
the "emcee" and his "hangout," but the main body of the program is taken up by film. Western films have been released
from the vaults of minor Hollywood studios and have been cut
and edited for television, and some new films are being produced. The market is flooded with ancient cartoon comedies of
the silent days, to which musical sound tracks have been added.
These are repeated over and over and children never seem
to tire of them. Disney, in his "Mickey Mouse Club," has, of
course, produced for children. The odd thing seems to be that
children resent the repetition of the high-quality Disney cartoons but will sit through dozens of repeats of the crude, ancient cartoons of doubtful taste which defy an editing job. The
problem that confronts the would-be producer of a live program is that the cheapest, easiest to produce, children's program is one of this type, and it also is the easiest to sell because it always draws a good rating.

What then is the recourse of the group vitally interested in
this field of programming, the group with experience in the
children's theatre field? Up to this time, plays produced for
the stage have been seen on television, or at least portions of
them, largely for promotion purposes. This presents many
problems: scripts must be changed, action reblocked, and
settings and costumes altered. There have been a few experiments over the country where scripts have been written primarily for television and the production has been staged for television alone. Unfortunately, kinescopes or films were not made

from these productions and there has been no way to evaluate them.

Both educational and commercial stations face the same problem with dramatic presentations: time for rehearsal in and out of the studio, and time particularly for complete camera rehearsal. Not only is this costly, particularly in the commercial station, but it does not fit into the regular program schedule. The local live show is not, generally speaking, a scripted show. It follows an outline and uses an ad lib technique which takes advantage of the intimate quality of the medium. The producer-director, working from his outline and with his knowledge of the content of the program, performs a truly creative job with his camera shots as the program unfolds. The rehearsal time before the show is spent in lighting, dressing the set, and doing a varying type of "dry run" (rehearsal without hot cameras). The dramatic, dance, or music programs upset this normal pattern. They call for a definite outline of shots and a complete rehearsal.

Educational Station Program Resources

Programs for leisure-time viewing have been developed by educational stations over the country. Many have tried new formats but none has attempted the dramatic format. "Children's Corner" was carried on N. B. C. for almost a year, and "The Finder" became "Let's Take a Trip" on the C. B. S. network. Some of these programs are part of the educational network and available for use on commercial stations by arrangement. At present, the Radio and Television Educational Center is experimenting with a new five-day-a-week framework for children's programs. Into the framework will go programs especially commissioned from various educational stations. Seven cities are to experiment with this program during 1959 and 1960.

Future

What possibilities are there for the future? We may be able to discover or develop new drama techniques, such as Chamber Theatre, that can fit into the schedules of the local station with greater ease. We can think in terms of simpler formats more suited to the medium. With the greater development of video tape we may be able to encourage experimentation in thirty-minute dramas planned especially for the medium in various centers; this experimentation might lead eventually to the possibility of a taped series which could be circulated by the educational network or used on commercial stations. In this way, material which will never be used in network production could find its way to wider exposure. This type of experimentation could also be directed more especially to certain age groups, not necessarily directed to the entire family.

How can we make the most of these communication arts by which children live and learn and grow? We can help children to be critical and choose with discrimination what they see and hear. We can share viewing and listening experiences with them. We must encourage the efforts in behalf of children by networks, local groups or stations, and national organizations; we must be alert to the changes and opportunities offered by both radio and television and cease to attribute to these mediums all the misdemeanors in children and youth. Let us accept television as part of our design for living, as we have radio in the past, and try to gain the greatest values from this appealing medium.

9 Films as a Medium for Children's Theatre

Burdette Fitzgerald and Ernest Rose ✒

Investigation into the mass medium of motion pictures for children's entertainment reveals that there are no films produced especially for juvenile audiences in the United States except by educational producers. American film producers, depending upon the number of paid admissions for financial success, are interested in pleasing the mass of viewers, not a minority.

Present Status of Film Producers

There exists no film movement either parallel or comparable to the children's theatre tradition which for many years has flourished in this country. The films that have appealed to children have been those that were designed with a much broader audience in mind and with inevitable compromises made in an effort to please everyone. The fact that children enjoy them is only incidental to the producer's motive of reaching the largest possible audience with the most paid admissions. As Joseph Reddy of the Walt Disney Productions states, "We do not make pictures here designed exclusively for children's patronage. Our pictures are all aimed to attract the family audience. I don't think any producer could remain in business if he made pictures only for the small fry. "[1] An effort is made to bring pictures to children, however, by means of the Saturday afternoon children's matinee at the neighborhood theatre. The program generally consists of a serial, six cartoons, a double feature Western, and many times a reissued horror film preview.

However, the motion picture industry has recognized the worth and popularity of children's classics. During the past ten years commercial producers from time to time have made available productions of classics including outstanding films of *David Copperfield, Little Women, Heidi,* and *Treasure Island.*

National Concern for Films for Children and Youth

The Children's Film Library was created in September, 1946, under the presidency of Marjorie Granger Dawson. It is directed by the National Children's Film Library Committee, comprised of twenty members. This major committee, the majority of which are women volunteers, is then divided into film selection committees. They represent such national, state, and local organizations as American Association of University Women; American Library Association; American Legion Auxiliary; National Society of the Daughters of the American Revolution; National Federation of Music Clubs; General Federation of Women's Clubs; National Board of Review; National Congress of the Parent-Teachers Association; National Council of Jewish Women; Protestant Motion Picture Council; Brooklyn Motion Picture Council; Cleveland Public Libraries; Long Island Federation of Women's Clubs; *Parents' Magazine;* Parents' Motion Picture Group of Greater New York; Queens Motion Picture Council; Schools Motion Picture Committee; Staten Island Motion Picture Council; United Daughters of the Confederacy; Vermont School System, among others.

These committees are assisted by an advisory council made up of child psychologists and other specialists in the field of mental health. Their purpose is to select films suitable for children of eight to twelve years and to make this list available to theatre managers who run Saturday matinees for children. More recently this has broadened to include other special children's programs, such as the Los Angeles Junior Programs which includes one film designed for children's entertainment in its annual series of eight events.

Pictures chosen by these committees for their entertainment

qualities and for their educational, moral, and social value
are retained in each film exchange area at the end of the general
release, as library subjects. Newly released films are obtained
directly from the distributors.

The committee does not advocate the making of recreational
films for American children above the age of eight years. However, the committee does suggest the need for sixteen milli-
meter feature films and short subjects for nontheatrical showing to children under the age of eight years. In a report of the
UNESCO Survey the committee states: "The children at this
age should not be exposed unaccompanied to theatrical pro-
grammes because too many of the ingredients of the Motion Picture experiences are frightening and bewildering to children
in this age group."[2]

Various other state and local organizations have shown concern for the selection of motion pictures for children. The
Catholic Legion of Decency publishes weekly a recommended
list of approved films. A *Playtime* service for parents was
an outgrowth of a five-year-study by the Seattle Junior Programs, Inc. In New York City, a "Cinema 16" has been established which presents a series of films designed especially for
children. This closely resembles the distribution of children's
films in other countries through the Cinema Clubs. Many of
the films used are from the "Club Cendrillon" in France.

Interest in Children's Films by Commercial Producers

While the motion picture industry itself has failed to recognize the possibilities of film production specifically designed
to entertain the young, and the National Film Library Association does not recommend the practice, it should be noted
that films for children occupy the major efforts of more than
a thousand film producers throughout the United States. These
people comprise the fast-growing ranks of the educational film
makers, whose annual output today dwarfs the combined product of all the Hollywood studios during their most productive
period. More and more of these new film makers are coming
to understand that "to educate the man, you must touch the
heart." Producers are learning that the fundamental elements

which hold attention in the Hollywood film can be effectively applied in other films as well, and that good, basic dramatic structure is an essential element in the teaching film.

Summary

There is no specifically designed theatre for children in moving pictures. However, since there are more than a thousand film producers whose major efforts are in educational film for children, it is recommended that cooperative study and research be made. Educational film producers need to recognize that the dramatic structure which holds the attention of adults in Hollywood films is essential in filming for children and that combined efforts of educational and Hollywood producers are desirable. Benefits to both groups of producers as well as to children's cinema should result.

10 Children's Theatre in Puppetry

George Latshaw ✒

Since puppetry in America is largely an entertainment for children, it is important to know the background of the art. Many of the traditional principles and practices have continued in the professional and semi-professional puppet theatres, though a number of changes have resulted from sociological and technological developments. As we know the background we may consider what directions of development may be advisable or expected in the future.

Traditional Practices

Although puppetry was an art native to the American Indian, it reached the world of entertainment in the United States as an import from Europe, bringing with it the traditional Punch and Judy, folk and fairy tales, and the variety numbers of the European theatre. "In repertory and technique the shows were largely traditional, transmitted by example from generation to generation."[1] At the end of the nineteenth century when amateurs had begun to invade the field, professional techniques of puppetry became carefully guarded secrets. However, puppetry as it is practiced in America today owes its revival to several groups who discovered technical material from European masters and disseminated it freely through example and the written word.

The dawn of the puppet revival was heralded in Europe in 1907 with the publication of Gordon Craig's "The Actor and the Uber-marionette" in *The Mask*. Increased interest in puppet creation and performance

75

throughout Europe followed. In 1914 and 1915 the influence of this revival reached three major cities in the United States: New York, Chicago, and Cleveland. The revival was no doubt aided by William Patten's article in the *New York Times* of May 4, 1913, "The Old Puppet Show Is to Be Restored." Mr. Patten urged "puppet shows in the schools and playgrounds, in the theatres and art galleries."[2]

In 1914 Londoner Tony Sarg found work as an illustrator in New York City and migrated to America. For the amusement of friends he frequently produced puppet shows in his home. A guest at one of the private showings was Winthrop Ames whose plans to bring the Munich Marionette Theatre to America were frustrated by war. He persuaded Sarg to undertake a professional production which was presented for a short season at the Neighborhood Playhouse in New York in November, 1917. A second performance followed at the Punch and Judy Theatre in April and May of 1919, and the show subsequently toured Detroit, Cleveland, and Boston.[3]

Except for the first performance, Sarg was not a manipulator of his puppets but acted as designer and supervisor, training others to perform the plays and frequently importing guest directors. Sarg's major contributions to the field, therefore, were bringing a sense of theatre to the world of puppetry and preparing others to work in the medium.[4] A New York contemporary of Sarg was Remo Bufano whose interests lay in the experimental approach. He was frequently called upon to create all manner of special effects, including puppets for the Walrus and Carpenter scene in Eva Le Gallienne's *Alice in Wonderland*. He also made life-sized puppets of Don Quixote, Sancho Panza, and Pedro's Boy for use with regular-sized puppets in a 1924 production of deFalla's opera at Town Hall, ten-foot puppets for a production in 1931 of Stravinsky's *Oedipus*, and a host of other unusual figures.[5]

At the same time that puppetry was coming alive in New York, its renaissance in Chicago was being effected by Ellen Van Volkenburg, wife of Maurice Brown, director of the Chicago Little Theatre. She went to Munich in 1915 to study puppetry and returned to Chicago to direct two seasons of puppet performances at the Little Theatre from 1915 to 1917. Since her company knew very little about the manipulation of puppets, she rehearsed the puppeteers by having them first act out the play themselves and then imitate the actions with the puppets.[6]

Also in 1915 Raymond O'Neill, director of the Cleveland Playhouse, suggested that puppetry become part of the activity of the theatre. Accordingly Helen Haiman Joseph produced and directed a shadow play, *Seven at a Blow*. The work of Mrs. Joseph at the Playhouse from 1915 to 1917 had a pronounced effect upon the use of puppets in education.[7] Winifred Mills, a teacher, and Louise Dunn, a museum director of education, wrote the first comprehensive book on puppet making.[8] Mrs. Joseph herself was stimulated to write the first English history of puppets.[9] Mrs. Joseph and Perry Dilley of New York were among the first puppeteers in the United States to forsake the string marionette for the hand puppet. It was not until the late thirties that an English hand puppeteer, Walter Wilkinson, visited the United States with his Pepp Show and influenced puppeteers like Burr Tillstrom, bringing on a real shift to the use of fist puppets.

Since 1925 the Association of Junior Leagues of America, Inc., has been important in the development of puppetry. The Portland, Oregon, league sponsored the first marionette show in 1925 followed in 1928 by similar sponsorship in Chattanooga. In 1929 the Roanoke league imported a case of hand puppets from France.[10] Other league groups have used puppets of various kinds to interpret civic programs and the work of community agencies. Recent statistics compiled by the national office of the league indicate extensive work of this group in puppetry. In 1957-58 there were eighty-eight Junior Leagues active in puppetry with a total of ninety-one projects involving 1,654 members in 140 productions. These shows resulted in 2,831 performances presented to a total audience of 426,752. Additional audiences were reached by one league which presented its entire program on television and by thirty-one leagues which used television to supplement their regular performances. Of these active groups seventy-one used hand puppets; eight used marionettes; eight used hand puppets and marionettes; and one group used magnet puppets. The most popular subjects were fairy tales, following the universal tradition in puppetry.

Although the puppeteers of the twenties and thirties performed for a time in their homes or in rented theatre space, most American puppet companies now are touring groups which have branched out into the road circuit. The puppet touring company developed in the mid-twenties with offshoots from the Tony Sarg troupe and school. Chief among the early groups were Rachel Sewall and Lillian Owen, Bobby Fulton, Harold and Robert Hestwood, Rufus and Margo Rose, Ellen Galpin, The Tatterman Marionettes (William Duncan and Edward Mabley), and the Yale Puppeteers (Harry Burnett, Forman Brown, and Richard Brandon). The thirties found puppetry growing, aided temporarily by the Federal Theatre Project. New companies joined the field: Basil Milovsoroff's Folk Tale Marionettes, The Proctor Puppets, Martin and Olga Stevens, Sue Hastings, Bernard Paul, Robert and Edith Williams, the Kingsland Marionettes, C. Roy Smith, and Franc Still.

While the majority of the groups toured their own plays, there were many which became an advertising medium for business and industrial organizations such as the Good Teeth Council, dairyman's councils, and Sight Savers as well as for department stores. Advertising became an important field for puppets.

The majority of pre-World War II puppeteers used marionettes, although the rod puppet and the hand puppet were becoming important near the end of the thirties. The coming of war in 1939 with the rationing of gasoline seriously affected the touring company, and when television and inflation followed close upon the armistice, many changes were already taking place in the practice of puppetry.

Present Practices

Two major changes have occurred in contemporary puppetry: the supremacy of the marionette has been challenged and the size of the troupe has diminished. Puppeteers who continued to troupe via public transportation during World War II found it easier to transport hand puppets and their stage rather than the complex equipment of a marionette theatre. With the increased expense of salaries it also became important to limit the number of manipulators required and, consequently, many husband-wife teams replaced large touring companies. Now the pup-

peteer spends his winters on the road and his summers creating
the next season's productions. Stories used are largely popular
fairy tales. The puppeteer usually writes his own script, builds
his own puppets, scenery, and backdrops. An occasional enlisting of professional talent does occur. Rufus Rose enlisted
the scriptwriting talents of Martin Stevens for his productions
of *Snow White* and *The Mouse in Noah's Ark*.

Although contemporary professional companies are still
largely marionette teams, the hand puppet has gained increased
prominence with semiprofessional and amateur groups. Rod
puppets are less frequently used and with the important exception of Pauline Benton's Redgate Shadow Players who present
authentic Chinese shadow plays, the shadow figure is virtually
unknown in America. Many of the older touring companies have
ceased to travel and have tried to develop a puppet theatre in
films or television, stimulated by the success of the advertising
show. A 1957 survey of puppet films show that 146 have been
produced throughout the world. While silhouette and shadow
puppets, marionettes, and hand puppets are used in films,
the motion picture has created a puppet type of its own.

Animated puppets are stiff-jointed mannikins which are set up and
photographed on only one frame of a motion picture film. Then the
figures are moved ever so slightly and photographed again. This goes
on until thousands of these single frame pictures have been taken of
the proposed "motion" of a puppet. When these pictures are run through
a motion picture projector, the puppets on the screen seem to move
of their own volition. [11]

Notable among the stop-action (animated) films are the works
of George Pal (The Puppetoons); Leo Bunin's "Alice in Wonderland"; and Michael Meyerberg's "Hansel and Gretel." Martin
Stevens' "The Toymaker" is an excellent example of hand puppet
filming. Beaton's "Spirit of Christmas" and Bil Baird's West-
inghouse "Fun with Numbers" series exemplify the use of marionettes in films. The single American shadow puppet film is
Jero Magon's "Shadowland."[12]

Television lures the puppeteer with a larger audience, personal recognition, and higher pay. In the experimental days
some of the first major television programs were puppet shows:
Burr Tillstrom's "Kukla, Fran and Ollie"; Leo Bunin's "Lucky

Pup"; and the "Howdy Doody Show." Unfortunately few performers had the theatrical training or creative imagination of Burr
Tillstrom to help them sustain the pace of television. Today
many commercial sponsors use the fantasy of puppetry to exploit the child.

The main concern of puppeteers is still one of technology
rather than performance. Colleges and universities have been
teaching puppetry in their art departments for the past twenty-
five years, but where puppetry has occasionally been offered
by theatre departments, it has not been a continuing program.
Two exceptions are the University of Washington, for a number of years sponsor of a touring company presently under
the direction of Aurora Valentinetti; and, more recently, the
University of California at Los Angeles, which in 1955 began
a puppetry program in the theatre department under the direction of Melvyn Helstein. This latter program consists of a two-
semester course dealing primarily with the making of hand
puppets and marionettes and the staging of plays. The course
includes two hours of lecture and four hours of laboratory
weekly and usually attracts six to ten students.

The United States lags seriously behind European and Asian
countries in its recognition of the puppet theatre as a propa-
ganda potential. While most European and South American
countries as well as Iron Curtain nations were represented by
performing companies at the International Doll and Puppet
Festival in Bucharest in 1958, the United States failed to send
a company and was represented officially only because the
Romanian government invited Marjorie Batchelder McPharlin
to serve as judge of the competition. [13]

Two organizations do serve the cause of puppetry. The Puppeteers of America founded in 1937 under the guidance of the
late Paul McPharlin holds an annual festival and workshop for
amateurs and professionals and publishes a bimonthly news
magazine. The puppetry yearbooks of Paul McPharlin, the
only recent historical record of American puppetry, were published by the author and released through the Puppeteers of
America. CTC has begun to take an interest in puppetry as a
theatrical form for children. It has formed a puppetry committee and includes puppet shows and workshops in its annual
conference.

One of the most encouraging steps forward for the puppet theatre is its recognition as a performing art by The Detroit Institute of Arts. Under the direction of its curator of Theatre Arts, Gil Oden, the gallery supports puppetry through the Paul McPharlin collection and archives, through its workshop program for children and adults, and through its commission of experimental work. In March, 1958, it cosponsored with the Detroit Symphony Orchestra a production of Copland's *Billy the Kid* using 9 to 12 foot puppets designed by George Latshaw. A second joint project with puppets designed by Latshaw took place in January, 1959, for the American premiere of Debussy's *La Boîte à Joujoux*.

Summary

Despite many changes in the practice of puppetry, the European tradition remains strong. We are still performing standard fairy tales with traditional types of puppets. American puppeteers have made few original contributions to the field, perhaps because the public is still so amazed that the puppets work that it does not demand better quality in puppet productions. Leaders of the twenties left a heritage of sound theatre technique, but many contemporary puppeteers are art-oriented rather than theatre-oriented with no formal training in showmanship and are slow to recognize themselves as performers.

The trend, though slow, is toward a greater affinity with children's theatre groups and dramatic principles and practices. As good theatre is more and more generally required of the puppet company, there will be a greater recognition of the puppeteer rather than the puppet as the performer. Puppetry has its own devotees who do not look upon constructive criticism with favor. If more knowledgeable theatre people can be interested in puppetry, as they were in the days of Tony Sarg, Ellen Von Volkenburg, and Helen Joseph, the standards can be raised. In this way the art form itself will move on to more mature work.

11 Producing Theatre for Child Audiences

Jed H. Davis 🙰

The production of plays for a child audience is one of the most rewarding experiences a theatre-lover can have. Whether he is a newcomer to the field or a producer well versed in the area of drama the experience is stimulating. Some may accept the rewards without question, but most children's theatre producers, acutely conscious of their brief heritage, hasten to assemble with others of similar inclination, to compare notes, to discuss problems, and to seek solutions which tend to further the progress of the movement as a whole.

This chapter, while it can only examine the surface of children's theatre production problems, is intended to serve as a summary of the major premises which have been advanced for the guidance of those who work in theatre for children. The section is centered on the main problems which are encountered along the way: organizing and managing, selecting plays, directing the actors, designing the scenery and the costumes, acting and publicizing—all in relation to the ultimate receiver, the child audience.

Organization and Management [1]

While the term "children's theatre" is applied to many different kinds of children's theatre organizations in the United States, these may be grouped as either sponsors or producers or both. A single group may function alternately or even simultaneously. The complexity of the structure is directly related to the

82

size of the program, to the number of community agencies involved, and to the degree to which responsibility for the various phases of operation is delegated.

Sponsoring Organizations

An ever-widening variety of civic, social, and educational agencies are choosing children's theatre sponsorship as a means of fostering cultural development within a community. These agencies include PTA or PTA councils, chapters of AAUW and AJLA, associations of elementary principals or school systems themselves, Child Study Clubs, Rotary, Kiwanis, and Lions clubs. Many groups of independent citizens have organized either separately or cooperatively for the purpose of bringing professional or nonprofessional companies to local auditoriums for the delight and stimulation of the community's junior residents. Much depends on how effectively the various responsibilities of sponsorship are carried out. Therefore the following principles and practices are recommended.

Compose the children's theatre committee so that each separate phase of the operation is well covered. A children's theatre chairman is appointed by the president of the parent organization. It is usually the chairman's responsibility to build the membership so that capable persons are in charge of publicity, ticket sales, school liaison, house management, transportation of school children, community relations, and even housing or meals for the visiting company, if these are involved. The chairman should see to it that certain members make arrangements for the stage, for any necessary union help, electrical service, janitors, sound amplification, and dressing room facilities. The local stage crew should be informed of the visiting company's arrival time and the specific staging requirements of the play. The success of the performance may well depend on how efficiently these matters are handled.

The children's theatre chairman must supervise all phases of the operation, yet remain relatively free of details to devote his main efforts to public relations. If possible, the chairman should continue in office more than one year. If a yearly change is a standard policy, a vice chairman should work closely with the chairman to insure continuation of contacts and policies and to carry out improvements.[2]

While setting up complete programs of a season's plays are worthy goals for established organizations, sponsoring a single play is safer for a starting group. It is important to make sure that an initial venture is successful from every point of view and to make sure that a ready appetite is whetted, a demand established. As the need develops, the single-play program can be expanded to include another or other plays in the season.

One of the first signs of an expanding program is evidence of the need to establish an all-community children's theatre board—a group which represents the many agencies in a locality concerned with children's welfare.[3] The board may be either purely advisory or, preferably, it will be an executive body which functions in much the same way as the children's theatre committee. This establishes the community children's theatre as an independent body. The contacts established during the climb to independence are jealously maintained and nurtured as the new corporation embarks on its full-blown children's theatre program.

Sound business management is essential for the stability of a children's theatre program. Although most children's theatre managers do not expect large profits, the continuing balance of income and expenses is no small accomplishment. It requires careful budgeting, progressive planning, and, most important, favorable public relations. A reserve fund on which the group can draw in case of emergency can be built from small seasonal profits or by contributions from parent or allied organizations.[4] The existence of the fund may provide just the reassurance the group needs to begin a healthy expansion of its program. Expense items such as auditorium rentals and attendant service fees and the printing of handbills, posters, newspaper advertising, and tickets, plus any amounts paid to bus companies for children's transportation will swell the costs of sponsorship well beyond whatever fees are paid to the producing group. While bookings may be handled on a "cost-plus" basis, on a flat rate, or by direct subsidy of the sponsor, production costs inevitably run high for well-

mounted plays. Sponsors should plan to balance these costs
with admission prices based on the ability of parents to pay,
the admission price to the local movie, and possibility of large
group attendance through the public schools. [5] The aim of any
children's theatre group is to have wholehearted cooperation
of the public schools in promoting its program; but should this
support be denied, other community resources must be tapped.
The local drug or department store, the library, the museum,
or the art gallery may welcome the sale of tickets.

Good house management provides for children's comfort
and safety. From the time they arrive at the theatre until they
leave, children are under the care of the house manager. They
should be shown quickly to their seats, encouraged to regard
their seats as theirs for the duration of the performance, and
should be allowed neither too much nor too little freedom.
Every effort should be made to assist the players in providing
a thoroughly gratifying theatre experience.

No children's theatre season is complete without an evaluation session. Sponsors should watch performances in the presence of child audiences in order to appraise degrees of success or failure. Care must be exercised lest the presence of
a full house become the only criterion for a satisfactory community response to the children's theatre.

Producing Organizations

The processes of play production are fundamentally the same
when bringing to life a children's theatre script as when working with adult drama; in fact, a large portion of children's
theatres are extensions of established adult theatre programs,
using the same directors, actors, designers, technicians, and
management personnel. Children's theatre producers are
usually obliged to assume some of the responsibilities already
outlined for sponsors because of the need to establish contact
with potential audiences. Children usually cannot undertake to
attend a given performance without the active help of parents,
community leaders, or school administrators. While it is not
necessary to restate the standard organization pattern for the
general production of plays—with all facets of the operation
under the ultimate control of the director—children's theatre

producers have found the following supplementary principles
helpful:

1. It is sometimes better to bring the play to the audience
than to bring the audience to the play. Even though staging
facilities encountered away from the "home" plant may be far
from ideal, the advantages of delegating duties of sponsorship
to a local group may be ample compensation.

2. Explore community resources. Most communities have
one or a number of agencies which may help producers of
children's plays. Bearing in mind that the aim of organization
is to facilitate, not complicate, production, a producer might
logically ally with a community arts group which incorporates
work for the cultural development of children. Likewise, a
museum or gallery may have such a program for which children's theatre would be a logical extension. Settlement houses,
music or drama studios may welcome the active participation
of their youngsters in productions. All of these might be of
assistance in providing child actors as well as in providing a
logical liaison for promotion of the children's theatre.

3. Organizational structure for production should be no more
complex than the situation demands. If the management and
promotion arrangement which exists for a going adult theatre
program is sufficient, there is no need for complicated alli-
ances. Contacts and involvements should be made only for
the purposes of casting, promotion, and public relations. Occasionally an alliance is made which accomplishes some necessary phase of operations such as transportation of children to
the theatre, but the danger of involving too many people in the
production of a play is very real. On the other hand, the organization which depends on the genius of a single person,
however talented, is neither efficient nor safe.

Selection of Plays

Whether a season consists of a single play or a series, a
producer keeps his knowledge of a child audience as the ultimate reference in selecting plays for the season's program.
While features such as suitability for touring, opportunities
to augment the cast, and number of sets may affect the choice

to some extent, these matters are really peripheral to the major question: *will this play satisfy the audience for which it is intended?*

While chronological age is certainly not the only factor determining their needs and preferences, children have been found to respond favorably to the subject matter of plays roughly according to this schedule: those under five (for whom few plays are intended) are interested in realistic situations which they know from their very limited experience; after five, most children begin to show some interest in fantasy characters not too far removed from reality, in kings and queens who had interesting things happen to them; around six or seven, if their sense of security is well enough established, they begin to find delight in classic fairy tales; sometimes, beginning as early as seven or eight, boys find strong interest in adventure and historical figures, the age of nine to eleven being considered the height of this preference; at twelve there is a liking for romanticism of the far away and long ago and this interest continues into adulthood. Thus the transition from child to adult drama is seen to be a smooth progression rather than a definite "stepping" from one interest to the next.

Happily, playwrights are now providing total works of art rather than "fairy tales," "adventure stories," or "romances." Plays of the modern children's theatre repertory, published by reputable firms, more and more contain a mixture of "age appeals." If the presentation takes place in out-of-school hours, the expected range will be considerably broader than for an in-school situation where the age can be controlled by grades. Producers should encourage playwrights to work on scripts founded on local legend, on original and imaginative themes, and on adaptations of unfamiliar as well as familiar stories suitable for the child audience. A number of groups sponsor playwriting contests. Winning scripts are often performed as part of the prize, and frequently these and other originals find their way to the "manuscript table" at annual CTC meetings where they are considered for production. While these methods encourage the writing of plays for children, and do augment the few manuscripts that are distributed privately by authors, the demand for new plays far exceeds the supply. Each pro-

ducer owes it to himself and to children's theatre to seek out
writing talent and guide it in the right direction.

Directing

While bringing to life a children's theatre script is not much
different from producing an adult drama, children's theatre
directors recognize that certain aspects of the process need
special attention if the play is to seize and hold the interest of
the child audience. First of all, a director must see a play
as a child sees it. A director must recognize that the story
is what children have come to see—not a display of histrionic
talent, dance routines, or directorial quirks. As far as children are concerned, a director hardly exists, actors are there
only to tell a story, and staging is important in so far as it
contributes to that story. A director should learn what parts
of the story are most important to children, and this he can
do by studying their behavior during a play as well as their
drawings, letters, and comments following performances. In
this way he can learn which scenes, events, details, or actions
are really important and which should be eliminated. He will
come to recognize that he can put nothing over on a child audience, that children comprise the most demanding audience he
will ever encounter.

Whether he works with children or adults, a director should
choose his actors so that characters are easily and completely
believable. The desired empathic quality is paramount in casting. Children must instinctively dislike the antagonist and want
the protagonist to succeed. While Snow White need not be a
raving beauty, she must exude a goodness which is unmistak-
able to the entire audience. The relative size of actors has a
great deal to do with a character's believability. Even with a
child cast, a short prince has two strikes against him as he
tries to win the princess who is five inches taller.

Children are oriented to action. Both in their own lives and
in plays, children much prefer doing things to talking about
them. Interesting action should seize attention right at the
start and carry the impact of the story. Movement will need
to be more extensive in a children's play than in adult drama.
Imaginative business and patterns of blocking should be in-

corporated to present to a child audience an almost constantly changing stage picture. All movement remains meaningful and fully motivated, nevertheless, as in all drama. A director must provide visual and auditory focus for a child audience. Every effort should be made to direct audience attention to the important sequence, character, bit of action, line, or word. Visually, a director arranges the pictures to emphasize the right thing, eliminating distracting nonessentials, grouping characters into lines of focus, framing and elevating characters of prime importance. He makes sure that actors deliver important speeches to the audience, that important action takes place downstage, that the diction of the actors is precise, and that volume levels are adequate for easy hearing.

The rhythm pattern built into the script should be emphasized by the director. Alternating tensions and releases are the means by which children's attention spans are accommodated within the dramatic framework. Directors should make sure sequences intended to arouse strong emotions are heightened in the playing, and those intended to release tension are played in a more relaxed manner. Neither scenes of tension nor scenes of release should be prolonged beyond the endurance of the audience. Overstimulation will result if excitement is undue, and a completely lost audience may result if quiet periods are long. The desired builds and releases can be greatly enhanced in children's plays by judicious use of musical background. Children are quick to respond to music underlining the emotional content of a scene or forming a bridge between successive scenes. Music introduced at a given point may strengthen release spots just enough to keep an audience involved in the story. In general, a lively pacing is best for most children's plays, but one can easily carry this principle to extremes and leave an audience far behind. A pace that is too slow will cause children to lose patience, and one that is too fast will cause them to miss the dialogue and its meaning. Each play should be gauged for its ability to sustain a fast or medium tempo, and scenes within a play should be interestingly varied to contribute to the general tension-release pattern.

Smoothly coordinated elements of production will contribute a memorable theatre experience for the youngsters. All phases

must work together with apparent effortlessness; and inter-
missions, as brief as possible, should be periods both of relaxation and of preparation. Children should not be expected
to forgive amateurish production flaws, mistaken cues, late
entrances, noisy scene shifting, or substandard stage management. The director is the one who sets the highest of standards
for his cast and production personnel. Anything less than their
best is unacceptable.

Designing and Technical Production [6]

The establishment and maintenance of high technical production standards has been a cause for which every children's
theatre leader has pleaded since the beginnings of the movement; and high technical standards remain one of the declared
purposes of CTC. [7] The following principles of design in children's theatre, based on characteristic responses of children
to artistic material, should serve as guideposts to an ever-
rising standard of technical production.

Visual elements—sets, lights, costumes, and properties—
assume a degree of importance second only to that of the script
and actors. Children attend very carefully to every detail of
staging. Their drawings are mercilessly accurate. Producers
cannot assume that shoddy methods will be acceptable because
children won't know the difference. If children's theatre is to
help cultivate the tastes of the coming generation, then only
the most artistic concepts should be allowed. Visual elements
perform four specific functions in children's theatre. [8] They
document by showing the children where, when, and under what
circumstances the action is taking place. They function dy-
namically as "machine for theatre," to help actors to tell a
story smoothly and effectively. They evoke images, ideas, and
emotions consistent with the mood of the play being presented.
And they compensate for children's unmet psychological needs,
for their uncertain comprehension of language, and even for a
child actor's small stature or relatively unskilled technique.

A play itself and the audience should determine the style
of production. Subject matter of the play, its tone, its structure, and style of its dialogue should be considered first in
deciding scenic style rather than the existence of stock sets

or a preconceived idea of what style is "best for children's theatre." Most presentational styles (stylization, expressionism, theatricalism, constructivism, and formalism) assume a high degree of artistic sophistication on the part of viewers for appreciation or even for correct interpretation. Children prefer representational styles (toward realism) when offered a choice.[9] Designers must realize that there are limits to the extent to which settings can be simplified if they are to remain satisfying to children. While simplification is necessary, usually, to accommodate the very extensive staging requirements of children's plays, enough of the settings must remain to fulfill the functions already mentioned. During the years in which they attend children's theatre, children either have already developed or are developing sensitivity to the standard principles of composition which are important in any art form. Both for education and for aesthetic satisfaction, therefore, it is important that these standard principles be applied to children's theatre design.

A relatively free use of bright color in scenic and costume design should probably be reserved for audiences of young children, a basically realistic relationship between objects and their colors should hold for audiences of the middle grades, and subtle color effects will be appreciated only by the older children. Warm, contrasting color combinations are apparently preferred by children of all ages. Costume colors should, in general, be the brightest in the stage picture, key properties next, and backgrounds should remain the least bright to maintain proper emphasis. Since color is likely to be the most noticeable element of composition, its use in design calls for the highest artistry.

Disproportionate masses can emphasize the relative importance of objects from the child's point of view, as well as compensate for the size of child actors. Key properties may sometimes need to be enlarged beyond pure realism to stress their part in the story. Mass and space complement each other, and the combined effect is critical as the designer attempts to convey scenes of intimacy or grandeur. An unmodified forty-foot proscenium is not likely to be convincing as the frame for a woodcutter's cottage.

Flexibly controlled lighting can do more than any single

element to project the essential quality of a script. Quietly and unobtrusively, light reveals the three-dimensionality of both actors and plastic scenic units. It alternately reveals and obscures various portions of the playing area, it subtly focuses children's attention where it should go, and it enhances or neutralizes pigment colors of sets, costumes, or properties. Beyond the array of spectacular effects often required in children's plays, lights quietly change moods with the actors and seem to live the life of the play.

Costuming [10]

Costuming a children's play is, again, no different from costuming an adult play. The costumer cannot be content with turning out "cute little outfits." He must recognize that his audience is a critical one, possessed of a surprising amount of worldly knowledge in spite of its limited experience.

If a play is concerned with an historical character or period, the costumes should be as accurate as sound stage practices permit. The educational purposes of children's theatre dictate that elements of historical design which have appeal to children be used consistently. Some exaggeration of detail is permissible in order to emphasize a certain childlike concept; but such distortion should not reach the level of stylization which usually ends up being an adult idea of "what children like" rather than the child's idea. A costumer must strive to maintain the integrity of the playwright's creation while trying to visualize the characters as a child would know them to be or accept them as being. Ask children to describe their favorite characters in order to discover how children visualize them. Children are imaginative, but they are even stronger realists. Costumers, too, must keep their creative imaginations within the realm of a child's reality. Unquestionably, a child's visualization of a character could be strongly influenced by illustrations which accompany his stories. Occasionally a story is so successfully illustrated that the artist's visualization becomes inseparable from the character as the author conceived him to be. In these cases the costume designer may be safer in duplicating the illustrations unless he feels that his own conceptions can be made equally believable.

Costumers can capitalize on children's nonconventional color harmony sense. As yet unspoiled by adult prejudices and conventions in the use of colors in combination, children delight in strong color and quite fantastic mixtures. Contrasts should be sharp, but balance should be employed; families and related characters should be tied together through repetition of certain colors. The use of color to focus attention is one of the costumer's chief responsibilities.

Evil characters should be costumed in accord with childlike concepts rather than "watered down." Witches costumed (and portrayed) as funny old women, ogres and giants as silly men, and evil fairies as somewhat unhappy sprites are not likely to satisfy the child's need to experience the delicious fear which these characters are intended to provoke. While adults seem very concerned about arousing serious fright in an audience, children themselves will usually contribute more lurid details about external features of these characters than most adults would consider decorous. Costumers have an obligation to capture and project as much of a childlike concept as seems consistent with the treatment of that character in the script.

Standard construction and good materials should be used for costumes in children's plays. It takes little longer to build a costume to last than to throw one together for a single performance. One which is made well can be altered and reused. The building of an adequate stock is the goal of economy-minded costumers who must make each hour and every nickel count.

Acting

A major portion of responsibility for bringing a children's play vividly and effectively to life ultimately rests with the actors. In preparing their roles and in presenting the finished production they must be concerned with meeting special requirements of their audience. Studies indicate that in his experiences with daily living the developing child is highly suggestible and is lacking in ability to distinguish clearly the external origin of stimuli that nevertheless may touch the core of his personality. Further, inner needs and tensions may lead to his indulging in uncontrolled behavior. In his experi-

ences with literature and in his own dramatic play, a child
has been found to surrender to a very real illusion. These
tendencies can be assumed to operate when a child is a member
of the theatre audience. A story brought to life upon the stage
by living actors supported by technical aids to theatrical production can be expected to evoke maximum response from a
child audience. It becomes the actors' responsibility to assure
that children's experiences in the theatre will be aesthetically
sound rather than merely superficially exciting, or, at the
other extreme, deeply frightening. An actor's attitude toward
the playscript and toward children's theatre in general are
critical factors. He must believe in what he is doing. His approach to his role must not be based upon a patronizing desire
to "bring culture to the kiddies," but rather upon a belief in
the children's theatre play as a challenging, worthy art form
deserving of his best creative efforts.

Children's theatre acting, like all good acting, finds its
basis in the playscript. In determining the acting style which
will serve best to provide an aesthetic experience for the child
audience, the actor finds numerous clues in his script. Analysis of the script should reveal that the thoughtful playwright
has exercised selectivity in drawing his characters, concen-
trating on certain traits that will individualize them to some
extent. [12]

There is reason to question the use of a representational
or naturalistic style of acting in children's theatre productions.
The nature of the playscript itself would seem to preclude such
an approach. Further, the representational style calls for the
actor to appear unaware of the presence of an audience. [13] There
is ample evidence that children's theatre productions should
be audience-centered and that the actors should take cues from
the audience to assist in bringing the audience into the play, in
tempering conflict, in building and controlling empathy and
tension, and in preventing boredom. In contrast to the representational, the presentational style of acting allows for the
awareness of the audience. "It finds its focus in the auditorium.
. . . It is frankly acting . . . which reaches out and takes the
audience into its confidence. "[14] This does not imply a super-
ficial approach to characterization; rather, sincerity of approach is its requisite. Actors must imagine they are charac-

ters in a play and identify with these characters, but they must always be aware that they are acting parts. [15] They should discover and display all that is worth presenting of their characters, thus creating an artistic reality, an event in the life of the theatre where actors and spectators come together to practice and to watch the art of make-believe.

In children's theatre productions selectivity in characterization takes into account children's inability to abstract from a mass of detail. Discovering the essential quality of their characters, actors provide outlines of illusion, sincerely suggesting what the characters are, and stimulating the audience to create with them. This selectivity also allows actors to comment upon their characters. By emphasizing essential traits, they continually point out to the audience those traits significant in relation to the total meaning of the play. [16] These comments begin with each initial entrance, when the characters in turn, through their comments, establish themselves as persons, letting the children know who they are, why they have come, and whether they are sympathetic or unsympathetic personalities. The actors' awareness of the audience and its responses can assist in controlling fatigue, tension, and boredom; in building and holding attention; in modifying conflict, suspense, and emotional tone according to audience response. By permitting actors to comment upon their characters, the presentational style assists antagonistic forces in controlling and tempering fear reactions. Generally speaking, characters in children's plays are developed to semiroundness or even to type. Presentational acting allows for selectivity and suggestion in bringing those characters vividly and clearly to life. Finally, this style of acting, which is based upon an awareness of the make-believe aspect of the dramatic event, appears to be eminently well suited to the average children's theatre playscript.

Publicizing

Publicity, designed to accomplish the immediate goals of selling either a single play or a season, should be clearly distinguished from promotion and public relations work. While sometimes these two facets of community contact are under a

single chairmanship, separate but complementary campaigns
should be carefully planned. The exact nature of a publicity
campaign will depend on whether the program is new or well
established, whether it is for a single play or a whole season,
the whether or not the children's theatre has the complete cooperation of the schools. Materials designed to incite interest
in the idea of a play for children will necessarily have to be
distributed along with materials about the play if the program
is new. The first play of a season will probably be stressed
at the beginning of a campaign. If theatre-going is to be an
integral part of the school program, publicity campaigns need
to be concentrated only on those people immediately concerned.

All publicity material should be attractive, but also in good
taste. It is unwise to cheapen a children's theatre program by
flamboyancy in advertising. Elaborate claims for any production may lead to embarrassment later on if expectations are
disappointed. While very novel schemes sometimes attract
considerable attention, the long-range goals of the children's
theatre may be seriously harmed if the sensibilities of the
community are offended even slightly. This principle extends
to both the form and the composition of materials. While children need to be interested in the prospect of attending a performance, it is equally important that parents be convinced
this would be a worthwhile experience for children. Customar-
ily, dodgers (or handbills), posters in the schools and libraries, pictures, and skits from the play in the classrooms are
the best means to reach the children who are likely to attend.
Parents, on the other hand, are most likely to respond to newspaper advertising and feature stories, speakers at PTA and
other group meetings, radio and television announcements
and interviews, and attractive posters displayed in business
establishments. The cooperation of teachers can be encouraged
by distributing "play guides" or teaching aids of background
material which they use in preparing children for a play-going
experience. Direct mail advertising is thought by many to be
more effective than other more popular methods.

Timing of publicity campaigns is especially important for a
child audience. Particularly active publicity effort or touring
of a dramatic scene should immediately precede the actual
sale of tickets. Information about dates and places of ticket

sales should be distributed, especially to parents. There should
not be a long period during which announcements could get
lost or money forgotten. Actual ticket sales should take place
when interest and enthusiasm are at their height, and the pos-
session of a ticket is assurance that a child will remember
his anticipated date with the living theatre.

Summary

The production of plays for a child audience is different from
production in the adult theatre in only a few specific ways. Organization patterns usually include the many agencies in a community concerned with children and their welfare. Plays must
frequently be brought to an audience far from the home producing plant. Plays themselves are selected to exploit characteristic responses of children, and they are directed, designed,
costumed, and acted so that children's interest is held and
focused on principal elements of the story. Those who work
in theatre for the child audience find it a most rewarding and
most challenging form of theatre art. It demands the best
they have to offer.

12 Writing Plays for Children

Sara Spencer ✑

In 1908 Mark Twain called children's theatre "one of the very, very great inventions of the twentieth century."[1] Since then a whole new school of children's theatre authors has emerged, whose efforts have resulted in the creation of a hundred-odd children's plays of publishable quality which are presented over and over again by producers of children's plays in this country. But even after fifty years of trying, the art of writing drama for children is still in its infancy, and the plays being written today are only a groping toward far greater possibilities. The basic principles applied to playwriting for children are therefore still fluid and largely immature, and we devoutly hope our current practices are not basic at all.

Basic Principles

It is significant that few playwrights of professional stature have undertaken to write a legitimate play for children. James Barrie's *Peter Pan* stands almost alone in a unique category. The awe with which practiced professional writers like Thornton Wilder and James Thurber regard the child audience shows that this is not an assignment to be entered into lightly. This alone should give pause to lesser authors, some of whom are all too eager to rush in where professionals fear to tread.

A good playwright for children has to begin by recognizing that children are innately artistic and—even without knowing why—are no less sensitive than their

98

elders to integrity of structure, authority of locale, sincerity in characterization, inevitability in plot development, honesty of language, appropriateness of style, and relation of the whole to theme. This is what M. Leon Chancerel was saying when he addressed the first International Conference on Theatre and Youth at Paris in 1952:

> When it is a matter of performance meant for children and young people, it is to the elite of poets, actors, musicians, stage designers, and producers that it is necessary to appeal. Whoever has had the redoubtable honour and the joy to conceive, to stage, and to play performances meant for children, knows what this public is—a public not yet sophisticated, new, unspoiled, sensitive, delicate, living hand in hand with poetry, ready to feel everything, to understand everything, to intuit everything, with infinitely more acuteness of judgment than the wisest among us here. [2]

The first basic principle, then, required in writing plays for children is a genuine respect for the child audience. In practice only a few literate authors have been uncovered who hold the child audience in proper regard and who still have the temerity to write for them. And of these few only one has brought to the work the artist's acceptance of responsibility for developing a high degree of professional craftsmanship. This was the late Charlotte B. Chorpenning. [3] Mrs. Chorpenning was a philosopher. It was she who conducted a single-handed study of the workings of the child mind within the framework of the theatre and discovered the need to weave long-range meanings into a play for children. She was under no illusions as to her playwriting talent, but she was in desperate need of actual dramatic material on which to base the experiments she was conducting in this new area. The plays she wrote for this purpose, while they play delightfully when interpreted with mature skill and sensitivity, were designed primarily as illustrations of techniques she wished to demonstrate. For she was a teacher, and she taught by anecdote.

Mrs. Chorpenning brought to the children's theatre a lifetime of experience in the theatre. Out of this experience came the knowledge, rudimentary to any practicing theatre artist, that any good play tries to say something to its audience, and that this meaning must be conveyed not by preachment, but by the story, through the characters. Perhaps the most important thing she said, in all her years, was "In the theatre children will not take in learning, unless it is first of all entertainment."[4] This is accepted now as a cardinal rule in the theatre. But it took a theatre-trained mind to translate its implications into children's theatre terms. What it means is that a serious author of plays for children is obliged to train himself, by every means possible, in all the techniques of entertainment—and this is the second basic principle required of a children's playwright—in a complete command of theatre craftsmanship. The Chorpenning example would seem to prove that one of the prime prerequisites for anyone who undertakes to work in the children's theatre should be a very thorough grounding in theatre. Progress in any art derives from a knowledge of the classic, even if only to depart from it; and in the children's theatre, as in any other profession, there is no way of bypassing the process of learning from the past.

For the children's theatre goes a dimension beyond the theatre requiring a spirit of adventure based on centuries of accumulated wisdom. This spirit of adventure is the third basic principle to be applied to this new realm of theatrical entertainment. This is the great challenge, since it demands a whole new level of thinking. The child's mind is a mysterious and wonderful place, a child lives hand in hand with poetry. To speak to him, one needs not only new story material. One needs new styles, new patterns of decor, new breeds of character, new planes of meaning, for a good play must give a child something to grow to.

As one author puts it,

When we consider the literature for children which has proved to be of permanent value and lasting importance, do we not find two complete and unbroken levels of meaning? The first is the child's level. On this level he has a complete and coherent experience, satisfying in itself, consistent with the principles set down by Mrs. Chorpenning. But at the same time there is another level, equally complete and equally satisfying in itself. This is the adult level. This second level is a counter-voice to the child's level. To ask which is the more important is like asking which is the more important of two voices in a Bach Two-Part Invention. Each voice is indispensable, and the supreme beauty of the total work is formed by the two voices playing ceaselessly against each other. In this way we should be able to give the child a richly rewarding experience on his own level. But in the process we must also try to give him a glimpse of and hunger for those things which are still beyond him. [5]

Practices

It is evident from an examination of the published plays written for the children's theatre that our current practices in writing plays for children fall short of these fine basic principles. The children's theatre does not lack authors, but it lacks authors who are fully learned in the background and techniques of the theatre, and it lacks authors with imagination and power to strike out on adventurous new paths. It takes an artist to penetrate the mists that hover always over the unknown, and to venture, not timidly but boldly, into unexplored space. "The genuinely creative artist," says Donald Weissmann, "expands judgment as he expands the nature and depth of art."[6] Such an artist was James Barrie, who brought the most advanced and sophisticated dramatist's skill to bear on the adventurous two-level idea of *The Boy Who Would Not Grow Up*.

Present-day children's theatre has only a few capable writers who have drawn their plots, their scenarios, their characters, their very dialogue, from time-proven fairy tales and stories. They have brought to children's theatre the elements of philosophy, the balance of emphasis, the social conscience that must be integral to a play for children. They have assumed the necessary duty of planting in young minds things worth believing in, worth living for—for "Every man," says Maxwell Anderson, "gives his life for what he believes."[7]

To this extent the authors of the present-day children's theatre repertoire have made a creditable contribution, and they have provided the material with which to develop the children's theatre medium. Unfortunately, their plays are seldom accorded the honor of a distinguished production. There are no top-ranking professional producers at work in the children's theatre field. School productions are beset by the well-known limitations of budget, minimum technical facilities, immature actors, and untrained staff. And college producers, with a few exceptions, relegate their children's plays to student di-

rectors, who are obliged to create with any actors, scenery,
costumes, and lights that may be left over from major productions. [8] Because of this the children's theatre medium remains underdeveloped and offers scant attraction to the artists
of the theatre. One has to see the consummate finesse, the
variety of skills, the fabulous technical perfection which the
Royal Ballet brings to a production of *The Sleeping Beauty* to
appreciate the inspiring possibilities of the children's theatre medium.

Summary

Those who work in the children's theatre strive constantly
for these possibilities. They are in a happy business, and out
of their great need for material they have created a hospitable
climate for playwrights. No children's theatre playwright goes
unread. Few lack for a producer. Three publishing houses vie
with one another to publish the best children's plays written. [9]
Producers bid eagerly for the right to try out new scripts. Five
established Children's Theatres offer substantial awards in annual Playwriting Competitions. [10] The Children's Theatre Conference seeks out unpublished manuscripts, and displays them
at its annual meetings. Yet the repertoire grows slowly. Good
playwrights are few, and their primary attention is claimed by
the necessity of making a living. The majority are teachers.
Some are actors, directors, lecturers, housewives. All have a
healthy interest in the aims and objectives of CTC and in some
cases have helped to shape them.

As a group, children's theatre authors seem inclined to draw
their conclusions more from observation of audience response,
than from a study of the theatre. Writing for the children's
theatre is a pleasant avocation to them, amounting in some
cases to actual philanthropy, for the returns are meager and
the work required prodigious. An author will spend sometimes
four years in research, accumulating material, steeping himself in the lore of his subject before he ever sets pen to paper.
When his play is finally written he will subject it to several
trial productions and patient revisions.

Even so, he does not aim high enough. He is very fond of
saying, "Only the best is good enough for children," [11] but

hounded by producers, beguiled by their plaudits and by favor-able press reviews, flattered by attention given his piece by little children, he settles too soon for success and leaves his work unperfected, characters underwritten, plot manipulated by expediency, meanings expounded instead of illustrated. The children do not complain. Like adults, they are easily delighted with theatrical entertainment that gives them no cause to think, to feel, to understand. A few years ago, a wise conference speaker warned: "Let me caution you, when a producer says, 'The children just loved it!', this is a bad word. You must seek more from your audience than a passing moment of pleasure."[12]

The task remains yet to be done.

13 Recommended Training for Children's Theatre Director

Frank M. Whiting ✍

In an effort to answer the question, "What kind of training does a director need?" I have sometimes challenged graduate students with the following rather fantastic problem: you are a teacher in a mythical kingdom. One day the King calls you before him and says, "Choose any new born baby in my realm. Subject him to a course of training that will, by the age of forty, make him one of the greatest stage directors of all time. You may have the power of life and death over him. For example, if war will help you may have war; if famine will help you may have famine. One thing and only one thing matters, by the age of forty your pupil must be a great director. If you succeed my kingdom is yours. If not, off with your head."

Outline the procedure you would follow in an effort to save your head!

As an examination device this problem would be improved if there were anyone wise enough to correct it; but at least it has provoked many stimulating discussions. If nothing else, it has tended to diminish some of the common assumptions on the subject. For example, I must admit with some embarrassment that not one of my best students has insisted that his pupil should enroll for my course in stage direction or for anyone else's course in stage direction. Instead almost all of them have focused their attention on providing their would-be directors with a rich and stimulating environment, particularly during early childhood. In general, this has been an environment that would provide much love but some hate, much joy

but some sorrow, much good but some evil, much security
but some fear. They have believed above all that the young
pupil should be exposed to the influence of many wise and
talented human beings, and to the stimulation of much inspiring theatre, although they have tended to balance even
these forces with an occasional fool and an occasional flop.
Briefly, the answers of outstanding graduate students would
tend to indicate that formal training, the study of stage direction in a textbook or a classroom, is not the major ingredient
in the development of a director.

Indirect Training

As indicated above, the director—like the writer, the teacher,
and the speaker—is first and foremost a total human being. No
training in a college classroom can replace such things as a
natural gift for leadership, a sensitive insight into human behavior, or a sense of rhythm and beauty. A director approaches
his first rehearsal with all he has inherited plus all he has
acquired in the process of living. Here are a few questions
that a beginning student might do well to consider:

1. Do I really love theatre, not myself in theatre?

A certain amount of pride and egocentricity may not be un-
common or alarming in the beginner, but if these traits per-
sist or continue to grow, as they unfortunately do even in
some great artists, the student should declare himself dis-
qualified as a director—especially as a children's theatre director. Directing, like teaching, is essentially a life of service.

2. Do I really enjoy children?

Some who love theatre most and are among the nation's finest
directors simply cannot bear to work with children. To them
theatre is a "great art" and the naturally undisciplined ir-
reverence of normal children toward such art is insufferable.

3. Have I a natural gift for leadership?

Sometimes in modest people the gift of leadership develops
later in life, after training and experience have bestowed the
right to be a leader. For the most part, however, those who
make good directors have already shown qualities of leadership:

at home, on the playground, in the school, in their church, or in other such areas.

4. Can I endure long hours of extra work without feeling like a martyr?

As much as we may regret it, theatre is not regarded as an essential in our civilization. The children's theatre exists only because there are many intelligent and talented people who are dedicated, who pour time and energy into their work because they love it and believe in it.

5. Have I, or can I acquire, an extraordinary appreciation of dramatic literature, especially children's literature?

How can we hope to inspire children unless we are a bit inspired ourselves? Dramatic literature is the very core of our work.

The above questions make no pretense at providing a complete self-inventory. They simply indicate the type of questions that a serious student should be able to answer satisfactorily before beginning conscious training toward a career as a director of children's theatre.

Formal or Conscious Training

I have laid much stress on the inherited and unconsciously acquired qualities that go into the making of a director because to do otherwise would be misleading and dishonest. Only the most crass of trade schools would pretend to train a person as sensitive and complex as an outstanding director in a few easy lessons. I have tried to make it clear that many of the most essential qualities have deep roots. Such things as judgment, patience, sensitivity, and good health (mental, moral, physical) are not to be acquired by a few pat formulas or from a few inspired lectures.

But once we have admitted the depth and importance of these factors that are largely acquired before the student enters college, there is still much that can be done. The only attitude worse than the belief that good enough training can make a director of anyone is the attitude that such training has no value at all. From 1925 to 1950 students of approximately equal "talent" enrolled in hundreds of universities throughout the nation and yet almost all who were to become outstanding in children's theatre graduated from only one, Northwestern University. No Ph. D. dissertation is required to discern the reason. Northwestern University was almost the only school offering training in children's theatre, and, even more important, the work was under the direction of Winifred Ward. Her work is an example of the fact that conscious training can still work wonders. Let us consider the potential contributions of such formal training by viewing education on three levels: (1) general education, (2) general education in the theatre, and (3) specialized education for directors of children's theatre.

General Education

Theatre, being an imitation of life, sprawls everywhere. It is difficult to imagine a single course in a college curriculum that could not under certain circumstances prove to be of value to the director of a children's theatre. Yet in spite of this rather obvious truth, college freshmen not infrequently bemoan the fact that they must take so many courses "outside" the theatre. They sometimes cancel out after one or two quarters to transfer to a professional dramatic school where they can study theatre and nothing but theatre. They are impatient. They want results, and they want them without delay. They fail to realize that living things seldom respond to such direct tactics. Stanislavski implies that those who are content with artificial flowers can manufacture them in a few hours using the direct approach: wire and crepe paper. [1] Those, however, who prefer real blossoms must follow a much slower, more complex, and devious route. They must prepare the soil, plant the seeds, remove the weeds, spray the pests, and finally with patience, wise effort, and good luck they may produce some prize-winning blooms. It would be foolish indeed to suppose that one of the more complex living organisms, a skillful children's theatre director, could be produced with less care, cultivation, and indirect control than a plant.

The student who slights his general education may well cripple and limit his future progress. Psychology, which many students try to avoid, digs at the very roots of human behavior off stage and on. Courses in art can do much to enhance skill and taste in the visual side of theatre production. Experience in music can greatly increase sensitivity to the auditory and rhythmic elements of production. Courses in physics can be fundamental to any mastery of light and sound. Training in business and advertising might make the difference between success and failure as one moves into the practical world of production. Skill in public speaking may pay dividends in dealing with actors and the public. Child welfare, educational psychology, and recreational leadership offer obvious values. Above all, literature—dramatic literature and children's literature—provides the foundation upon which our work rests. A would-be children's theatre director simply cannot be too wise or too well informed. Accordingly a broad and thorough foundation in general education is devoutly to be desired.

General Education in the Theatre

Most of the things already said about the values of general education still apply as we narrow the field to a theatre education. Years of experience in teaching stage direction have convinced me that the outstanding students of direction are almost certain to be those who have already proved to be outstanding in other phases of theatre. I sometimes say that directing is something one soaks up by osmosis. Place the student in a healthy, stimulating, theatre environment, let him soak for a few years, and he is likely to come out saturated with what it takes to make a director.

A lack of well-balanced theatrical skill and know-how seems to be the major weakness of far too many directors of children's theatres. If directors are to win and hold respect as responsible and professional leaders they must know the theatre and know it well. At present the height of theatrical achievement is to become a director on Broadway or in Hollywood; success in a college or community theatre comes next, while success as a director of a children's theatre receives polite and condescending acquiescence. Actually it would be more rational and civilized if this attitude could be reversed, for the college director needs everything that the professional director needs plus the kind of character, personality, training, and understanding that makes him a worthy member of an academic community and an effective teacher of young men and women, while the children's theatre director in turn needs all that the college director needs plus special aptitude, skill, and training in handling the most difficult and challenging of human beings, young children. It is a field that calls for the best.

Specialized Training in Stage Directing

Let us assume that a given student has been well equipped at birth, that his early environment has been rich and rewarding, his general education well rounded, and his general experience in theatre excellent. Theoretically he is now equipped to assume the role of a leader by becoming a director. Chances are, however, that he will handle his new assignment much more effectively and with far fewer errors if he takes a good course in stage direction at some reputable college or university. I have already made it clear that such specialized training is not indispensable; also that it would be folly to expect the impossible of such a course. On the other hand a good course in stage direction can offer many values, among them:

1. It can give the beginning director the courage to use what he already has. This may be a rather negative approach and yet it seems to be fundamental. I have known so many students of direction who at the beginning simply lacked the courage of their convictions, who were afraid to give rein either to dramatic impulses or common sense, afraid to use action, honest expression, or have fun. Faint heart ne'er directed fair play! Especially a children's play. The first and most valuable shock that a student of direction should get is the discovery of how much more the great director can see in a scene than the student dared to see. The first touch of enthusiasm usually comes when he dares to free his own imaginative powers.

2. It can offer a chance to learn by doing. During some twenty years of teaching direction I have come to rely less and less on lecture and more and more on doing. During fall quarter our students now direct two or more scenes from plays;[2] during winter quarter each directs two one-act plays (one an original); while during spring quarter each directs a full-length play. Theory and knowledge can be gained from reading and from the discussions that grow quite naturally out of the productions themselves. Students cannot survive such a course without acquiring much skill in directing.

3. It can stimulate learning by means of healthy competition.

Fortunately students can learn from the successes and failures of others. The knack of good direction seems to be contagious. The epidemic often spreads through an entire class.

4. It can offer a chance for constructive criticism and wise counseling. Unfortunately these are usually denied the director when he gets into the field. The polite practice following a show is to indulge in clever or flattering comments. Honest and soul-searching evaluation has its best chance when the student is able to sit down and discuss his production with other student directors and especially with a teacher who has had years of experience.

A good course in stage direction can offer many other values than those outlined above, but even these four should be enough to convince the student that at least one such course is highly desirable.

Finally there are several specialties that the would-be children's director should cultivate above and beyond those of his other classmates. Perhaps these require an additional course of study or perhaps they can be learned in a basic stage direction course if the teacher and student are able to make the necessary shifts in emphasis. But however he acquires them there are certain unique qualities that the director of or for children will need, or need to a greater degree, than his classmate who plans to direct in college or on Broadway.

1. He should recognize a different emphasis in the objectives of children's theatre and adult theatre. To have any excuse for existence, both children's theatre and adult theatre must achieve excellent standards. A children's play, however, approaches such a standard when it tells a wonderful story with highly effective entertainment, fun, and excitement. In much of the greatest adult theatre, "entertainment" is only a means to an end, an end which consists of probing into the meaning and mystery of human existence.

2. He should try to develop skill in keeping the story line strong and motivation at a maximum. This quality is fundamental on all levels of theatre, but the children's theatre director will be especially wise to stick to this most useful of all fundamentals. It is related to a strong sense of communication: alert listening and a desire to convince. A rehearsal technique that is sometimes effective with children is to seat

them on opposite sides of a table and let them beat one another with the ideas. In extreme instances they can even beat each other over the heads with pillows as well as ideas. This does not guarantee a good show, but it will cure the most deadly of all sins, the stilted reciting of words. Everything said and done must spring from a desire to say it or do it.[3] In other words apply the "Stanislavski method" but do so on the child's own level with fun and enthusiasm.

3. He should try to develop a keen sense of action. Action if free, natural, and well motivated is probably the director's best weapon in counteracting stiffness, stage fright, strained voices and the like. Healthy children are naturally active, un-inhibited, and expressive. The children's theatre director should capitalize on these qualities, not fight against them.

4. He should try to develop a sense of fun and excitement. This need not be shallow. With a good group the play acting can become very serious and convincing, but beware of forcing standards of art that the child is not ready to understand or accept.

5. He should try to develop in himself a healthy aversion to long, boring rehearsals. In working with children both the individual rehearsals and the total rehearsal schedule should probably be shorter than when working with adults. True, the child has more to learn, but he also has a tendency to lose interest and enthusiasm if the work becomes tedious or de-tailed. A feeling of progress, growth, and accomplishment is very necessary. Long, strenuous, polishing rehearsals are likely to destroy more than they add.

6. He should try to develop a passion for teamwork, not stardom. This may not be important to a given play, but it is crucial to the director's function as an educator. Adults, classmates, and doting parents can quickly turn a healthy, normal child into the most terrifying of all creatures, the child prodigy. Pray you avoid this mistake.

Summary

The stage director, especially in the children's theatre, is above all a total human being, a complex combination of heredity plus environment; and specialized training in directing is but a part of this environment. Yet recognition of this complexity need cause no despair, for environment can be shaped and controlled. Undoubtedly thousands of freshmen who enter colleges and universities this year will have acquired qualities from heredity and early environment that could with experience and skillful training transform them into outstanding directors of children's theatres. Such training, however, would include much more than specialized work in stage direction. It would include a broad general education and a well-rounded theatre education as well. Nor can we say which is the more important: a love and understanding of children, or a love and understanding of theatre. Both are essential if children's theatre is ever to assume the importance and prestige in our culture that it so richly deserves.

PART III

*. . . It is to turn pumpkins into
coaches, and mice into horses,
lowness into loftiness, and nothing
into everything, for each child has
its fairy godmother in its own soul.*
            - Francis Thompson

Hansel and Gretel. School of Drama, University of Washington
(Photograph by James O. Sneddon)

14 Development of Creative Dramatics in the United States

James E. Popovich

To trace the history and development of any art form is a difficult task. A study of the development of creative dramatics is particularly frustrating because the various and dissimilar attempts and experiments—resulting in the development of an activity known today as creative dramatics—do not fall into neat, orderly, and necessarily related patterns. Creative dramatics, like any other art, depends upon a fluid technique which results in highly individualistic teaching methods. In a narrow sense there are probably as many different creative dramatic techniques as there have been individuals teaching drama. Yet, very few have written about their methods or their development. An accurate historical review of the development of creative dramatics presents some difficulties because of this fluidity of technique and dearth of information.

However, certain trends which generated policies and influenced other educators are recognizable as significant in the parade of various educational experimentations which led to current creative dramatics practices. The purpose of this chapter is (1) to discover the specific contributions which were made to the development of creative dramatics by various educators and by pedagogical trends; (2) to explore these contributions by scrutinizing the rise, results, and extent of each of these contributions; and (3) to

---

*Monograph drawn from Ph. D. dissertation: James E. Popovich, A Study of Significant Contributions to the Development of Creative Dramatics in American Education (Northwestern University, 1955).

interpret these findings and point out by comparisons the relative importance and significance of each contribution.

Edward Sheldon and "Object Lessons"

The first evidence of creativity in American classrooms which utilized any degree of spontaneous activities, including some crude efforts in dramatics, is observable in the educational innovations made by Edward Austin Sheldon, head of the Normal School and superintendent of the public schools in Oswego, New York.[1] Dissatisfied with existing methods of teaching, Sheldon—searching for possible solutions—traveled extensively and corresponded with other educators. In this search, he discovered publications extolling the Pestalozzian theories of education. Pestalozzi, who led a revolt in the late eighteenth century against the current teaching practices in Europe, emphasized exercises in sense impression and language. These exercises became known later as "object lessons" and were intended to teach the child to observe and discuss. Sheldon experimented with these methods in the late eighteen hundreds and found them successful. He wrote two books, *A Manual of Elementary Instruction,* and *Lessons on Objects,* on the extended use he made of oral discussion by children, and the enactment and performance of their ideas. There are, however, serious objections to the object-lesson theories, when one views them from a creative teaching standpoint. Many lessons taught by the object-lesson method and based on child participation were concluded by a parroting of the lesson learned, which, paradoxically enough, worked against the fundamental principles inherent in the new philosophy. The contribution of Sheldon to the development of creative dramatics in America was indeed great, for leading educators were greatly influenced by his concept of adapting the elementary school curriculum to the needs of the child. Among these educators were John Dewey, Colonel Francis W. Parker, and William Wirt.

Francis W. Parker School

A great contribution to the field of creative dramatics was made by the Francis W. Parker School during the first half of

the twentieth century. The school, founded by Colonel Francis
W. Parker in 1901, pioneered in successfully implementing
new precepts of educational philosophy which had been advanced by Pestalozzi and Sheldon. Parker became a leading
spokesman for the new education, conducting summer institutes
and making many speeches. During the summers of the early
1880's Parker served as head of the Department of Didactics
at Martha's Vineyard Summer Institutes. In these lectures
Parker emphasized the significance of oral expression. He
also emphasized that lessons taught graphically are those best
learned by children. Parker urged simple improvised activities as an excellent technique. Although recommending improvised actions of children in teaching language, he stopped
short of recommending it as a technique for teaching literature.

In 1899 the daughter of Cyrus McCormick, Mrs. Emmons
Blaine, offered to endow a school which would allow Parker
a freer hand in realizing his educational theories. Although
Parker was soon involved in the building of the University of
Chicago (becoming its first director of the School of Education),
one of Parker's most gifted followers, Flora J. Cooke, was
selected to head the Parker School. Emphasis on correlated
projects utilizing techniques of dramatization was one of her
early innovations. To accomplish this end, exceptionally gifted
men and women served as instructors in the upper and lower
schools. Among them was John Merrill, a graduate of Emerson College where he had been thoroughly trained in speech
and drama. Merrill worked in all twelve grades of the school
as a special teacher. His main purpose in teaching was to
acquaint his young students with world literature. The pre-
occupation at the Parker School with group activities as related to the educative process manifested itself in a series of
ten pamphlet publications called "Studies in Education." A
large portion of the first yearbook[2] gave attention to the role
dramatics and oral expression played in implementing and
socializing education. Two years later, Merrill wrote a long
tract on the dramatic instinct and its value and place in the
education of children.

Sometime between 1925 and 1930 Merrill collaborated with
Martha Fleming on a book which synthesized their ideas on

dramatics. Their volume, *Play-making and Plays,* appeared
in 1930. Curiously enough, in the spring of the same year,
Winifred Ward's *Creative Dramatics* had been published; both
books were written and published independently. As in all of
Merrill's other writing, *Play-making and Plays* never actually
used the term "creative dramatics," and less than one sixth
of the book concerned itself with the creative technique. In
1939 Merrill retired from teaching. Not until 1954 did he write
his autobiography, and in this book, strangely enough, he de-
votes only one fourth of the space to teaching. Yet, although
Merrill himself has not properly evaluated his contributions
in this field, the imprint of his teaching and philosophy is
evident still. Parker School continues to emphasize social
learning through correlated projects utilizing techniques of
dramatization. Although the school Merrill founded did not
actually invent or formularize the techniques of creative dramatics, it pioneered in experimenting with those theories which
became the bases of creative dramatics.

Dewey and the Progressive Education Movement

Advent of the progressive education movement was a great
impetus in furthering theories upon which creative dramatics
are based. It evolved from the dynamic philosophies which had
been voiced abroad by Pestalozzi and popularized in America
by Sheldon in the Oswego schools, Parker in Chicago, and Wirt
in the platoon schools in Gary.

Although there has been no exact definition of the term "progressive education," it is usually applied to a variety of pedagogical procedures which have been adapted and influenced by
different educational followers of John Dewey. Dewey (1859-
1952) started a laboratory school at the University of Chicago
in 1896 which was designed to accommodate the experimental
work he and his associates were then undertaking. The school
centered its activities and its learning processes around the
child. Dewey stated:

> . . . the primary root of all educative activity is in the instinctive,
> impulsive attitudes and activities of the child, and not in the presen-
> tation and application of external material, whether through the ideas

of others or through the senses; and that, accordingly, numberless
spontaneous activities of children, plays, games, mimic efforts . . .
are capable of educational use, nay, are the foundation-stones of educational method. [3]

There are numerous examples throughout the reports of
the Dewey Laboratory School of the manner and frequency
with which dramatization was utilized. Dewey's Laboratory
School served as a model for several others, notably the elementary school of the University of Missouri and the Porter
School near Kirksville, Missouri. Marie Harvey's work at
Porter School was heralded by educators. As early as 1919
Mrs. Harvey employed free dramatization of fables and stories, going ". . . through the story several times in a morning with different children taking the parts. "[4] In addition to
Porter School, six other experimental schools, patterned
after Dewey's Laboratory School, were founded between 1900
and 1915.

By 1919 the progressive education movement had become
so popular that new theorists of education decided to incorporate themselves into an organization; their journal, founded
to disseminate information about progressive education activities, did much to promote emphasis on group activities, the
correlated project method, and other teaching techniques using
some amount of free dramatization. The complete issue of
the January, 1931, *Progressive Education* was devoted to the
role of dramatics in progressive education. Contributors from
Missouri, New York, Illinois, and other widely separated
places attested to spreading use of educational dramatics. The
special edition devoted to creative expression through dramatics was a milestone in education. Representing the official
view of a national association of educators, it formally declared that dramatics as an educational tool and art was now
recognized as an important force in education.

William Wirt and the Gary, Indiana, Plan

Another contribution to the development of creative dramatics
was made by innovations in the schools of Gary, Indiana, during
the first quarter of the twentieth century. The founder and ex-

ecutor of these experiments was William Wirt (1874-1938), an unusually dynamic educator who was dissatisfied with the narrow, rigid discipline which then pervaded late nineteenth-century schools. He organized the schools of Gary on three fundamental principles: (1) that they should provide opportunities for work, study, and supervised play for children in urban areas, (2) that school facilities should be used to their maximum efficiency, and (3) that children should come in contact with a varied and enriched curriculum.

One of the significant features of that school organization was the emphasis put upon the auditorium and its related activities. The Gary schools, which were the first to employ the auditorium idea, developed its use and thoroughly integrated its activities. In 1920 Mildred Harter joined the staff of the Gary schools as a special teacher of speech in one of its largest schools. By 1926 fifteen teachers were employed in the Gary system as auditorium teachers; that year, Miss Harter became the director of auditorium teachers and influenced growth of that phase of the work-study-play concept of education.[5] Early in her work in the Gary schools, Miss Harter insisted that one of the main objectives of auditorium work was the training of children in oral communication through related dramatic activities.

The auditorium idea was an inherent part of the platoon or work-study-play type of school organization. Although many educators had different aims, methods, and procedures in incorporating the work of the auditorium into the total curriculum, the movement toward more group dramatic activities was inevitable. This became a significant contribution to the development of creative dramatics in elementary schools because (1) the platoon school system, by its organization, gave emphasis to group dramatic activities by assigning all students to a fixed auditorium period each day; (2) the platoon school administrators sought to employ trained speech and drama teachers as directors of the auditorium work; and (3) the auditorium teachers of platoon schools seized upon creative dramatics as an excellent method of synthesizing work in the auditorium, thereby helping to popularize and promote work in creative drama.

Winifred Ward and Experiments at Evanston

Efforts of Winifred Ward in the public schools of Evanston, Illinois, and at Northwestern University during the second quarter of the twentieth century were among the most significant in the development of creative dramatics. Joining the faculty of Northwestern in 1918, Miss Ward taught, in addition to other classes, a course in Advanced Story Telling. During the years between 1920 and 1923, Miss Ward became increasingly interested in the teaching of storytelling and she experimented freely with the idea of dramatizing formal productions from stories. In 1923 the dean of the School of Speech became a member of the Evanston board of education. Knowing of Miss Ward's interest in and experiments with dramatizing stories and of her wish to incorporate this approach into the child's total education, he suggested that the elementary schools of Evanston might be a laboratory where she could realize these aims. During the school year of 1923-24, Miss Ward began her work inconspicuously in one class of an elementary school. In 1924 she was named supervisor of the dramatics program for the elementary schools.

By the late twenties, the teaching of dramatics in the Evanston schools had met with enthusiastic support and was offered in two large new intermediate schools; six dramatics teachers were employed, assisted by several practice teachers from the university. Miss Ward undertook to record her theories and procedures in *Creative Dramatics,* published in 1930. Less than half of the book was devoted to an explanation of creative dramatics; the remainder was a detailed account of production procedures of formal plays with children.[6] Publication of the book drew the attention of children's theatre directors as well as elementary school teachers, especially to the new concept of creative dramatization which made up the first portion of the book. A great many became curious about the work in the Evanston schools, and Miss Ward's classes (during both the academic year and the summer session) began to attract much attention. In 1947 she sought to develop her ideas on creative dramatics at greater length than she had in her first book. She also incorporated into this book those changes in theory which evolved as a result of her experience in the Evanston schools and at Northwestern since the publication of *Creative Dramatics,* seventeen years before. The new volume was released in 1947 under the title of *Playmaking with Children;* it has since been revised extensively.

In June, 1950, after serving simultaneously over a thirty-year period as supervisor of the creative dramatics program in the elementary schools of Evanston, as director of the Children's Theatre of Evanston, and as an instructor in the School of Speech at Northwestern, Miss Ward retired. Since her retirement she has continued to make notable contributions: she served as theatre resource specialist at the UNESCO Conference in 1949, as a member of the national board of the American National Theatre and Academy in 1952 and 1953, and as a member of the educational commission of the Methodist Church. She taught summer classes in creative dramatics at the University of Minnesota, San Jose State College, National College of Education, Michigan State University, and Kent University in Ohio. She had conducted short workshops and institutes at various places. In one year alone she led seventeen institutes. She has held workshops and made speeches in nearly thirty states and more than twenty leading cities in the United States. Besides taking care of her extensive speaking schedule, Miss Ward carefully collected and edited a volume of materials suitable for creative dramatization. [7]

Development of Creative Dramatics in Colleges

At present a significant and growing contribution to the creative dramatics movement is being made by American colleges and universities in training students to employ techniques of teaching creative dramatics. In 1955 a study was made of curricular offerings by examining college catalogues and by use of detailed questionnaires. [8] The results of this survey were very revealing; ninety-two colleges in America offer at least one course in creative dramatics and an additional seventy-nine colleges offer courses in which creative dramatics is a portion of the class work. The popularity of creative dramatics courses in American colleges and the opportunity for observation and practice teaching in some programs make a considerable and significant contribution to the creative dramatics movement.

With over ninety-two colleges offering at least one course specifically devoted to a study of creative dramatics, the training of almost two thousand future leaders of creative dramatics activities is being made possible each year. In addition to these significant numbers, seventy-nine additional schools offer courses in which a portion of the study is concerned with creative dramatics. Although practice teaching and observation opportunities are extremely limited, the scope of these courses and their election by thousands of elementary education majors each year make for an impressively widespread knowledge among elementary school teachers of the significance and concepts of creative dramatics.

Summary

New educational philosophies of the late nineteenth and twentieth centuries constituted a fundamental contribution which made possible later a general acceptance of creative dramatics. Sheldon, Parker, Dewey, and Wirt all played significant roles in popularizing and advancing these concepts so important to the bases upon which creative dramatics rests. Winifred Ward's experiments in the Evanston schools were the most significant of all contributions to the development of the creative dramatics movement. Miss Ward has become a most important influence in the teaching of creative dramatics methods. Although of varying degrees of worth, all made significant contributions to the development of creative dramatics in American education. The creative dramatics trend owes its heritage to educators, but its principles, techniques, and popularity to an educational dramatist, Winifred Ward.

15 Values to Children from Creative Dramatics

Eleanor Chase York ✑

A four-year-old when asked why she liked to participate in creative dramatics replied simply, "It's good."
Her reply is typical of children's reactions to dynamic
experiencing in this art.

Creative dramatics is informal drama which exists
primarily for the enjoyment and benefit of the players
themselves. The precise and objective measurement
of specific benefits received by children from participation in this art is a difficult and complex process. At
the present time we have very little in the way of exact
research to substantiate our belief in the values received. However, over a period of thirty years outstanding creative dramatics leaders have reached certain conclusions about values of creative dramatics to
the individual child. These conclusions have come as
the result of having observed children in classes and
of having considered evaluations of other teachers,
parents, and the participants themselves. These conclusions are presented here.

Creativity

Teachers recognize in this art one means of preserving in individuals the creative spark which is their
natural endowment. Those who have observed children
of preschool and kindergarten age have seen this ir-
repressible creative spirit which is evident in their
freedom to do, to make, to be. Teachers have seen
the confidence with which children of this age attempt
any expression of themselves; they have seen the freedom of their expression unhampered by fear of failure

or doubt of approval; they have witnessed the individuality and originality of the play of these children. "When a child makes his entrance into the world, he comes with a gift of imagination, with the power to create, and a desire to express himself."[1]

Too often in older children this power has dwindled into timidity in undertaking a new venture, inhibited expression which is uncomfortable without patterns to follow, self-consciousness which leads to such things as exhibitionism or withdrawing. In our desire to educate children to live comfortably within the rigid patterns of our culture, to make them "well-adjusted," somehow we rob them of their freedom to create. We emphasize conformity rather than individuality; we direct rather than stimulate; and too eagerly we supply the patterns to be copied. Ruth Sawyer says,

> Midway in childhood something begins to happen. There must be adjustment to a factual, material world. Children begin to conform. Adults help the process along, that adjustment may be made as swift and resistless as possible. Children's minds are railroaded from this station to that, all plainly marked on the map called Education. That space so boundless in babyhood, that heavenly pasture for play and joy unbounded, becomes narrowed down with each year, each grade, until it becomes no wider than your thumb.[2]

Opportunities for experience in creative dramatics under skilled and sensitive leadership may help overcome some of the "narrowing down" of which Ruth Sawyer speaks.

Winifred Ward says "There is no school activity which gives better opportunity for creativity than playmaking."[3] She lists as an important value of creative dramatics "to encourage and guide the child's creative imagination," and stresses the point that the imagination must be constantly exercised "if the individual is to become a creative thinker."[4] In a discussion of creative dramatics values Geraldine Siks asserts that creative dramatics "develops confidence and creative expression."[5] Isabel Burger lists "an active creative imagination" as an outgrowth of creative dramatics.[6] Each of these teachers and many others have recorded moments of true creative expression from children in their classes—those moments when individual children, having lost themselves in complete concentration on an idea, experience the freedom to express without

self-consciousness the thoughts, the feelings, the beliefs which
come from deep within themselves. A brief examination of
how creative dramatics develops significant attributes of creativity will make this clear. [7]

Sensitivity

A creative person is one who is sensitive to the world in
which he lives. He responds with keen awareness to sights,
sounds, textures, scents, and the thoughts and feelings of
others. Leaders of creative dramatics find many opportunities
to guide children to develop sensitivity. Perhaps a child is
asked to recall a bit of action from real life in order to pantomime it, or he depends upon his observations of nature in
order to create an imaginary setting in which to play, or he
listens intently to music in order to discover its rhythmic
patterns, its mood, its story. When children play together in
improvised drama, they are called upon to listen and respond
sensitively to others. When they study the motivations and
feelings of the characters whom they play, they acquire an
understanding of people which contributes to their becoming
sensitive, sympathetic individuals. Siks writes concerning
creative dramatics and sensitivity: "Creative dramatics stimulates a child's awareness. It causes him to learn, to look,
and listen, and from this to see, hear, and feel. It strengthens
his sensibilities and builds a receptiveness to the world around
him—to the world of people, nature, things—to moods, beauties,
wonderings. "[8]

Fluency

Viktor Lowenfeld explains that fluency of ideas is an indication of creativity. This fluency may be observed in the person
who is able to move quickly from one idea to another, who can
see many possibilities in one situation. A very young child who
has not yet lost his creativity demonstrates fluency of ideas
when he creates in rapid succession—from the same cardboard
carton—a boat, a plane, a tower, a house. In almost every
creative dramatics activity there are opportunities for practice
in fluency of ideas. The problem may lie in the planning of different ways of giving exposition in a story dramatization, or
in devising several possible endings for an original plot. Or

the exercise may have to do with discovering many uses for a simple object—a crooked stick may be a witch's broom, a giant's club, a motionless snake, and may serve in several different dramatic scenes. In all of these creative dramatics activities the participant finds himself searching for many solutions to the same problem and thereby increasing his ability to think with fluency.

Flexibility

A creative individual is flexible in his thinking and doing. This third attribute requires a kind of thinking which can adapt to change, can redirect its course. Spontaneous, improvised drama which comes from a group of children playing together, taking a basic idea and developing it as they play, demands that they constantly adapt their thinking to the suggestions and direction of other individuals. For example, perhaps the story begins with the finding of a mysterious box. One child takes the lead and discovers that the box is locked and cannot be opened, but another child steps in and changes the course of the story by finding a magic spring which opens the box. The first child now redirects his thinking and follows the course suggested by the second. A third takes over and determines the contents of the box, and the others must adapt their thinking to his. The story progresses with six or eight children all helping to move it forward and each constantly adapting and redirecting his thinking in order to build on the ideas of the others. The agility in thinking—the ability to seize upon a new idea and use it to progress to another—which can be observed in a group of children playing together in this way is amazing. They are acquiring a flexibility which, Lowenfeld tells us, will contribute toward their being creative people.

Originality

A creative person has originality. Originality is possible only when an individual has confidence in his own ideas, when he feels free to be different in his thinking. Geraldine Siks says, "Creative dramatics encourages the growth of individual spirit in the presence of a group."[9] In a good creative dramatics class every child knows that the ideas he expresses will be considered.

If we were to consider creative dramatics as only a means of preserving creativity through fostering sensitivity, fluency of ideas, flexibility of thinking, and originality, these alone would be reason enough for making this art a part of the everyday life of all children. For educators from all fields have come to acknowledge that the shaping of the future will demand minds which think creatively and which have the vision and imagination not only to seek the answers but to ask the questions which science and technology cannot ask. Albert Einstein somewhere says "The mere formulation of a problem is far more often essential than its solution, which may be merely a matter of mathematical or experimental skill. To raise new questions, new possibilities, to regard old problems from a new angle requires creative imagination and marks real advances in science."

Emotional Stability

There is much that creative dramatics can do for children in addition to developing creativity. Ward emphasizes the value of controlled emotional outlet[10] while Siks speaks of developing emotional stability. Ward says "Better than any other school experience, the arts offer opportunities for channeling emotions into constructive uses."[11] The activity may be free rhythmic movement with physical response to varying moods of music and ideas which release tensions otherwise suppressed or expressed by means of irritation and unpleasant actions; or it may be participation in a dramatic conflict through which the child finds legitimate release for antagonisms or for the vicarious experiencing of lofty emotions which leave him enriched and elevated in spirits. Through the emotion of drama he may discover the dignity in sorrow, the strength in power, the warmth in sympathy, and the freedom in joy as well as the degradation in hate and greed.

Creative dramatics leaders are somewhat cautious about asserting therapeutic aspects of the art, partly because it is easy to lose sight of the fact that it is an art and not a tool. Yet all creative dramatics authorities recognize that participation in this, as in any art, can have a therapeutic effect, and all leaders have seen individuals and groups move toward more stable emotional and mental health through participation in creative drama. Although Lowenfeld was writing specifically on the graphic arts, what he has to say applies equally well to this form of dramatic art. He says, "Because perceiving, thinking, and feeling are equally stressed in any creative process, art may well be the necessary balance for the child's intellect and his emotions."[12]

Social Cooperation

Creative dramatics is a group art. Certain social values have been observed as a direct result of creative dramatics experiences. In order to achieve success an individual must learn to work with the other members of his group. He must learn not only to express his own ideas in communicative fashion, but to listen to and accept ideas of others. He learns where he fits into a group and how he can best make a contribution. He learns to wait his turn, to share, to lead, and to follow. Peter Slade, leading exponent of creative dramatics in England, points out that through creative dramatics "a bond of friendship and trust between children and adults may be established."[13]

Because drama is the art dealing most directly with the motivations and actions of man, the child who plays many roles gains in understanding others and in his ability to live successfully in his environment. "Experience in drama makes a child more sensitive to the thoughts and feelings of others because these are the very essence of his study."[14]

Moral Attitudes

The degree to which an individual achieves his potential depends in large part upon the attitudes which he develops as he grows up. The art of creative dramatics is ideally adapted to the developing of healthy attitudes toward oneself and others. The very nature of the activity proclaims the importance of "what's on the inside" as it minimizes the externals. Another attitude which can be an influence in directing a child's life is inherent in the playing of drama just for the sake of the playing, without any thought of future plaudits from an audience. The real values of truth, sincerity, honesty, belief in

oneself are constantly before the child who is a part of creative dramatics and as he plays with all the sincerity, honesty,
and belief of which he is capable these attitudes may become
a permanent part of his personality. The doing of the thing
for the sake of the doing is a refreshing attitude to find in our
materialistic society where too often the chief concern is with
"what will it get me?"

Through the material which is used for creative dramatics
a teacher may present high ethical and moral standards, and
it is a well-recognized fact among educators that ideas are
deeply impressed when experienced dramatically. Hughes
Mearns explains, "The fine playing of even an evil role can
be done only by those who are at the same time inwardly re-
pudiating evil. We know, if others do not, that the play better
than precept establishes permanently an allegiance to the moral
life."[15]

Siks refers to this building of attitudes as contributing toward a philosophy of living. She says of the child in creative
dramatics, "He cogitates and thinks upon things far greater
and more glorious than his immediate sphere of living. He
strengthens his social and aesthetic attitudes and appreciations. In indirect but vivid ways creative dramatics introduces children to a philosophy by which to live."[16]

Physical Poise

Through the rhythmic movement involved in every form of
creative dramatics and through the disciplining of his body to
express ideas, feelings, characters, the child acquires physical coordination, grace, and poise.

Skill in Communicating

In the process of this art a child acquires skill in expressing
his ideas. He gains confidence in his own thinking as he contributes to the planning of a creative play, and when he plays
a role. Because dialogue is always improvised, he must learn
to think quickly and to be readily articulate. Ward has found
that older children often think first of this objective when evaluating their experience in creative dramatics.

Appreciation of Drama

In addition to the many personal values, creative dramatics also provides a way of introducing children to the art of theatre. More experiences will develop an increased appreciation of this art and make children a more discerning theatre audience in the future. In addition, appreciation of children's literature and, ultimately, of dramatic literature is built. In fact, since drama is the meeting place of all of the arts, finer appreciations for the visual arts, music, and dance may also grow from experience in creative dramatics.

How can we afford to withhold from our children this facet of their education through which they can gain in physical coordination, emotional stability, intellectual expansion, and spiritual depth?

16 Creative Dramatics in Elementary and Junior High Schools

Winifred Ward ❧

Once upon a time, but not so very long ago, some boys were playing an exciting game in an alley. To a woman who watched the game from a window the place was an ordinary alley; but to the boys it had been transformed by their imaginations into good, green Sherwood Forest, and they themselves were Robin Hood and his band of merry outlaws. The woman, impressed by the utter absorption of the boys in their make-believe, began to realize that if this natural dramatic impulse had potential value in education, it was a great waste of power to ignore it. She ventured to experiment in her classroom by giving her pupils opportunity for free dramatization of scenes from history and literature. Other teachers here and there over the country were encouraged by the new trends in education to explore creative dramatics' possibilities also, and to discover that here was an art through which many children might find their own best avenue of expression.

This might well have been the beginning of creative dramatics in the schools. For it was the children who taught us this free, informal drama. All we had to do was to work out the *way* to use it, and then to convince the administrators that it belonged. Then the children took over, and they did the rest. The time for its universal acceptance has not yet come, but during the past twenty years many of the foremost educators of the country have expressed their belief that it has a fundamental contribution to make to a child's development.

132

Present Status of Creative Dramatics
in Schools

In general, creative dramatics is not a subject in the public school curriculum as are music and the graphic arts. Because it is a latecomer in education, having been introduced many years after these other arts were well established, it has few departments or supervisors. This is due, partially, to the present trend away from specialization, toward the "self-contained classroom" where one person is expected to teach all subjects as was the case in the schools of many years ago. Thousands of classroom teachers, however, are making use of creative dramatics techniques in their classrooms. Many have taken courses in this art in colleges or universities, or in workshops offered by the public schools or local children's theatres. Others have been inspired to experiment with it merely by seeing demonstrations of its techniques by an expert working with groups of children.

Kindergarten and Primary Grades

Such teachers have discovered that the introduction of informal dramatics can make the ugliest classroom a fascinating place. On a rainy day, when her first graders are restless, instead of having them stand up and stretch, the teacher may perhaps ask them if they would like to take the elevator up to the top of the building to see what they could see! Delighted, they step into the make-believe elevator in the "pretend" basement, crouch down on the floor, and, as the elevator goes up, they slowly straighten their knees until the teacher calls out, "First floor!" Then on and on up to the top of a tall building they go, taking care to stretch up very gradually to "Second floor!" "Third floor!" "Fourth floor!"

Part of the fun is in saving enough stretch to last until they reach the top floor, by which time every child is on tiptoe, with arms stretched high. Then they all step onto the roof and run to look out over the city. What they see depends largely upon experiences they have recently had. Up in the sky they see dark clouds, jet planes, birds flying north; down below they may see "little tiny people with umbrellas," "lions in the zoo," "my mommy working in the garden," "my baby sister playing in her sandbox. " Soon they all get into the elevator again, and go down, down, down until they are crouched in the basement. Then they straighten up and jump out—and by this time they are ready for work again!

In the kindergarten and primary grades, dramatic play and creative rhythmic movement, puppetry, and story dramatization all become a natural part of the program. Because of the nature of primary education today, every school that encourages creativity must use imaginative play if it is to carry out the purposes of education. The very equipment of the kindergarten room speaks of make-believe to the five-year-old, and whether or not the teacher initiates such play much of it goes on.

In the ensuing years the teacher's encouragement is more needed, for there is less and less equipment to stir the imagination and suggest dramatic play. Rhythmic movement, begun with children the first day of school, usually continues in the first grade and in the better schools for several years longer. After the basic rhythms in kindergarten, such as clapping, walking, running, skipping, galloping, the children are ready for a creative use of rhythms. They all have seen parades, so that it only requires marching music to set the mood for the rhythmical marching of a spirited brass band. The hopping of rabbits, the galloping of horses, the whirling of autumn leaves, the swaying of trees in the wind—these and many other creative rhythmic movements are used in most primary schools so that little children may have a kinesthetic sense of rhythm along with the joy of creativity.

Education to strengthen awareness of sense impressions, basic in any form of dramatic training, receives scant attention in most elementary classrooms. Only the kindergartens give appreciable training in this important phase of a child's development. Here, however, teachers are opening doors to many live experiences such as visits to farms and forest preserves, the planting of flower gardens, the observation of the process of evolution from cocoon to butterfly. Such experiences are prepared for and followed by questions and suggestions motivating sense awareness. Teachers call to the children's notice beautiful clouds and shadows, the sound of voices pleasant and unpleasant, the feel of textures, and tastes and smells. The children sometimes play out a trip they have taken in order to re-experience the sense impressions of which it made them aware.

The creating of very simple plays from stories is a favorite activity in kindergarten. Familiar Mother Goose rhymes, "The Three Bears," "The Billy Goats Gruff," "The Elf and the Dormouse," are the springboards for many dramatizations. After such beginning experiences, children of the first, second, and third grades are ready for less simple stories such as some of the old fairy and folk tales—perhaps "Cinderella," "The Sleeping Beauty," "The Three Wishes"—as well as modern stories like "The 500 Hats of Bartholomew Cubbins" or "Mrs. Mallaby's Birthday."

Middle Grades

Though most widely used with kindergarten and primary children, informal drama has been discovered by teachers of older children to motivate and bring alive the social studies, and especially to develop ability in oral communication which is a part of the language arts. Several illustrations of the "integrated" plays which grow out of social studies will be found in the second part of this section. In schools where dramatics is a special subject in the curriculum, it is used chiefly as an art, like music, creative rhythmic movement, and the graphic arts.

Junior High Schools

When a school is so organized that seventh, eighth, and ninth grades constitute a junior high school, there is a definite break from the sixth to seventh grade. Departmental organization usually takes the place of the self-contained classroom, and unless the school has a special dramatics teacher, there is little chance that students will have any experience in creative drama. Even in schools where the break comes at the end of eighth grade, opportunities for informal drama are few. Pressure to complete requirements for senior high school, lack of preparation on the part of the teacher, and self-consciousness which affects boys and girls of thirteen and fourteen years cause a great falling off in this creative work at a time when it is so badly needed.

Drama as a Tool

Because children can be counted on to enjoy whatever is dramatic, it is a common practice to use dramatic techniques for the purpose of making factual material more interesting, or even as a means of ascertaining whether the pupils have grasped the meaning of what they read. Historical and geographical facts are put into dialogue form without regard for human dimensions, with the result that though dramatization may make clear whether or not children have understood subject matter, the art itself will lose interest for them.

Lack of teacher education in the philosophy and techniques of creative dramatics is the cause of the two extremes which are common in its use in this country: as a tool to teach facts, and as public exhibition. Though few of its protagonists question the value of dramatic techniques in presenting subject matter such as is illustrated in the second part of this section, they insist that the first purpose of any art is to bring happiness and enrichment to life. Therefore, if joy is lacking, the procedure prostitutes an art in somewhat the same way that an adult play loses its value as an art if its thesis overbalances its entertaining qualities.

The other extreme lies in creative dramatics' use as a public exhibition. Though it is not considered questionable to share a creative play occasionally with parents and school, the nature of improvised work is such that if exhibition is its objective, its educational purpose is largely defeated. Costume, scenery, and the necessity of much teacher-directing if the play is to be performed publicly, take it out of the hands of the children to a large extent, and change improvisation to formal production.

Workshops in creative drama are a partial solution to the problem of teachers untrained in this art, and the number of workshops has multiplied in recent years. Some inservice workshops have been only a few days in length; others have been offered for a week or two; and university extension courses meet, as a rule, for two hours on one evening a week during a semester. Such workshops are more often offered by a college or university than by the public schools themselves. As administrative and curriculum heads have come to realize the potentialities of creative drama, many local, county, state, and national educational meetings are giving it a place on their programs and encouraging the use of it in their schools. Though few supervisors are provided as yet, many teachers' colleges offer a course in the subject, and in some universities it is required of all students majoring in elementary education.

Schools with Trained Specialists

A large number of private elementary schools over the country have trained specialists teaching dramatics, both formal and informal. The more progressive of such schools, in many cases the "country day" type, believing in creative teaching in all areas, consider creative dramatics ideal for the elementary age level. Practices from several of such schools are given in the second part of this section.

Among public schools having regular dramatic departments with a supervisor and trained dramatic teachers are the elementary schools in Evanston, Illinois, a city of 75,000. Since 1924 this school system has offered children of the seventh and eighth grades electives in informal drama, the classes meeting either two or three times weekly during the regular elective hours of forty-five minutes each. After several years, the work was extended to the middle grades as a regular subject for two thirty or forty-five-minute periods a week. Whatever dramatic activity goes on in the primary grades is guided by the classroom teachers. The dramatic teachers of the middle grades confer often with the classroom teachers, and base many of the creative plays on material chosen from literature or social studies in the regular course of study. For instance, one might see a fifth grade class, which had just seen a film of Hawaii as a part of its study of that new state, experiencing, with Hawaiian music, such rhythmic movements as paddling an outrigger canoe, riding a surf board, dancing a hula, harvesting sugar cane and pineapples.

In the seventh and eighth grades (which are organized into "intermediate schools"), dramatics is one of many electives, some of which meet for two forty-five minute periods a week, some for three. Every pupil may take two electives each semester. These grades are departmental, so that dramatic courses are not correlated with other subjects.

However, in Skiles, one of the new Evanston schools, experiments are being carried on in fusing all arts and sciences into unified learning experiences for the children. The dramatic department is headed by a supervisor who is also a faculty member of Northwestern University School of Speech, teaching creative dramatics and children's theatre to university students.[1] There are at present in the elementary school dramatic department twelve dramatic teachers, all graduates of speech and theatre schools.

Winnetka, Illinois, is another community which places much emphasis on dramatic expression. Carleton Washburne, for many years superintendent of the Winnetka schools, has voiced his belief in the worth of creative dramatics.[2] From the early twenties every elementary school in the community has had a specialist as coordinator of creative activities. This teacher helps to plan creative activities of the school, demonstrates techniques for classroom teachers who have not had special training, and gives the creative arts status in the school and community.

"Platoon" schools, of which there were many in the earlier part of this century, placed much emphasis on communication. Daily auditorium periods were one of the features of these famous "work, study, play" schools originated by William Wirt, superintendent for many years of the Gary, Indiana schools. Several grade levels met together each day with trained specialists, for an hour of music appreciation and experience in speech and drama. Objectives were both cultural and educational, the audiences being as important as the programs where all might share in the most interesting and exciting learning experiences of each classroom. Gradually, the trend back to the "self-contained classroom" undermined the distinctive Gary system until at present all elementary auditoriums have disappeared and speech is taught only in senior high schools. There are still a number of elementary schools over the country based on the Gary plan, but probably none which so thoroughly exemplifies the creative ideas of William Wirt as did the Gary schools.

Flint, Michigan, has approximately a thousand children in after-school classes in creative dramatics, children's theatre, and puppetry, in a program sponsored by the public schools and financed by the Mott Foundation. The coordinator of the program is Helen Brown, who chooses teachers, supervises their work, and arranges for workshops and extension courses from Michigan State University for their training.

The Akron, Ohio, elementary schools for a number of years have had a speech department headed by Dorothy Kester, with a staff of specialists who teach remedial speech, as well as choric speaking and creative dramatics. Arlington, Virginia, Madison, Wisconsin, Freeport, Illinois, and other public schools scattered over the country offer some work in creative dramatics with trained teachers in the elementary or junior high school. Most of such schools are in the Middle West, which has been the most progressive area in this respect in the entire country. The influence of Northwestern University, which has offered courses in creative dramatics and children's theatre since 1924, has been at least partially responsible for this trend. The state of Washington, however, has become a live center of creative dramatics in the last few years. Under the leadership of the University of Washington, the Northwest is being educated to the need for this art through courses at the university headed by Agnes Haaga and observation classes, workshops, lectures and extension courses by Miss Haaga and Geraldine Brain Siks. Margaret Woods, formerly on the University of Washington staff, has offered workshops, extension classes, and inservice training in this art.

Practices in Elementary and Junior High Schools

Creative teachers are always highly individual. They do not fit neatly into categories because conformity to pattern is inconsistent with creative teaching. Therefore, though leaders in creative dramatics have certain basic principles in common, their practices differ widely. The following illustrations from public and private elementary schools in different parts of the country are typical of this variation.

Kindergarten and Primary Classrooms

On the very first day of school, when many kindergarten children are too shy to be audible in telling their names to the group, one teacher introduces them to one another with a

bit of make-believe that never fails to set them at their ease.[3]
With a puppet clown to ask each child his name, she quickly
puts an end to their uncomfortable shyness by having the puppet
make ridiculous mistakes in repeating the names. When one
child answered faintly, "Christine Ivy," he cocked his head
to listen and then said cheerfully, "Oh, Christmas Ivy!"

"No, no!" shouted the whole group laughingly. "Christine
Ivy!" After he had made several other comical mistakes in
the names, the children felt pleasantly superior and acquainted
with one another. Their complete acceptance of the make-
believe, in spite of the fact that the teacher was standing in
plain view with the puppet on her hand, was evidenced by the
little girl who exclaimed gaily as she went out the door that
afternoon, "He'll never remember them until tomorrow!"

Out of the free imaginative play in housekeeping and block
corners of every kindergarten room come the beginnings of
many kinds of creative expression. Boats and trains, shops
and churches built with the big blocks inspire the "families"
of little girls and dolls to take trips to shopping centers and
to go to church schools, while the boys do all kinds of intricate
mechanical work on boats and planes. What children teach
about themselves while they are trying on the lives of grownups is a constant source of learning to teachers and psychologists who are fostering their growth. In the words of one
of them, "To read the language of play is to read the minds
and hearts of children."[4]

From kindergarten to the end of the eighth grade, children
in the National College of Education[5] have a challenging course
in creative rhythmic movement. Under the leadership of Jean
Duffy they are given a thorough foundation in basic movements
before any emphasis is placed on dramatic rhythms. After
children have experienced a piece of music kinesthetically,
Mrs. Duffy may ask them to sit down, close their eyes, and
see if it makes them think of anything they have ever experienced. A running, turning movement became for one boy a
dog chasing his tail. For a girl it was a circular sprinkler;
while still another child thought of it as the movement of a
planet. For some vigorous boys in the second grade, a complex movement of leaping and falling evolved into a deer leaping
as he was pursued by a pioneer hunter, and falling when he

was killed. Rachel Field's eight-line poem "A Summer Morning"[6] gave great opportunity to older girls, since it has a different kind of movement with each line. Scarves helped them characterize the dawn creeping, gulls flying, the sea putting on its dress of "midsummer loveliness," the trees stirring, the wind calling to a child to "Get up, my dear, it is today."

Live experiences with sense impressions, and a teacher who questions children about beautiful things they see and hear, touch, smell, and taste, may be a prelude to what Geraldine Siks calls "Hyacinth Time." Quoting from the ancient Persian poet who wrote, "If thou hast two pennies, spend one for bread; with the other buy hyacinths for thy soul," she tells of classroom teachers who begin and end each school day with "Hyacinth-time."[7] An awareness question is asked at the close of the day. When the children return the next morning they either take a few minutes to share "hyacinths" or each child writes or draws his idea. Such questions may be, "What do you see that tells you it is spring?" "What is yellow?" "What was the biggest thing you saw this week?"

Creative plays based on simple stories and rhymes may be seen in many, many kindergarten and primary classrooms. A first-grade teacher in Kansas City finds that her most successful arrangements for a story dramatization is "theatre-in-the-round."[8] When the children are seated in a circle the action flows in and out among them so that they seem a part of the play. If another character is needed, he can be brought immediately into the action. When the mother goat and her kids need bushes to hide in, they drop down behind some of the audience; and the comments and enthusiasm of those who are not playing are close at hand, a part of what is going on.

Third through Sixth Grade

"You promised to bring a pixie," reminded a third grade class as the dramatics teacher came into the room one morning.[9] "I did!" she replied. "Get out your magic spectacles!" And as the children drew them out of pockets and put them expectantly on their noses, she walked to the door, knelt down, and returned with her hand held carefully before her, palm up. The children gathered around her, eyes dancing. "Isn't he the cutest little fellow you ever saw?" she began. "With

the tiny, pointed red cap, his green jacket—" "And his shoes
that are too long for him," finished a little boy.

The teacher held the pixie close to her ear for a moment,
and then said, "He thinks he would like you, and he wants to
walk over onto Jimmie's hand." Out went Jimmie's hand and
over walked the pixie. "I think he wants to tell you something,"
she said. And after a moment, "What did he say?"

Jimmie looked a bit baffled until the teacher helped him
out. "Was it a secret?" A quick nod of relief from Jimmie.
And then the teacher took the pixie to the open window, saying
that it would have to fly away to Pixieland. A waving of hands
as the tiny pixie flew away, a calling out of good-bys—and
they all turned eagerly to the play they were about to create.
What had the pixie incident done for them? It had built a delightful rapport between teacher and class, stirred imaginations, set a mood for the little play which they worked together
to develop, and brought a sparkle to the commonplace classroom.

More than any other one aspect of creative dramatics, the
pantomime of activities may be seen in fourth, fifth, and sixth
grade classrooms. Sometimes it is purely for relaxation and
recreation, on a stormy day, perhaps, when the children cannot go out-of-doors for recess. With little required from the
teacher, it becomes a kind of game in which volunteers pantomime their own experiences for other children to guess. On
the day of a blizzard one group pantomimed all the things people
were doing because of the storm. Favorite sports, adventures
they would like to have, incidents from books, and any number
of other bits of dramatic action are played as guessing games
or charades.

Improvised plays from stories are favorite practices in creative dramatics among probably all boys and girls during this
period, and they are always a strong incentive for group cooperation. The following is a brief account of the good guidance
to be seen in many classrooms. This experience included also
poetry reading, creative rhythmic movement, and graphic art. [10]

A swirling snowstorm served as a springboard for imagination in the playing, by fourth graders, of George Cooper's
poem "The Wonderful Weaver." Because the snow set the mood,

only the inner quiet of the teacher and her relaxed voice were
needed further for the introduction of the poem.

> There's a wonderful weaver
>   High up in the air,
> And he weaves a white mantle
>   For cold earth to wear,
> With the wind for his shuttle,
>   The cloud for his loom,
> How he weaves! How he weaves!
>   In the light, in the gloom.
>
> Oh, with finest of laces
>   He decks bush and tree,
> On the bare, flinty meadows
>   A cover lays he.
> Then a quaint cap he places
>   On pillar and post,
> And he changes the pump
>   To a grim, silent ghost.
>
> But this wonderful weaver
>   Grows weary at last,
> And the shuttle lies idle
>   That once flew so fast;
> Then the sun peeps abroad
>   On the work that is done;
> And he smiles: "I'll unravel
>   It all just for fun!"[11]

At the end of the reading the teacher paused for a moment,
and then ventured:
"Who is this weaver, do you think?"
"He's Jack Frost." "He's a weaver." "He could be anything."
"How does he move up there in the sky?"
"He moves lightly. " "Gently. " "He has to move lightly because what he is weaving is light. " "May I show you how he
moves?"
Others volunteered also until it looked as if a snow storm
were on the way. As the teacher and part of the group began
reading with hushed voices, the others dipped and swayed and,
caught up in the witchery of the poem, arms, hands, heads,

bodies, legs, and spirits were released. Movements were large, light, free. Linda lightly threaded her wind-shuttle with a cloud, turning her head to see the wispy trail of snow behind. After they had floated to their seats, the teacher asked, "What did you like about the weavers up there?"

"They were light." "You couldn't hear them." "I liked Linda's loom."

"May we have a turn?" "May we be weavers?" asked the ones who had been in their seats. Weavers and readers exchanged roles so that all had had a turn at reading and playing out the first stanza before the period ended. For the next session the teacher brought the record of "Clair de Lune," by Debussy. The children listened carefully, and on the second playing, "as each began to feel inside like a weaver," they left their seats and let themselves be carried with the music. The same record later motivated interesting abstract crayon designs.

"Now that the weaver has woven so much beautiful lacy material," said the teacher when they met the next time, "let's think of all the places he'll put it"; and after she had read again the second stanza plenty of suggestions came forth. A cast was chosen from the volunteers, with a weaver who began to weave "with the wind for his shuttle, a cloud for his loom," and to lay his fragile lace on trees, bushes, on a park bench, stop-and-go lights, a playhouse, a fence post (on which he lightly placed a cap of snow and tied it in a bowknot under the post's chin)! Finally they played the three stanzas, with the teacher as the sun; and as she came up, she began to improvise: "The world is cold and dark. Everything is stiff and frozen. But here comes the sun and it's getting warmer. Look what is happening to the snow on this park bench!" (Jeff, the snow on the bench, by now was unfreezing. He slowly slid to the floor.) "I do declare, I'm turning the snow to water." By now all the children were lying on the floor—inert, boneless. They were melting. Eyes were closing. They were limpid water.

This use of "The Wonderful Weaver" indicates how easily and happily different arts are woven together in a creative experience. One motivates and heightens enjoyment in another, according to classroom teachers who tell of the surprising improvement in art expression, for instance, when it is preceded by dramatic play.

In a Canton, Ohio, school, Stephine McCue finds that creative writing has strong motivation for her group of gifted fifth
grade children when they know that the story they write will
later be dramatized if it is good enough. A music teacher in
Kansas City worked out with a group of children a play based
on the life of Mozart, using the composer's music. [12] Children
with the guidance of a physical education teacher in Overland
Park, Kansas, developed a creative dance from "Our Lady's
Juggler. "[13] One teacher who guided her children in creating a
pantomime with costumes and masks, showing how art, music,
and dramatic play can be combined to create a mood in rhythm,
says "the children put the most feeling and grace, however,
into a performance when they are free of masks, costumes,
and most properties. My children can use the gym floor for
rhythms and songs, and without costume or property can create
anything from a flowing river to a queen on her throne. "[14]

Creative Dramatics Techniques in Academic Subjects

If the joy of the art is not lessened by its practical use, creative dramatics techniques can illuminate and enrich whatever
is studied. Here is a first-grade teacher who motivates skill
in reading by letting a child choose a cast to pantomime the
story as he reads it. [15] "If he bogs down in the reading," the
teacher says, "the cry goes up from the stalled performers,
'Read! Read!' How this drives them to study like beavers to
master their stories!"

A third grade teacher in Boston, in selecting from a long al-
phabetical list ten new words a week for spelling, chooses those
which have enough relationship one to another so that children
can weave them into a story. [16] Studying these words, written
on the board to see how they can be made into a playable tale,
children not only learn the spelling, but by using them in a
dramatization gain a real understanding of their meaning.

Examples of the use of social studies as material may be
found wherever creative dramatics experiences are encouraged
by the teacher. A typical example comes from a Seattle school-
room where the course of study in the fourth grade includes
the history of Seattle. Documentaries in television as well as
a great amount of research in the library gave children background for dramatic scenes they developed. Norma Roblee,

their teacher, was interested to see how many fields they
could include in this project; and, indeed, with episodes which
concerned making camp, stories told around a campfire, a
birthday party, square dancing, and various other pioneer
experiences, they needed to draw on practically every subject
in the curriculum.

Science, language arts, and social studies played the major
part in an elaborate dramatic project on the sea called "High,
Wide, and Deep," developed by sixth grade children in Huey-
town, Alabama. The work was guided by Lucile W. Flynn,
with Dorothy Schwartz as consultant, and was presented as a
demonstration at a meeting of the department of classroom
teachers of the Alabama Education Association, in Birmingham.
Following an extensive period of research, children created
costumes, sets, and properties for the play which they developed. Achievement tests showed that during the year in which
this project was developed the children made most unusual
progress in paragraph comprehension, word meaning, and
spelling.

An interesting example of children's independent use of
creative dramatics in the study of French shows how natural
its techniques are to boys and girls. After a group at the Villa
de Chantal School in Rock Island, Illinois, had translated a
story, the teacher was surprised and amused to overhear on
the playground a lively dramatic version of the story going
on with improvised dialogue, all in French.

Integrated Projects

The Keith Country Day School of Rockford College, in Rockford, Illinois, gives its pupils many experiences in developing
projects in which creative plays are the center of a broad study
involving language arts, social studies, scientific research,
arts and crafts—in fact, every aspect of the curriculum. One of
the most interesting and valuable of such studies was a recent
African project carried out with a fourth grade by Neva Balmer,
the classroom teacher, and Wilma McNees, their teacher of
creative dramatics. It began with a geographical and social
study of the continent, and gradually centered on Zululand, the
location of the story chosen as the basis of the play they developed. This was the story of "The Seven Grandmothers,"[17]

which, though not highly dramatic, gave them a wonderful opportunity to use all that they had learned.

During a period of several months the children read seven books about Africa, heard poems and primitive music characteristic of the country, learned songs and dances, saw a film, "The Musical Forest," and heard a travel talk on Africa. As the play was growing, they made two murals of animal and plant scenes; made pouches of powder for medicines, masks, chicken-bone necklaces enameled with bright colors; painted tempera scenes; and, most interesting of all, each child made a drum from a nail keg laced with goatskin and decoratively enameled. The boys and girls were proud of the play which they presented for school and parents; and their teachers felt that besides building a keen interest in Africa and Africans, the play had served to unify and build high the morale of a group of children whom the teacher had not been able to reach in any other way.

A Play Based on the Idea of *Time*

Sometimes, on rare occasions, the miracle of the theatre happens even in a children's informal play. Rapport between a skilled and sensitive teacher and a group of children who have experienced creative drama for several years may bring about a play in which imagination takes wing. Such a play was one based on the idea of *time*. It was developed by two sixth grade classes at Miller School in Evanston, Illinois, guided by their dramatic teacher, Ann Heekin, and their two classroom teachers, Armin Beck and Amelia Vorhees.

At the very beginning, the children talked about time: what it was, what it meant to them. "Time is everything that has been and will be," ventured one boy. "Men have always been trying to find better ways to measure time," said another. One girl wrote her idea into a poem which she later set to music:

> Time to me is a great white bird,
> Spreading its wings through the sky.
> Eager hands reach up to grasp it,
> As it flies relentlessly by.

The play which came out of their first gropings and their

later study in history, science, poetry, music, and art showed
man in his measurement and his use of time, from the Egyptian
with his slow rhythm of life down to the swift jazz beat of modern man "who has put Time on the assembly line." Humor,
pathos, satire, and a kind of childish wisdom characterized
this play, which ended on a note of exaltation as the young
"Year" started forth to carry to earth his message: "You cannot
grasp Time, you cannot hoard it. You must spend it freely,
joyously. One minute wisely spent can be worth a thousand
years."

Junior High Schools

In Cosmopolis, Washington, Elsie Nagrodski uses creative
dramatics extensively in correlated projects, believing that it
is especially valuable in guiding a teenage child to understand
himself through this transition period. After a discussion of
their state's program of highway improvement, the students
played the folktale "The Stone in the Road." During the evaluation period, one of the students said, "When you have a problem, it's kind of like a stone in the road—you keep going
around it because you don't know what else to do." This led
into a discussion of stones in their own roads, which prompted
several students to come to the teacher with personal problems
which she and they talked over and tried together to solve.

Nan Elkins, of Austin, Texas, who teaches in the Allen
Junior High School, uses creative dramatics as a "loosening
up" device before pupils go into formal drama or public speaking. She finds that they consider this improvised drama a re-
ward for doing other things required in their speech-drama
course.

Boys and girls in the eighth grade elective in drama in the
Evanston, Illinois, schools are introduced to Shakespeare's
plays in the way they were intended to reach people: by giving
students a chance to see and take part in them. Because the
language is very difficult for them, the creative approach is
especially valid; and therefore, after they have had background
material on Shakespeare and Elizabethan England, students
hear the story of one of the plays, discuss plot and characters,
decide on episodes they would like to do creatively, hear the

text of one of these scenes read by the teacher in order to sense the flavor of the dialogue, and then "try on" the characters in various situations. Gradually they develop the scene, keeping it as true to Shakespeare as they are able, and using many expressions from the plays. Favorite among the stories they have developed creatively have been *The Taming of the Shrew, A Midsummer Night's Dream,* and *Macbeth.* With such an introduction to Shakespeare—offered only by skilled teachers and to young people who have had several years' experience in creative dramatics—students approach their high school study of the plays with interest and confidence.

Basic Principles of Creative Dramatics

Most teachers who guide boys and girls in creative dramatic experiences follow, in general, these basic principles:

1. Though creative dramatics, like all other arts, should first of all be enjoyable, its objective in education is the individual and social development of every child who participates.

2. The teacher is a guide rather than a director. The play is the children's, and it is the role of the leader to make the process of development significant to them.

3. Stories chosen as material for creative dramatics should be of good literary quality and be suited to the age and interests of the children who are to use them. They should have conflict, action, clearly defined plot, interesting characters, and a worthy idea.

4. They should be introduced in such a way as to relate them to the past experience of the children who are to use them as a basis for creative plays.

5. A play is created character by character, scene by scene, before the entire story is played from beginning to end.

6. Children are motivated to observe people so that characters may be true; and to "be" rather than "pretend" so that characterization may come from inside.

7. A part of the group becomes an audience for the playing of each scene so that the players can communicate, and the audience may appreciate and evaluate their ideas in creating the drama.

8. The play is kept fluid by continual free improvisation. Because it is never fixed by being written, it constantly challenges creative thinking.

9. The teacher guides the children by skillful questions to think of more possibilities in the story than they at first see, and to understand meanings and values.

10. If a play developed by creative drama techniques is shared with an audience other than a part of the group, such a presentation is usually in the nature of a demonstration; or it may be an informal sharing with another group of children. Costumes, scenery, and make-up are rarely used unless it is an ambitious integrated play in which these production aspects are a part of the creative process.

Summary

The trend toward "self-contained classrooms" results in fewer special teachers in public school systems, with the result that practically all subjects must be taught by the classroom teacher. In most good schools there are supervisors, consultants, or special teachers for music and the graphic arts, but seldom for creative dramatics. Knowledge of the philosophy and techniques of creative dramatics is steadily growing, however, because of college courses, workshops, demonstrations, and textbooks. Even in this age of science and technology, there is increased appreciation of creative arts and widespread recognition of the contribution of creative drama as a language art. Though it is still too much used as a tool to make facts palatable, there is hopeful growth toward understanding its value as an art—an art which can vitalize social studies and literature, enrich school experiences, help in guidance, and make children more sensitive to beauty and truth, more aware of human and artistic values.

The need is for creative dramatics supervisors or consultants in creative dramatics to teach elementary teachers who have had no training, to help them in their more ambitious projects, and to give real status to this art. Before creative dramatics can win the place it merits in the school curriculum, parents, administrators, and curriculum directors must be educated to recognize its significance in a child's development. One of the best ways to spread far and wide the knowledge of this art will be highly effective films showing the progress of groups of children experiencing creative dramatics over a period of time. Other ways are articles in magazines read by parents and administrators; discussion by leaders in county, state, and national educational meetings; demonstrations by children for smaller groups; and constantly better teaching of creative dramatics in universities, teachers' colleges, and elementary schools. All of these steps are being taken or contemplated by CTC. The impact on education will depend largely on how rapid and how dynamic are the forces which can be summoned to work toward this significant aspect of a child's growth and development.

17 Creative Dramatics in Programs for Exceptional Children

Barbara M. McIntyre ✐

The Committee of the National Society for the Study of Education defines exceptional children as "those who deviate from what is supposed to be average in physical, mental, emotional, or social characteristics to such an extent that they receive special educational services in order to develop to their maximum capacity."[1] This committee made a conservative estimate that from 10 to 12 per cent of children of elementary and secondary school age would be considered exceptional and in need of special educational services.[2] Included in the exceptional group are the physically handicapped, the partially sighted and blind, those with speech and hearing disorders, the mentally handicapped, and the mentally gifted. All these children require special help in order that they may reach their highest potential development.

In October, 1954, Dr. Leonard Mayo, Director of the Association for the Aid of Crippled Children, presented a *Creed for Exceptional Children* to the Conference on the Qualifications and Preparation of Teachers of Exceptional Children. His final section summed up the philosophy which is pertinent to our present investigation.

> Above all, we believe in the exceptional child himself; in his capacity for development so frequently retarded by the limits of present knowledge; in his right to a full life too often denied him through lack of imagination and ingenuity on the part of his elders; in his passion for freedom and independence that can be his only when those who guide and teach him have learned the lessons of humility, and in whom there resides an effective confluence of the trained mind and the warm heart.[3]

This expression of belief in the ability of the exceptional child correlates readily with the basic philosophy of creative dramatics for all children. Because of this interdependence and because of the great numbers of children who are exceptional, this monograph will deal with creative dramatics for the exceptional groups—the physically handicapped, the mentally retarded (emphasis on the educable), the speech-and-hearing-handicapped, the visually handicapped, and the mentally gifted.

Harry J. Baker, Director of the Psychological Clinic, Detroit schools, believes "that one of the greatest obstacles to a better and more complete program of education for exceptional children arises from the wide-spread misconception that they are a class separate and distinct from normal children."[4] Bearing this in mind, we therefore need to recognize that creative dramatics has its basic principles and practices which hold true for all children. Modifications must be sought in the light of the individual gift or handicap but the essentials remain the same.

General Investigation

How far is creative dramatics being used in programs for the exceptional child? What are the basic principles and practices in this field? A brief evaluation was made of the curricula of special schools for exceptional children. This was followed by an examination of the curricula references listed in the *Directory for Exceptional Children.*[5] A survey of the Teacher Training Curricula for Teachers of Exceptional Children was undertaken.[6] A questionnaire requesting information concerning programs of creative dramatics for the exceptional child was sent to fifty of the colleges and universities appearing in the *Directory of Colleges and Universities Offering Training in Children's Theatre and Creative Dramatics.*[7] Finally this same questionnaire was sent to individuals, teachers, clinicians, and organizations all known to be interested in activities for the exceptional child.

The examination of the curricula references for the children attending special schools proved negative. Although there were frequent references to music activities, speech activities, and arts and crafts, not one school referred to dramatics.

This was, however, condensed material and it was noted that in a few of the cases where some dramatic activity was known to be carried out no mention of it was made. It may be assumed that, although there is probably some dramatic activity in some of the schools, it is very slight and not emphasized.

Examination of detailed curricula for the training of teachers for the exceptional child in ten of our leading universities also proved negative. It was noted, however, that in many of the course listings reference was made which could conceivably include some instruction in creative dramatics. Such courses as Techniques of Language Development, Classroom Methods, Techniques of Speech, Vocabulary Development, and Curriculum Development may have dealt at least briefly with the subject. In some instances reference was also made to the opportunity for elective courses. Although these elective courses were not listed it is reasonable to assume that creative dramatics may be one of them. Creative dramatics as such appears to receive little, if any, emphasis in the over-all training of teachers for exceptional children.

Results of the questionnaire sent to colleges and universities offering courses in creative dramatics proved more fruitful. Twenty-seven completed forms were returned. Of these, seventeen institutions indicated that their institution placed no special emphasis on creative dramatics for the exceptional child. Of the eight institutions where creative dramatics for the exceptional child was considered, four made use of it in the speech clinic as well as in the teacher training program, two conducted special classes for the exceptional child, and two included exceptional children within their regular programs. Two of the colleges reported cooperation with the school district in a program of creative dramatics for the exceptional child, with special emphasis on gifted children.

Results of the questionnaire sent to individuals and organizations known to be interested in activities for the exceptional child were encouraging. Four teachers and three clinicians completed the form. All seven reported that the inclusion of creative dramatics within their programs had been very successful. All suggested that creative dramatics should be part of the training for all those working with the exceptional child. The two organizations, a community theatre and a recreation department, reported successful creative dramatics programs for exceptional children.

From an analysis of the completed questionnaires a picture developed. It revealed that very little was being done to provide creative dramatics for the handicapped exceptional child. It suggested, however, that there was a definite awakening of interest in creative dramatics for the gifted. It showed that in the few instances where creative dramatics had been incorporated as an activity for the exceptional child, the results proved rewarding. It appeared that creative dramatics programs were incorporated most frequently in work with the speech- and hearing-handicapped, while such programs for the mentally retarded, physically handicapped, and visually handicapped were incorporated less frequently.

Speech- and Hearing-Handicapped

Speech- and hearing-handicapped children were most frequently involved in creative dramatics in the speech clinic as part of the therapy, or in school programs as part of the speech improvement class. Creative dramatics in the speech clinic appeared to be used as an adjunct to therapy in order to provide a successful speaking experience, as a technique to stimulate auditory training, or as a type of play therapy. In some instances it appeared that creative dramatics may have been confused with role playing and sociodrama.

Mentally Retarded Children

Several successfully conducted classes for the mentally retarded were reported. In most cases the objective was to stimulate language and social development. Dramatic play, rhythm, and pantomime formed the core of the activity. Benefits derived were listed as enlarged vocabulary, increased social and emotional poise, and happy stimulating fun. Such an activity was usually sponsored through a school program or community theatre at the request of a parent group seeking activities for its children. It was noted also that creative dramatics appeared to be used in classrooms for the educable mentally retarded when the teacher was aware of its use. Such

teachers were generally those who had witnessed creative
dramatics with normal children and had adapted the technique
to the needs of these special children.

Physically Handicapped Children

Physically handicapped children of normal mental ability
presented a different problem. However, it was reported that
adaptations were easily made depending on the type and degree
of the physical handicap. Hospitalized children were reported
to have profited from creative dramatics activities. These
were carried on according to the individual needs of the children ranging from simple pantomimes in storytelling for the
more seriously ill to creative group activity carried on by the
less ill children within a ward. At least one master's thesis
was reported in progress, dealing with the use of creative
dramatics within the hospital.

Visually Handicapped Children

Visually handicapped children were reported to have been
integrated within regular creative dramatics programs. Where
partially sighted children were reported to be part of a regular
group, successful programs resulted. The sighted children
appeared to make the necessary adjustment to the handicap
without apparent effort, and regular principles and practices
prevailed. An interesting "buddy" system whereby blind children were aided by their sighted classmates was described
by one teacher who integrated several blind children into a
normal group. From this it would appear that this group of
exceptional children can most readily be integrated into participation in regular groups.

Gifted Children

Today a great deal of emphasis is being placed on the upper
two per cent of the population—the gifted child. Often the exceptional abilities of these children go unrecognized and un-
challenged. These children need to be given every opportunity
to develop their individual aptitudes and self-expression not

only for their own betterment but for the good of the whole population. Participation in creative dramatics may provide such opportunity. "Major-work" classes in Cleveland and Detroit have been pioneer groups with the gifted. Enrichment in curriculum has provided many advantages for these children. Dramatic activities have formed an important part of these programs. More recently a Report of the Program for Gifted Children in the Portland, Oregon Public Schools, by Robert C. Wilson of Reed College, was given to the Research Conference on the "Identification of Creative Scientific Talent." This report emphasizes the development of seven special talents in the elementary and the high school. These were listed as "art, creative dance, creative dramatics, creative writing, music, social leadership, and mechanical talent."

Reports of the creative dramatics activities in such programs for the gifted child as the one found in Colfax School in Pittsburgh include creative playwriting and production. Through the introduction of this material it appears that the gifted child may progress beyond traditional child activities into the realm more often reserved for the adult. Gifted children need disciplined freedom in order that they may expand and express their exceptional talents. Creative dramatics with its careful guidance and opportunity for self-expression may offer a unique opportunity for the gifted child. As yet, little experimentation in this area has been reported. Recent increased interest points to future graduate study and investigation.

Summary

Although this investigation does not present a complete picture of creative dramatics for the exceptional child, three basic factors emerge. First, very little has been accomplished in the area of creative dramatics for the exceptional child. However, where creative dramatics has been included as an activity for these children, reports of beneficial success have been noted. Further, most programs have been conducted along the same basic principles as those laid down for the average child.

Second, what creative dramatic activity there has been appears to have stemmed from observation of regular creative dramatics programs for the average child or from participation in university courses involving creative dramatics. Here teachers have noted this activity and have adapted it to their specific use with their special children. Therefore, the value of including creative dramatics in the training of teachers of exceptional children is the second basic factor to be stressed.

Third, research and experimentation with the exceptional child has barely begun. This area needs to be stimulated and encouraged in order to provide creative dramatics for all children.

18 Creative Dramatics in Religious Education

Emily Gillies ✑

The superintendent of schools in a large city recently confronted a group of business executives, educators, and doctors with the following question: "A boy has just received a high school diploma. What does that mean to you?"

No two of the persons questioned could agree. Opinions varied from the implication that finishing high school simply meant an endurance contest requiring no special academic skill, to the conclusion that the boy had reached a point in life where he would now choose between working or continuing his education.

In examining creative dramatics in religious education, one finds himself in a similar quandary. It appears that among specialists who have made a thoughtful study of creative dramatics in a religious setting, there are many disagreements and conflicts regarding definitions and directions. Marvin P. Halverson takes issue with a basic problem not of creative dramatics in religious education, but of religious education itself.[1] Mr. Halverson says, "The term 'religious drama' is justified in being used when it refers to a body of dramatic literature possessing insight into the human situation and the overcoming of man's dilemma. The tendency in religious education is to teach values, morals, etc., and is in conflict with the church itself which tries to teach what goes beyond . . . that life is to be lived by faith, not works."[2]

Summarizing the attitude of the drama staff at Union Theological Seminary, Robert E. Seaver objects to the term "religious drama."[3] He states, ". . . We feel

159

it is wrong to think in terms of the detachment of religion and life. If we call ourselves and live by the knowledge of our creed as Christians and/or Jews, the main question we must ask is 'What does it say in *all of life* to us?' If religious life is confined to Sunday School, it is not enough, and gives a queer connotation to the term 'religious drama'. "[4]

To clarify where such statements stand in relationship to this present study, a reflective religious educator, Francis W. Voelcker, says,

> As I think about the statements by Mr. Seaver and Mr. Halverson . . . both, I think, are objecting to a rigid classification of religious drama because this suggests dealing with religious ideas in traditional language. These two gentlemen reflect the more widely held understanding of theology today, which sees the profound problems and relationships of man with man as essentially religious despite the language used to describe them. [5]

Accepting the fact that there will be many disagreements in definition of terms, we shall attempt the following objectivity: For the purpose of this study we shall consider "religious education" as meaning classes for children in Sunday School, Church School, or Bible School programs, whether run as part of weekly worship, after-school or vacation programs. Our purpose has been not to provide statistics, since few which prove anything clearly are available, but to show a sampling of some of the work being done in various denominations, particularly when the work points the way to certain new directions. The limitations felt in this kind of work are mountainous, for possibly some of the most interesting developments of all have not been reported only because information was not available.

Lay Teacher's Use of Creative Dramatics

Some of the most imaginative teaching in this field was done in the early thirties. At that time the late Hulda Niebuhr was using creative dramatic techniques at the interdenominational Riverside Church in New York City. Some of the scenes developed creatively were then presented as part of worship services for various groups within the church. Material for these plays evolved from such events as the home visits of missionaries from foreign countries. [6]

Today use of creative dramatics in building scenes to be shared at children's worship services is a common practice in many religious denominations. An effective illustration can be found in Kansas City, Missouri, in a Disciples of Christ Church. Here the husband-and-wife team of Ann and Albert Viola work with junior and senior high school students creatively developing worship services which last fifteen to twenty minutes. The scenes correlate story material, music, and religious art. Recently students were taken to a Hebrew Temple where they observed a worship service; they later built their own fine service based on Hebrew ritual.

Individual Sunday School teachers in many denominations throughout the United States have been experimenting with creative dramatics on many different age levels. On the East Coast at the Congregational Church in New Canaan, Connecticut, Nancy Cole, beginning in the fall of 1957, inaugurated an active creative dramatics program. [7] As part of the after-school youth program of the church, creative dramatics classes were arranged on Thursday afternoons for those who had the greatest needs among approximately 200 children, from first through ninth grade. In the fall of 1958 three creative scenes based on "animals in Christmas" were developed and were used as part of the Christmas program presented in the chancel; later, in the study of Sophia Fahs's *Jesus, the Carpenter's Son,* several groups worked out improvisations and pantomimes amplifying their Sunday School work.

In the West at the University Lutheran Church in Seattle, Barbara Salisbury used creative dramatics in a different way. As superintendent of the junior department for her church and school and as substitute teacher she used her teaching opportunities to introduce creative dramatics, working on Old Testament personalities such as Joseph, Elijah, and Elisha. In the summer of 1956 it was possible for her to concentrate for ten weeks on creative dramatics with a group of eleven children aged nine to eleven. She reported that the results of this experience were rewarding, particularly in interest and in inspirational growth.

Teachers of some denominations feel the pressure of too

little time and too little space in which to try creative dramatics, but others use creative dramatics extensively. Apparently
the relaxation felt by the slower pace of summer allows more
of this kind of teaching, especially in vacation church schools.
The First Baptist Church of Los Angeles tried creative dramatics during the summer of 1958 both in the primary and junior
departments, and expanded and extended teaching sessions
have been introduced in this same church. In several denominations, carrying the teachings of church and temple to children in religious education classes by means of puppets and
shadow plays has been found effective. A puppet show was
created for huge groups of children for a special church occa-
sion at Trinity Episcopal Cathedral in Cleveland. With sensitivity and careful research, Ohio puppeteer George Latshaw inter-
viewed and worked with an architect, an organist, a stained-
glass maker, and the Episcopal bishop of the diocese, the
Right Rev. Nelson M. Burroughs, to produce a show of real
excellence. Each of these persons was worked into a fluid and
imaginative script which explained in children's language the
background, traditions, functions, and history of a cathedral.
Then on April 26, 1958, during a children's pilgrimage, the
production was presented to two extensive audiences totaling
over 1,700 children. The presentation concluded with a worship
service aided by an 168-voice choir of fourth to sixth graders.
Hundreds of thank-you letters sent to Bishop Burroughs recorded the deep impression made on the boys and girls by this
fresh approach. [8]

Some work is now beginning in the making of slides, film-
strips, and movies in which children have done creative dramatics, with adults from the parish cooperating in the technical
filming or photographing. The Glenview Community Church
in Glenview, Illinois, recently used fifth and sixth grade classes
to work out the Biblical story of Joseph in creative scenes.
Parish adults filmed the final scenes in color, with a syn-
chronized tape recording of the voice of one of the ministers
telling the story. The imagination in the project was very
apparent. The church approved the project to the extent of
making another color film, this one of "The Good Samaritan"
in two versions, one Biblical and one modern.

In most cases, teachers have started creative dramatics

work in their own individual churches and temples. Sometimes a leader has helped train other teachers or even all the teachers in one Sunday School to use this technique. Of course, rarest of all is the introduction of creative dramatics in any one faith on any widespread level. However, in at least two faiths there is extensive use of creative dramatics: The first is in the Church of Jesus Christ of Latter-Day Saints (Mormon) throughout the state of Utah. As one of the prime functions of the Mutual Improvement Association (MIA), division of young people twelve years old and up, a creative form of folk dramatization called "Roadshow" is used in every unit or ward of the church throughout the state. Songs, dances, scenes, and pantomimes are created by each group to form acts, the best of which travel to different parts of the state to be viewed by other larger groups. Although the material used is not always Biblical in origin, the spirit of dedication among those both acting in and presenting the shows is so apparent that productions sometimes are a key moment for spiritual growth among the persons participating.

One branch of the church made up of deaf and dumb members recently presented a "Roadshow" which achieved one of the real dimensions of Christianity, for the participants later told the director that they felt for the first time in their lives that they were accepted as human beings. In any one year, approximately 61,000 young people participate in "Roadshow" on stage, with around 17,000 persons forming crews off stage.[9] The primary department of the church, for children up to twelve years, uses creative drama and role playing in Sunday School work also.

The other striking example of the use of large numbers of well-trained creative dramatics teachers throughout one denomination is that of the Jewish Education Committee of New York. Its school dramatics department acts as a vast resource-house, a teacher-training laboratory, and the stimulator of the use of many fine, forward-looking creative techniques in drama. More than 700 Jewish schools in the New York area alone use the services of this department. Countless others, nationwide, write in for information and materials. Among other services, the department conducts in-service courses in the use of creative dramatics as a teaching aid;

publishes dramatic materials, monographs on methodology, places and supervises professional drama teachers in approximately fifty schools in Metropolitan New York; and provides consultation in the use of creative dramatics in the classroom.

Scarcely any of the drama teachers in Jewish religious schools are volunteers, owing to the increasingly strict licensing of teachers. One of the thoroughly exciting new developments in the field of creative drama has come about through the work of Samuel J. Citron, director of the department, who had developed a technique for the use of role-playing in the teaching of the Bible. Mr. Citron also conducts workshops, training teachers to invent their own contemporary parallels of Biblical stories, encouraging the children to role-play these modern versions, and then searching in their discussions not only for the actual Biblical references, but for the moral values behind them. This new technique thus "brings to the fore the timelessness, the immediacy, the vitality of the Bible."[10]

Adult Training Programs

Having glanced briefly into what the individual lay teacher is doing in her individual classroom, we cross into the second main area of the training of adults in creative dramatics. This training is necessary before any widespread use of creative dramatics in religious education is either possible or desirable. Many of the teachers already described are resourceful persons who double not only as classroom teachers but as teacher-trainers and supervisors. Competent teachers who successfully demonstrate good creative dramatics teaching with children often are selected to offer courses in creative dramatics at leadership schools, religious drama workshops, and the like. Barbara Anderson,[11] Linnie Mae Brobston,[12] William H. Cleveland,[13] and Ella B. Magee[14] are among these persons.

It is easier to point to locations where creative dramatics is offered in religious education leadership training schools and their equivalents than it is to find colleges, seminaries, or schools of theology where a course in the application of creative dramatics to religious education has become rooted.

Among a few notable exceptions are these: McCormick Theological Seminary (Presbyterian), Chicago, Illinois, where
Hulda Niebuhr has offered work in this area for a number of
years; Union Theological Seminary (Interdenominational), New
York, where Winifred Ward taught as visiting lecturer in the
field of creative dramatics during the winter of 1957, and again
during the summer session of 1958, both times as part of the
religious drama program; University of Kansas City, Missouri,
where a course in this field is offered through extension; and
Northwest Christian College, Eugene, Oregon, which describes
its course as "informal drama in religious education," offered
by Marguerite Dallas. A number of Roman Catholic colleges
are listed as offering courses which either entirely or partially
cover creative drama, but no information could be obtained as
to how much stress was laid on its application to the religious
education field. [15]

An unusual trend is reported from the Boston University
School of Theology by Harold Ehrensperger, who says "In our
new degree program a Master's in Fine Arts in Religious
Drama given through our School of Fine Arts in cooperation
with the School of Theology has a course in creative dramatics
as a prerequisite for the degree. We do not yet have anyone
to teach it. "[16]

Creative Dramatics Publications in Religious Education

Although no references were made in Winifred Ward's first
book, *Creative Dramatics,* regarding possible application of
creative dramatics to religious education, this book became
one of the first important references throughout America for
religious education leaders. [17] Twenty years later, Isabel B.
Burger's book, *Creative Play Acting,* was published; and again,
although it contained no references to religious education,
many Sunday School teachers used it extensively. [18] Several
books published since 1950 have included material designed to
aid religious education leaders. [19] In addition to treatment in
textbooks, creative dramatics articles and reports of varying
quality are frequently published in bulletins, journals, and
magazines of various faiths. Occasionally an entire issue of a

magazine is devoted to creative drama. One example is a 1957
issue of *Children's Religion.*[20]

Discussion Groups

In response to the growing application of creative dramatics
to the field of religious education, the board of CTC added a
committee on religious education to its annual conference committees. The first group met in August, 1955. By August,
1958, the number of persons participating in this part of the
annual meeting program had doubled, with representatives
from a wide range of religious faiths. Members of this group
expressed a need for more trained leaders; many were asking
how to introduce the technique into their Sunday School programs; many seemed aware that their curricula were trying
to win acceptance of this teaching method by those who had had
no training.

Summary

Introduction of creative dramatics into the field of religious
education has been due largely to skilled creative dramatics
teachers, who carried it into their own churches, rather than
to the insight of national boards or educational heads of various
denominations. The well-trained creative dramatics teacher
doubles in many roles, such as teaching in workshops, leadership schools, and in-service training courses, many of them
interdenominational. Interestingly, a few denominations which
in the past historically broke away from art, drama, and rituals
have reversed their former trend and, influenced by the contemporary religious education movement as well as by modern
psychology, have reintroduced these forms into their educational programs. The Philadelphia yearly meeting of the Religious Society of Friends (Quakers) is, for instance, now "very
receptive to the use of creative dramatics in religious education."[21]

Even among experienced creative dramatics leaders, however, little critical attempt has been made to clarify the goals
behind their work or to evaluate their teaching. Also, among
experienced creative dramatics leaders there exists a sense

of disdain for those religious educators working to encourage examination of the soundness and the theology of currently used religious dramatic materials. Conversely, many directors of religious education fail to understand the deep skills needed for training a teacher sufficiently in this discipline. Directors of religious education have a tendency to oversimplify creative dramatics techniques in their Sunday School curricula and study guides, and they frequently downgrade the need for adequate training in this art. If mature growth is to come, the leaders of both fields must be willing to set aside former standards for religious education and creative dramatics and to create new goals and definitions which could satisfy both. If we can become of one mind and one spirit and put down old ways to search for new ones, we will not feel ourselves classed with Adeimantus when Socrates asked him: "Well, and don't you know that in every task the most important thing is the beginning, and especially when you have to deal with anything young and tender?"[22]

19 Survey of Creative Dramatics in Correctional Institutions

Werdna Finley 🙵

In endeavoring to explore the use of creative dramatics in correctional institutions for children, we have met problems similar to those Columbus must have encountered as he set out on his famous voyage. We, too, set out on uncharted seas. We, also, had hoped to find one thing and wound up discovering another. We think the parallel goes even further—that, in a way still to be seen, finally, we, like Columbus, have discovered a new world.

By "we" are meant all the people who helped with this survey: Helen C. Shank, Superintendent of Maple Lane School; Edna Goodrich, Principal of the Education Department at that institution; the girls themselves who did the typing, mimeographing, and mailing of questionnaire and cover letters. Mrs. Shank helped formulate the questionnaire and provided mailing lists of institutions.

The questionnaire used deserves mention in that it was specially designed to arouse interest in creative dramatics where knowledge of that subject was limited or lacking. We purposely omitted a definition, hoping to find from the questionnaire how many people knew the term and could differentiate it from psychodrama and sociodrama. For instance, we asked, regarding material used, questions which were phrased in such a way that the value of creative dramatics was apparent to the reader without discourse or definition. Most of the recipients of the questionnaire were social workers or persons engaged in public welfare of a custodial and correctional type. Since such people are generally overworked and extremely busy, we guarded against having our questionnaires repose, unanswered and unread, in wastebaskets throughout the country: we asked Mrs. Shank to write a cover letter on letterhead from her nationally known institution. The prestige of her name and institution evidently stimulated response. We received 130 returns from the 250 questionnaires mailed out.

Eighty-five of the institutions sending returns indicated interest in having creative dramatics programs. Thirteen institutions have such programs. Seven others have some type of drama program; several are in the process of introducing dramatics of one type or another.

Maple Lane School

In considering the significance of these figures, we shall take a close-up picture of one institution. Because it is close to this writer and because it has had a creative dramatics program for five years, we shall use Maple Lane School. This is the name of a training school for girls between the ages of ten and eighteen. It is located at Grand Mound, Washington, and generally houses about 140 girls. Helen C. Shank, who has been superintendent at the school for the past eight years, is nationally known in the child welfare and social work fields. Under her leadership the school has become a model for institutions of its kind. The school grounds are referred to as a "campus." And with its pleasant mingling of old and new buildings it does resemble a private school—that is, until we notice that some of the windows are barred. Physically, it has much in common with most of the institutions contacted through our questionnaires.

Insight into Institutional Child

A description of the type of child residing at Maple Lane is important because it is a description applicable to each of the approximately 50,000 children between the ages of six and eighteen living in such institutions throughout our country.[1] This number includes both boys and girls, though they are housed separately. All are not delinquent; some just have nowhere else to go. Regardless of age or degree of delinquency, their lives are as alike in many respects as though they all inhabited the same lost and forlorn city.

Almost always the children are emotionally damaged. They are the product of a defective or destructive background. They have lost the ability to communicate in the normal world because the world in which they live is so different, bounded on the one side by institutional living, and hedged in on the others by trouble, courts and judges, parental problems, and a thousand related factors. In the words of Helen Shank,

> The girls who are committed by the courts to Maple Lane School are delinquents because they have been rejected and deprived to the point of being mentally ill. Their backgrounds are varied but in almost every case there is a broken home, stepmother or father (two, three, or four), and poverty, although not in every case. And they have experienced such things as beatings, malnutrition, drunkenness, prostitution, and even incest. All of this adds up to an urge to seek attention in unorthodox ways by stealing, truancy, and sex delinquency. By the time they reach the school they have been so damaged that their faith in people has been destroyed.

Why is CTC interested in such children? Perhaps because there are 50,000 of them, and 50,000 people will touch a far greater number of lives in succeeding generations. Perhaps, too, because the picture of drama, particularly creative dramatics, begins to emerge with a great potential for such children.

To continue, these are simply children. For many different reasons, usually involving some fault in the individual world into which each was born, they live in correctional institutions. The institutions are crowded, understaffed, hard pressed to provide more than food, clothing, supervision, and a bare minimum of educational advantages. More often than not, the multiple problems are exaggerated by too little funds for the total operation. Ordinarily it is unthinkable to hope for a salaried teacher in any of the art fields. Rehabilitation of children under such limitations is a long and difficult process, often impossible.

A thesis or a dissertation should be written on institutional living, and not the Oliver Twist sort of thing. Rather the writing should concentrate on today's institution which tends to be enlightened, wherein the educated supervisor is confronted with the doleful difference between what public moneys will provide and what she knows is necessary for true rehabilitation. Building upkeep, properly trained staff in sufficient numbers, food, teachers, clothing, medical, dental, and psychiatric care— these take the bulk of the funds. The wise administrator concentrates on healthful necessities; when funds run out as many nonessentials as possible are obtained through volunteer help and through donations and gifts. The dedicated superintendent is forever on the lookout for "extras" that will help create a feeling of normalcy.

This need of normalcy is emphasized for the child by the routine of institutions. How does it feel never to be really alone? Never to be free to explore where childish curiosity leads? If each person has some innate creativeness, how does it flourish in day after day of regimentation? There is a recreation program, of course, but where is the sustained program which will provide a little understanding of the arts and foster a love of them? In a place like Maple Lane this is one of the "extras."

Development of Creative Dramatics Program

In the fall of 1953 Mrs. Shank requested that the University of Washington send a teacher to train the staff and the cottage parents in creative dramatics. Agnes Haaga journeyed ninety miles each week from the university to conduct an extension course. At the same time she held one class with a "pilot" group of girls. Under Miss Haaga's direction, her former student, Mrs. T. R. Richards of Olympia Junior Programs, Inc., also began classes with another group of girls at the school. The initial training took three months, but the classes have continued ever since with Mrs. Richards as volunteer leader.

It is not our purpose to become involved in a discussion of the relative merits of sociodrama, psychodrama, and creative dramatics; or to indulge in arguments revolving around the words therapy, therapeutic, art, or degrees of meanings of these words. The course at Maple Lane School has been purely one of creative dramatics. Yet, in a letter written in

March, 1954, Dr. Harlan McNutt, Consultant Psychiatrist at
Maple Lane, termed it therapeutic for the girls who, he said,
"represent, indeed a wide spectrum of psychopathology."
At the same time Mrs. Shank made this observation:

> In addition to being many wonderful things, creative dramatics is
> democratic. When it is part of a recreational program, girls learn
> to cooperate as they play together. Each one is given responsibility
> for her part in the total effort of creating a play that will be success-
> ful. Creative dramatics can be just as exciting and satisfying an out-
> let for pent-up rebellious attitudes as a baseball game. Since we have
> had the classes we are convinced creative dramatics should be a part
> of every recreational program in a boys' and girls' training school.
> We should like to be able to demonstrate its value to other institu-
> tions.

Values of Creative Dramatics

The administrative staff at Maple Lane has watched closely
the results of the classes over the past five years. There are
significant findings:

1. A social worker is sometimes *never* able to bring into
the open the child's true feelings toward neglecting parents or
to uncover the nature of the block she knows is there. However,
regardless of story material, where a "prop" is used the child's
deprivation always comes out—it is her missing parents who
come to the door in "Imaginings" (her drunken father or prosti-
tute mother).[2]

2. As significant to the social worker as the revelation of
the blocking is that in their dramatizing the children give a
picture of their dreams, of what they wish were true. As the
story is played out, the mother becomes a kind, generous,
loving person who gives parties for her daughter; the father
is revealed as understanding, loving, generous. The deprivation always shrinks to a core of sadness, loss, hostility which
loses or eases its tension in the "playing out." Dreams are
always of the good (or what we classify as normal, average,
everyday): a high school diploma; a small, neat house with a
neat, loving mother and a father who works at some honest
job every day; marriage to a nice young man; good clothes;
parties. Not often do they stretch toward such unrealities as
wealth, fame, and prestige.

3. The social worker can use the creative dramatics class as a school barometer. When the campus is upset, there is always the deprivation theme at the base. Hostilities against society come out when the children are restless. When everyone is happy, the classes reflect the children's appreciation for the good things in their lives; they reveal their innate longings for the good. It is not unusual at such times for them to indulge in prayer during class time, as a part of the "play." It is important to note that after a session on restless or upset days, the participants in the class are relieved of tension. They are often relaxed and amiable after a creative dramatics class which they entered sullenly.

4. Material used with these children is the same as that used for children of a normal world, yet these children will interpret it differently, according to their individual experiences. For instance, a *window* to the average group may hold many a delightful thought; to the institutional child, it usually is reminiscent of running or escaping.

From our questionnaire to Maple Lane, we learned that the classes are composed of an average of fifteen girls who meet for two hours once a week; only those who are interested and who sign up for the course may take it. Good literature is preferred over role-playing situations though it is a permissive program and the girls develop their own ideas and are allowed freedom in choice of material and interpretation of ideas. Material that was successful with one group might fail to appeal to another. Bible stories have been used with unusual success. After five years Maple Lane is convinced that the best results are obtained through a small, voluntary group, regularly in attendance. It is felt that having the staff trained in creative dramatics has been of inestimable value.

National Emphasis

Answers from the other twelve institutions which had creative dramatics programs were substantially the same, although no other institution seemed to have had its staff trained in creative dramatics. All thirteen agencies outlined in varying words the same reasons for having such a program: "therapeutic," "builds self confidence," "teaches meaning of good entertainment,"

"develops poise, " "self-control," "teaches to work in groups,"
"prepares them to go back into the community and accept responsibilities, " "rehabilitates, " "allows for individual expression," "releases tension," "gives enjoyment," "allows the
child to vocalize," "gives sense of belonging," "builds up
individual ego," "gives joy of production of something worthwhile," "shows that the experience of helping and serving others
in a wholesome way is means to true happiness," "means of
teaching self-discipline," "morale booster," and like phrases.
Those institutions which listed other types of drama programs,
or which were in the process of setting up programs, were
alike in their reasons for doing so. And those reasons were
very similar to the above.

Of interest were two questionnaires from institutions which
were not of a correctional nature but which had creative dramatics programs. One was a state school for the deaf, the other
a school for the mentally retarded. The values to the children
in these schools as listed by those in charge were the same as
those listed in correctional institutions although the techniques
employed may have been different.

It is easy to see why such a large percentage of questionnaires indicated that a program of creative dramatics was
desired. It is not a criticism of an art form if an experience
in the art turns out to be therapeutic. One child's individual
creative expression may be another's "legitimate emotional-
constructive outlet. "

Summary

Rather than an analysis of principles and practices, this
chapter appears to be a logging of the initial voyage. Some
charting has been done; some soundings taken. The returns
show strong trends but few mathematical exactitudes. There
seems to be no past history upon which to build comparisons.
We are dealing with such intangibles as people's varied opinions. Who knows exactly how helpful creative dramatics will
prove to be in the future to individuals who will have had it
in one institution or another? Who can say whether we should
even examine it from a "helpful" or "therapeutic" viewpoint?
It is the belief of most of us that creative dramatics is a vital

force in the development of appreciation-for-living in all children, an unveiling of wonder, a preparation for maximum living. But this survey creates a suspicion that creative dramatics is almost a necessity for children in institutions.

This, then, is our discovery of a new world—a world where children are in real need of what we have to offer. "Children should be understood and loved—in them lies the regeneration of the world," said Dr. Arnold Gesell in 1949 (to delegates attending the fourth annual CTC in New York).[3] Today, a decade later, our questionnaire seems to bring the full-circle thought that "creative dramatics should be understood and loved—therein lies the regeneration of the problem child." Recognition of the situation underlines the need for teachers, volunteer or professional, who understand this type of child and who can use creative dramatics in this kind of environment. Many pioneers will be required to explore this new world.

20 Creative Dramatics in Community Programs

Margaret S. Woods ❧

In many neighborhoods today, one sees children experiencing magic moments in the lives of Sleeping Beauty, Cinderella, Tom Sawyer, and other special people in children's classics. Adults who have become aware of such rich creative experiences resulting from participation in dramatics have caught the challenging spirit of Winifred Ward. Communities have provided classes for children and adults through summer enrichment classes and programs offered the year around. A growing interest is evidenced by the increasing number of community organizations engaged in sponsoring classes in creative dramatics and the related arts. An intensive investigation reveals the following practices in community programs throughout the country. [1]

Basic Practices

Community programs sponsored by such organizations as YMCA, Junior Programs, park departments, PTA, museums, and Junior Leagues reveal certain practices concerned with organization and development, leadership, training, and the stimulation of the related arts.

Organization and Development

West Coast Programs. While there is evidence of new community programs springing up each year throughout the United States, the study indicates an unusually high degree of concentration in the West. As far back as World War II, little children in Seattle,

176

Washington, enjoyed dramatic play experiences in nursery
schools provided for war-working mothers through the services of a program consultant for the public schools, Nancy
Taft Smuck.[2] At the same time, additional contributions of
Mrs. Smuck, on a volunteer basis, included public library
classes in creative dramatics and puppetry to assist parents in acquiring special techniques in creative drama.

Another individual, Ruth Lease, "a storyteller with a love
and understanding of drama," shared this talent and enthusiasm
with youngsters who had come to Seattle with their parents
who worked in wartime industries.[3] Enlisting the support of
Seattle Junior Programs, Inc., the project was adopted by
Seattle Junior League in 1946, and ". . . with the cooperation of Junior Programs, Public Schools, Park Board, Art
Museum, City Council, and the Council of Social Agencies,
creative dramatics was made available to even greater numbers of children. As the program grew, so did the need for
trained leaders. Hence in 1947 the University of Washington
was approached by the Junior League. With the cooperation
. . . of the School of Drama and . . . the Adult Education
division and Extension Services, creative dramatics was added
to the curriculum, and a director was appointed to teach at
the university. . . . Within a year the university assumed full
responsibility for the program."[4]

As the need for leaders became apparent, additional instructors were added and an intensive program of interpretation
to communities throughout the state was carried on. From the
small beginning, originating in the community in 1941, the
growth of the training program at the university provided communities throughout the state of Washington with qualified
leaders. These programs have been developed and organized in
a variety of ways.

One such program, which had its inception in a single community, spread to forty areas throughout the city of Seattle
during a period of ten years. Sponsored by PTA, three classes
for sixty children in 1948 increased to seventy-five classes
the second year, with 120 classes available by 1950 in a city-
wide program for children from the ages of four through fourteen. That the program was not a hit and miss project was
indicated by Bam Whitebrook when she said, "the PTA does

all the organization of the classes; the University of Washington
recommends the teachers, the Seattle Public Schools give the
buildings. As soon as class is over it is not forgotten as the
teachers must turn in a report of each class."[5] Through the
efforts of the PTA Council chairmen in cooperation with the
city-wide PTA Council chairmen, classes were organized
in as many as forty communities with 120 classes for some
2,500 children. Registration blanks were sent home with school
children. A registration fee of $3.00 for ten one-hour sessions
was collected by PTA chairmen at registration desks set up
in local school buildings. A maximum number of twenty children in each class was grouped according to age: five and six
years, seven and eight years, nine, ten, and eleven years,
and junior high students.

A special program for the young child, "Let's Pretend with
the Fours and Fives," has been in operation in Seattle from
1953 to 1959. Sponsored by the Pre-School Associations of
PTA in cooperation with the children's department of the Seattle
Public Library, classes are provided for the purpose of developing an interest in good literature through dramatization.
Classes limited to seventeen four- and five-year-olds reach
as many as 700 preschoolers in one year. Classes are held
in as many libraries as have space. Where libraries cannot
accommodate children, mothers arrange for space in private
homes or in church buildings, and provide picture books as
well. A fee of $3.50 for ten one-hour sessions provides the
salary of a six-dollars-an-hour stipend for the teachers. The
creative dramatics leader informs the children's librarian
of the theme for each class session. Books pertaining to the
theme are made available to children following one half-hour
of dramatic play. As a result, children reacquaint themselves
with the characters dramatically played; thus an appreciation
of worthwhile literature is stimulated. During the class, most
parents remain in the library to browse through books. One
leader, Ann Pirtle, indicates that significant learning takes
place in addition to real moments of pleasure which the child
experiences.[6] Ruth Hewitt Hamilton, supervisor of the children's work for the Seattle Public Library, believes the program has greatly stimulated the use of the children's section,

and has introduced many mothers to the library.[7] With the growth of PTA-sponsored programs in creative dramatics, a new chairmanship, that of Creative Arts, was added to the board of the Washington Congress of PTA in 1956, for the purpose of acquainting units with the philosophy of creativity and participation in the arts.

In 1957 at Olympia, Washington, a program was organized not only for children but also for mothers. After children play-acted favorite stories, mothers enjoyed similar experiences in an adjoining room. The leader, Jean Richards, indicated that parents seem to be in a better position to understand and develop children's imaginations following observation of pre-school classes in dramatic play. In Yakima, Washington, service groups have paved the way for classes in creative dramatics. As a result of training classes in creative dramatics sponsored by the Extension Department of the University of Washington, a leader was available to guide children. With a minimum registration fee and contributions from Kiwanis and Rotary organizations, Yakima Junior Programs assumed responsibility for organization of classes held in public school buildings. In California, the Palo Alto Recreation Department makes available classes in creative dramatics and story play to children from five to ten years of age for a minimum registration fee of one dollar per quarter.

Programs Throughout the Nation

Although many programs in creative dramatics are scattered throughout the midwest, three are cited here as examples: the Dunes Art Foundation in Michigan City, Indiana, provides opportunities for teen-age participation in creative dramatics for the purpose of writing plays or entering formal drama classes.[8] At the University of Minnesota in Minneapolis an after-school program gives student teachers an opportunity for leadership experiences under guidance of a creative dramatics supervisor. In Shrevesport, Louisiana, professional leadership is available for four classes in creative dramatics sponsored by Junior Programs for children from ten to sixteen years of age. A fee of one dollar is the charge for a one-hour session.[9] Classes are held in the YMCA building. In Baltimore, Maryland, the Recreation and Education division of the Baltimore Council of Social Agencies has developed a youth program to meet requests from PTA and Scout groups. [10]

Throughout the country, community programs appear to have been developed by either an individual or an organization. Basic practices of limiting the size of children's classes and limiting registration fees are similar. A chief difference in practices lies in housing of the program. Public school buildings, libraries, churches, museums, and homes have been made available in accordance with community resources.

Leadership Training

As parents become informed and as children participate in satisfying creative dramatics the demand for trained leaders follows. Training is made available to potential leaders through beginning and advanced classes in more than one hundred institutions of higher education throughout the United States. [11] Quality leadership is maintained through workshops and in-service training for religious education and recreation leaders, Girl Scout and Camp Fire leaders, and workers with children of limited abilities. A listing of credit or noncredit workshops scheduled for summer programs in institutions of higher learning is available through CTC. Re-enforcement of dramatic techniques in leadership training is an important trend. Junior Leagues have not only encouraged creative dramatics with allocated funds for classes but have sponsored workshops for the purpose of training community leaders, their fees being paid by community organizations. [12]

In many different cities and communities creative dramatics leaders throughout the United States are exposed to periodic refresher courses through in-service programs. Although basic requirements for qualified leaders vary from training through in-service programs to actual student teaching, many leaders have a college degree in speech and have had training in creative dramatics. In other areas, certification in education is required; lack of understanding of the needs and interests of children frequently causes discipline problems in the class.

Stimulation in Related Arts

Participation in the arts is a powerful factor in the perpetuation of a true democracy. This tenet has spurred community leaders to provide experiences in a variety of arts for children. Parents, teachers, and community leaders through cooperative undertakings have spread the philosophy of creativity, and influenced the need for training programs.

One such continuing program began in 1937 in what is known today as the Children's Centre for Creative Arts. Initiated and sponsored by Adelphi College, Garden City, New York, a weekday and after-school program provides opportunities for some 300 children to enjoy participation in a variety of the arts. A director and an assistant director, with the help of fifteen skilled artist teachers and six volunteer adults from the community, work toward achieving the objective of child development through participation in the arts. Each child pays a tuition fee of $60.00 for ninety hours of classes throughout the year. [13]

The Seattle Creative Activities Center opened its doors in January, 1957, with the aim of developing the exceptional in each child. The Center provides quality experiences in a variety of creative arts. Sponsored and operated by a board of trustees, an advisory board, and executive director, it takes care of an approximately $12,000 yearly budget including a $150 monthly rental fee for the dwelling which houses Center activities. The board of trustees, composed of twenty-five lay and professional people, meets monthly to direct the plans for the Center. Board members assume responsibility for various phases of the program such as publicity, membership, projects, and volunteers. An advisory board meets to make recommendations on special matters. Supported by gifts, special fund-raising projects, and a three dollar registration fee per quarter (ten one-hour sessions), the Center includes a total of twenty-five classes each quarter in art, dance, drama, music, and puppetry. [14]

A program of a similar nature but one which included integration of the arts found its beginning in 1956 with experiments conducted in two Seattle communities. Sponsored by the Washington Congress of PTA and the local creative arts chairmen, the program provided opportunities to participate

in creative dramatics followed by experience in one of the
other arts. Successful results served as the basis for inclusion of five creative arts centers offered in conjunction with
the city-wide PTA-sponsored program in creative dramatics.
A leader skilled in two or more of the arts media guides children through a two-hour experience of creative dramatics and
some other art.

Other programs providing opportunities for creative arts
participation have had their beginnings in one or more of the
arts; some of these include the following: an after-school enrichment program in creative dramatics and creative writing
sponsored by the PTA in Lafayette, California, [15] and the Music
and Art Foundation's Creative Art School in Seattle which provides opportunities for fifty children to participate in one of
the art media. A lengthy waiting list seems to be good indication of the success of the school in developing creative potential. The Mott Foundation of the Flint Board of Education in
Flint, Michigan, provides some fifty classes, tuition-free,
for approximately one thousand boys and girls from the ages
of four through twenty. [16]

Workshops and conferences at national, regional, and local
levels in the creative arts have strengthened leadership and
spread creative arts programs in communities. One such workshop of national scope provided stimulation in creative thinking for 500 lay and professional leaders from the United States
and other lands. Fifteen experts, nationally recognized in the
field of creativity, guided participants through two experiences in related arts, including lecture, participation, and
discussion of creativity and its implications. [17] There is evidence of creative arts interest, nation-wide, in the theme
chosen by the American Association of School Administrators for their 1959 annual meeting: "Education and the Creative Arts." The Country and Rural Area Superintendents included creative arts as one of six major areas of emphasis at
their national convention held in Seattle in 1959. [18] Discussion
groups of ACEI set aside one day of their 1959 conference to
give delegates an opportunity to participate in one of the creative arts. Further evidence of creative arts growth is noted in
recent appointments of creative arts chairmanships at various

local, regional, and national levels. Pertinent appointments include state and regional chairmen of creative arts for AAUW; state and local creative arts chairmen for PTAs; a National Cultural Arts chairman for the National Congress of Parents and Teachers; and establishment of a new subcommittee on cultural and environmental influences for the 1960 White House Conference on Children and Youth. Such appointments with their respective organizations re-enforce Howard Hanson's belief that "the arts by developing greater perceptivity of the eyes and ears as well as the mind, will increase the sensitivity of the human spirit. And man, thru that sensitization, may be helped to find his own soul."[19]

Summary

Parents, community leaders, and organizations play a vital role in the encouragement or discouragement of children's creative power. As a result of participation in creative experiences, adults begin to realize that although every child may not become an artist, he can use art forms creatively in daily living for his own enjoyment. As a result of this investigation certain trends are revealed:

1. Community programs frequently develop when individuals and organizations inform and inspire parents and members of community groups with the philosophy of creative arts in shaping the lives of children.

2. Community programs in creative dramatics seem to be prevalent in areas of close proximity to a training center in an institution of higher learning.

3. Community programs tend to include an integration of the arts rather than an offering of a specific art.

Three recommendations emerge from this study:

1. Parents and youth leaders need to "catch" the philosophy of the creative arts to ignite a spark in every home and to expend effort to provide centers in every community in every nation throughout the world.

2. Community programs will grow when trained leaders feel the need for re-enforcing philosophy and techniques of creative dramatics by frequent workshops and in-service training.

3. Requests for creative arts programs must come from parents in the community; hence there is a need to motivate action by public relations programs.

The urge to create through the arts will endure. Through the help of creative artists, the democratic process remains strong. Its strength lies in identification with worthwhile human experiences. Since participation in creative dramatics and other creative arts benefits members of a community, results will be far-reaching, for art knows no national barriers.

21 Creative Dramatics: An Approach to Children's Theatre

Isabel B. Burger 🙡

Many leaders, recognizing the close relationship between creative dramatics and children's theatre, include both in their programs in order to provide maximum benefits for young participants. Winifred Ward finds "no conflict in ideology between them; rather do they complement each other. Children's theatre is primarily for child audiences; creative dramatics is primarily for children who participate."[1] The same view is taken by Geraldine Siks who says, "These two forms are in harmony as they provide for enjoyment and child growth. Children's theatre provides strong impressions. Creative dramatics provides for strong expressions. A child must have both. He must take in and he must give out."[2] Marie Dienesch, a French pioneer in creative drama techniques *(jeux dramatiques)*, agrees on this point. She comments, "Let us say at once that these two forms are in no way opposed to each other, but so far from being incompatible, they appear to us complementary."[3]

Research in this area has revealed that creative dramatics has been used effectively as an approach to children's theatre in terms of (1) a preparation for acting, (2) tryouts and casting, (3) developing a scene in a scripted play, (4) the building of discriminating future audiences for children's theatre. The principles and practices considered in the following paragraphs have been established through research, interviews, and correspondence with children's theatre directors throughout the country.

Preparation for Acting

Only an actor who believes and is believed in can create the
magic moment which will stir young hearts to empathize with
a Heidi or a Sara Crewe, and provide an "experience that builds
into [the child] dreams, desires . . . perceptions."[4] Such an
actor's movements must be fluid, eloquent, and honestly motivated; his speech must sing its message straight to the child's
mind. This ideal performer is rare, but when he does appear
one often discovers in his biographical record a rich background of creative dramatics. Mary Fluhrer Nighswander
comments on the work of her actors who have had training in
creative dramatics as follows: "I feel very strongly about the
transition from creative drama to formal drama. I have been
happily amazed at the results! Coming, as I do, from a strict
professional background, this amounts to a right-about-face
for me. Results have been most rewarding."[5]

Everywhere directors report assigning the more demanding
roles to young actors who have had creative dramatics experience. Replies to one of the questions on the *Child Drama Questionnaire* circulated in the United State in 1958 bear out this
point. To the inquiry: "Is the work of those who have had creative drama experience more convincing?" Only affirmative
responses have been received.[6] Constance Welsh, in discussing
creative dramatics as a preparation for acting says,

> The school age child often retires within himself, to be safe from
> the stings of adult criticism; his communications become monosyllabic
> and awkward. As he becomes relaxed and confident, in the permissive
> atmosphere of the creative dramatics group, his imagination is quick-
> ened and he finds himself able to express thoughts and feelings in natu-
> ral coordinated action, accompanied by sincere, meaningful speech.
> The essential attributes of the convincing actor, aesthetic sensitivity
> and awareness, are soon in evidence; the creative dramatics experi-
> ence is responsible.[7]

Winifred Ward and Rita Criste also consider the preliminary
work essential for those participating in their plays. They write,
"In the Children's Theatre of Evanston, we use only children
in casts who have a creative drama background. It is required

for every child cast in a formal play. "[8] Other directors indicate a similar practice. Ella Heimbrodt says, "During the
first year with us, children work only in creative dramatics.
At the end of this period, they are ready to try a one-act play."[9]

Patt Merrick recalls an instance when resourcefulness
learned in creative dramatics saved a show.

> During a dramatic moment when the climax depended upon Aladdin
> taking the lamp which the magician was trying to steal, Aladdin, much
> to our dismay, ran offstage without it! All supposed that the Magician
> would naturally pick up the lamp and follow him off, which would have
> put an end to the show and reversed its meaning. But the scene was
> saved by the resourcefulness of those young actors. With barely a
> second's delay the Magician raced in front of the closed curtains where
> the lamp lay, and Aladdin followed in mad pursuit. At the end of a
> realistic chase, accompanied by convincing dialogue, Aladdin re-
> gained possession of the lamp and the play continued serenely to the
> proper denouement. [10]

Method for Tryouts

An ever increasing number of directors are finding creative
dramatics or improvisation a useful tryout technique. The
book-in-hand, eye-on-page method often inhibits honest expression and gives an unfair picture of the actor's body and
voice potentials. Says John De Puglio, "One can seldom determine abilities in a new group of young people at a reading
tryout. Concentration, resourcefulness, imagination, ability
to listen and to move comfortably cannot be accurately observed. If incidents in which the play characters are involved
can be used to motivate original improvisations, a youngster's
true potentials can be discovered at once."[11]

Patt Merrick's plan is similar. "I ask my students," she
writes, "after they have heard the story, either to improvise
a scene from the play itself, or an imaginary scene concerning
one of the characters." "In Evanston," says Miss Ward, "after
children trying out have heard the story and know something
about the characters, a short scene involving much action may
be read to them. First one group and then another will try it
out creatively either in pantomime or with improvised dialogue." Miss Criste adds: "In certain cases music is used to

motivate characterizations at try-outs. The imaginations of those to appear in *The Blue Bird* were aroused by 'The Dance of the Hours.'"

Developing a Scene of a Play

Some directors adhere strictly to the script of a children's play; others find the use of creative dramatics techniques adds spontaneity and credibility to a final performance. Although methods of application vary, they fall generally into two categories: (1) creatively developing crowd or group scenes, especially where young children are involved, (1) creating a whole play based on the study of a place, a period, or a familiar incident in history. The latter practice occurs most frequently in schools and church schools. Several directors report successful methods of treating crowd scenes. Most directors refer to such groups as school children, court ladies, penguins, and the like, where little differentiation of character is indicated.

Dan Lipschutz describes a recent experience in directing "Mr. Popper's Penguins" for the Children's Theatre of Evanston:

Out of fifty fifth and sixth grade children, I selected eighteen penguins. By using improvisation in try-outs, I was able to discover which children were naturally endowed with the qualities needed to portray the roles: imagination, ease of movement, ability to relate to others, and response to quick changes of mood. All of the penguin scenes, which should be most compelling for a young audience, were developed at rehearsals creatively. I first motivated actions by establishing the dramatic conflict, Mr. Popper's need to raise money and their desire to help him. Questions such as these brought interesting responses: "What could the birds do to make an exciting theatre show?" "How could they entertain an audience?" "They could do acrobatics," said one. "Maybe they could march, because they always walk in lines anyway," added another. They had gathered this knowledge from our trips to the zoo and study of pictures. "They could dance, rock'n roll maybe" was another suggestion. Through group discussion concerning the period of the play, which we placed in the 1920's, and some acting out, we unanimously agreed to eliminate the rock'n roll suggestion and substitute a square dance. The spontaneity and sincere quality of the work was a direct result of the total participation in the creative development of the scenes. A unique experience, testifying to the validity of the creative approach, is worthy of recording. Selections from the original story, not used in the play version, were told to the cast, for improvisation purposes. A new scene, thus created, was so expertly handled that it was incorporated in the final production and surpassed many of the other parts in vitality and natural humor. [12]

Certain scenes from Dickens' *A Christmas Carol*, the annual December bill of the Children's Theatre Association in Baltimore, are built in this way. A report reads:

Creative dramatics is the secret of successfully catching the natural, fresh spirit of the scene glimpsed by Ebenezer Scrooge of his school days long past. The original story gives few details, but suggests that when the Christmas holiday came, the children all went happily off to their homes, leaving the lonely little Ebenezer to spend his fortnight in a barren school with its sour-faced master. The cast listens to a dramatic telling of the story. The plot framework seems to suggest three obvious subjects: (1) the joy of the anticipated holiday, (2) sympathy for little Ebenezer whose family will not accept him at home, (3) the arrival of the coach with its new trappings. Before the end of the second rehearsal period, each child has decided upon his own dialogue contribution in the three areas. To avoid confusion, each is given a number from one to six thus establishing a speech order. (Sometimes names are used.) The spontaneity of the scene and the genuine empathy it evokes have never ceased to amaze teachers who have come to observe this effective application of creative drama to the preparation of the formal play. [13]

Burdette Fitzgerald writes of an interesting project conducted at Idyllwild during the summer of 1958.

It resulted from a reading of the Orpheus story to a group of twenty-seven twelve- to fifteen-year-olds. Completely on their own, they developed two scenes creatively. They made simple settings, costumes, and properties and carried out an interesting light plot in reds and greens representing Hades, etc. I stress "on their own" because I experimented to see just how far they could go without adult help. The Orpheus incidental music was the only uncreative aspect. The audience was deeply moved. [14]

In developing a formal play creatively, most authorities feel that the leader assumes a role somewhat different from that which he has played in the creative dramatics class. He must be especially adept at accepting and refining the children's suggestions, always conscious of his responsibility for giving a fine theatre experience to the audience. On this point Winifred Ward says,

> Any creative play developed by children needs some directing if it is to be effective for the audience. The young actors now have a different kind of learning experience, one which stresses the sharing of their creation. . . . They will be happier if they feel that they have accomplished something out of the ordinary, a play of which they can be proud. The assurance on the part of the teacher which comes from acquaintance with the basic principles of dramatic construction will do much to make the experience of guiding children rewarding. [15]

Geraldine Siks' comment shows agreement: "If a creative dramatics leader is to help children create a play, she must know what makes a play . . . and understand the fundamental drama elements that go into the making of a play." [16]

Building Audience Appreciation

Most directors who practice creative dramatics ascribe to this technique another significant value: its power to build a discriminating theatre audience of the future. The creative dramatics class provides ample opportunities for the analysis of character relationships, motivated action, and the need for balance, contrast, and emphasis in the effective stage picture. These experiences sharpen aesthetic sensitivities, deepen appreciation, and develop sound criteria for judging theatre art.

From children's theatre directors come such statements as these: "After creating their own plays, I find my children avidly saving pennies to attend the professional theatre and, with real wisdom, discussing the merits of the performance at a post-mortem session." "It is exciting to see how sensitive creative dramatics classes have become to play structure and dialogue to which they are exposed in movies and TV programs." "A real understanding of what makes good theatre is growing in our teen-age creative drama groups. Let us hope that their opinions, courageously expressed, will raise the standards of professional theatre and build discriminating audiences of the future. "[17] These comments would seem to provide strong additional arguments for the practice of creative dramatics with young people as it can affect the quality of theatre in days to come.

Summary

Research and written statements seem to offer irrefutable proof that wherever creative dramatics has been used by a sensitive, skilled leader in producing the children's play, results have testified to the effectiveness of the practice. Whether it is used as a training exercise to equip the young actor, as a tryout method, a technique to develop convincing group scenes, or a whole play based on an original theme, it would seem to merit further study, experimentation, and far wider use. The following recommendations are suggested:

1. More specific help and guidance should be offered to new workers in the field of children's theatre. A small group composed of those directors who are experienced in this special phase of creative dramatics might prepare a joint publication in the form of a workbook on "Creative Dramatics and the Formal Play for Children. "

2. Institutions offering training in creative dramatics and children's theatre should carefully consider the personal qualifications of the applicant, which are essential to success in this highly specialized field, before recommending him as a candidate for graduate study.

3. Preparatory work of all specialists in children's theatre and creative dramatics should expand in scope to include more field work with children and young people under expert supervision and enriched courses of study in child psychology, human development, social group work practices, and, above all, theatre.

22 Creative Dramatics in Recreation Programs

Virginia Musselman

The acceptance of creative dramatics as a specific art form and an important activity in public recreation programs is relatively new, even though drama itself has long played an important role in such programs.

Developmental Background

The major impetus was the result of action taken at a National Recreation Congress in Seattle in 1952. At this congress, a small group of leaders felt that emphasis on Community Theatre was not enough and that creative dramatics for children should receive major emphasis in recreational programs. Leaders, headed by Grace Walker and Edna Braucher of the National Recreation Association and Agnes Haaga of the University of Washington, formed themselves into an informal committee on creative dramatics. This committee asked for more recognition of the art by the National Recreation Association. The move met with enthusiastic support. Immediately a bibliography was compiled and sent to all National Recreational Association membership.

In addition the association, in the process of forming a National Advisory Committee on Recreation Programs and Activities, considered it logical to organize a Drama Committee. They used the informal committee as a nucleus. This committee has functioned since 1953.

One of this committee's major contributions has been its influence on the National Recreation Congresses held annually. In congresses held in Philadelphia,

Denver, St. Louis, Long Beach, and Atlantic City, demonstrations and workshops on creative dramatics have been given.
This programming has resulted in similar workshops and demonstrations at regional and district conferences. Another
significant contribution has been in the publication of articles
in *Recreation*, the association publication, which reaches
twelve thousand readers.

This is not to say that creative dramatics in public recreation was born in 1952. Long before this date, Agnes Haaga,
Isabel Burger, Grace Stanistreet, and other leaders who had
been trained or influenced by Winifred Ward had brought this
activity into their programs. Lexington, Kentucky; Portland,
Oregon; Baltimore, Maryland; Milwaukee, Wisconsin; and
Long Beach, California, had such drama programs. However,
in comparison with Community Theatre activity, creative
dramatics in recreation is still new and is still limited in
scope.

To offset this, the National Recreation Association has tried,
in addition to its own promotion of creative dramatics, to work
more closely with CTC. Members of the association have attended CTC meetings; have invited leaders in CTC to serve on
the National Recreation Association Drama Committee; and
have attempted to interest CTC in working more closely with
the recreation movement at local, regional, and national levels.

Present Status

To date, no clear picture of the place of creative dramatics
in recreation has emerged. No over-all survey has been made.
Figures for it do not appear in the Recreation and Park Yearbook, the major survey of public recreation made every five
years by the National Recreation Association.[1] The last survey
made in 1955 revealed the spread of Children's Theatre, Little
Theatre, festivals, pageants, plays, puppets and marionettes,
and storytelling, but it did not list creative dramatics as a
specific entry. The 1960 survey will correct this omission.

Until this report appears, information will be sparse and
limited to reports, correspondence, word of mouth, and magazine articles. The association believes, however, that a definite trend toward cultural activities is apparent. As a reac-

tion against the increased emphasis on science and technology and as a result of increased leisure time, attention in public recreation throughout the country is being directed toward creative and fine arts programs. In an effort to appraise this trend the association took a survey of the performing arts in public recreation programs.[2] This survey, while in no way qualitative, indicated that drama in all its forms ranked close to dance and music but was third in place. Opera and poetry trailed far behind. In this survey, thirty-eight different types of dramatic activities were written in, creative dramatics being one. Other terms such as improvisations, pantomimes, skits, story plays for children, playground dramatics, may have been used synonomously.

From the limited sources of information concerning creative dramatics for children and youth, it seems quite evident that it is still regarded as a "sometime thing"; that it is found primarily in summer playground programs; that confusion concerning its nature is still prevalent; that leadership is scarce and frequently nonspecialized; and that its scope as a continuing activity is not generally understood.

Current Practices

Leadership is the primary problem. There are over eight thousand recreation leaders employed full time, year 'round, in public recreation. However, there are over 76,000 leaders in all, the difference being primarily in the vast number of summer playground leaders used for seasonal work. These playground leaders are primarily college students, who may or may not have had any training in any form of drama. Brief pre-service and in-service training cannot give them the skills and techniques, or the feeling of security in an area of work outside their previous training. Even in those cities with full-time drama supervisors, this handicap is tremendous. Also, trained drama specialists may themselves have had no experience outside formal drama, and therefore may regard creative dramatics as a fringe activity, or ignore it completely in their plans for playground programming.

This need not be true. At Whitefish Bay, Wisconsin, in the summer of 1958, a drama specialist was employed to train leaders and to supervise a very simple creative dramatics program. Three full days of pre-service training of *all* staff members and the choosing of a leader from each playground to conduct the program under supervision resulted in so successful a program that it was awarded a permanent place in succeeding years. The leaders were most enthusiastic after their first experiences. "Some stepped out with confidence and plunged into it with composure and self-assurance. Others were nervous and unsure of themselves, but they were soon swept ahead by the enthusiasm of the children."[3] This reaction and this program bear out the following statement of national drama specialists: "The bulk of children's drama activities should be made up of creative drama. It has a place of its own in the on-going program of the recreation agency."[4]

Fred Cunningham, Assistant Superintendent of Recreation in Beverly Hills, California, explains what can happen when a public recreation department has the advantages of trained, professional leadership in creative dramatics: "Our creative drama program is offered to all youngsters from six through eleven years of age. We run this special program in fall, winter, and spring sessions. It is taught and directed by faculty members from the Theatre Arts Department of the University of California at Los Angeles. Burdette Fitzgerald, Chairman of Children's Theatre, is supervisor and her staff is made up of faculty members with masters and higher degrees.

"As creative drama is a special form of informal playmaking and is different in many respects from 'putting on a play,' it takes specially trained and educated instructors. Creative drama is an immediate experience and its values are for the players rather than for an audience. We have had fantastic acceptance of this program since we opened our new building and had a place to offer it to our children."

With growing interest in the performing, creative arts, a natural outgrowth is the emergence of creative programs that coordinate them. These seem to be taking the forms of Art Councils, Creative Workshops, or Creative Arts Centers. In these rhythms, creative dramatics, art, music, and dance are correlated. Requiring regular attendance to be effective, such programs are often scheduled for concentrated sessions on Saturdays. Washington, D. C. ; Waterloo, Iowa; Winston-

Salem, North Carolina; Portland, Oregon; Richmond, Virginia;
and Oakland, California, are among the cities using this method
of providing creative experiences for children. Here again
specific and detailed information and interpretation of results
are not available.

Recommendations

It is evident that much needs to be done before creative
dramatics receives full support in recreation programs and
takes its proper place as an accepted and valued part of the on-
going program.

First of all, there is need of a simple, graphic interpretation of the activity. Even among drama specialists there seems
to be confusion and conflict over semantics. Many books and
articles have been written, but even in them there are differences of opinion and a confusion between techniques and philosophies. Leaders in the field of creative dramatics could
perform a great service by agreeing upon the publication of
a simple handbook on this art in recreation that would serve
to reduce confusion.

Second, it is evident that professional training in recreational leadership on the college undergraduate level should
include creative dramatics, and that specialized drama courses
should be given more emphasis in the recreational program.

Third, more workshops and demonstrations should be conducted at local or state levels, since many leaders in program activities are not given travel expenses to attend national
meetings.

Fourth, for wider creative experiences for children, more
efforts should be made to stimulate interest in correlated and
coordinated creative arts programs at local levels, and on
a continuing basis.

Above all CTC and its leaders should make concerted efforts
to be more active in recreational programs. Qualified and
trained leaders should accept the ever-increasing challenge
of providing leadership, literature, and guidance in creative
dramatics for both children and youth in recreation. Preoc-
cupation with standards of training and performance, important
as these are, can result in sterility. Participation with all

its mistakes and pains is vital to growth. Learning comes
from doing.

23 Recommended Training for Creative Dramatics Leader

Agnes Haaga ✺

The art of creative dramatics is a complex art. The art of developing its leaders is no less complex. There is no ideal training course for there is no one ideal situation into which our students will advance once they have left the college or university. Just as schools of drama and speech at institutions of higher learning throughout the country have developed in ways unique to particular environments, needs, and personalities, so have the programs in children's drama both formal and informal.

We shall examine where training is being offered, to whom, and in one particular instance how. We will also consider where the trained potential leader will practice his art and skill and with whom. This will necessitate touching upon the philosophy of the art, the type of person or persons best suited or gifted to practice it, and the type of general education as well as specific drama background that will enrich leadership.

Individual Differences

When the College Curriculum Survey Committee of CTC made a survey of colleges and universities in the United States in an attempt to ascertain the quantity, nature, and extent of children's drama curricular activities, it was found that 220 institutions had programs, partial programs, or occasional programs. [1] Fifty institutions are listed as offering courses in creative dramatics; thirty-seven are listed as offering courses in children's theatre; thirty-seven are listed as offering both children's theatre and creative dramatics courses.

These programs in children's drama are offered by a variety of schools or departments within the institutions: seventy are under the auspices of speech departments; twenty-nine under drama or theatre departments; fifty-five under drama and speech departments; fifteen under education departments; eight under departments of English; four under language arts departments; four under English and speech departments; three under schools of fine (or creative) arts; three under extension divisions alone; three under language and speech departments; two under English and education departments; two under public relations and communications; two under English and psychology departments; one each under an English, speech and drama division; an arts and education division; a theatre and radio school; a department of humanities; graduate school alone; and an education and speech division.

Ninety-three of these institutions offer graduate courses in the area of children's drama. Ninety-eight offer laboratory programs with children for observation and/or practice teaching experience.

So it is evident that individual differences in program offerings do exist—influenced, as has been stated, by individual environments, needs, and personnel. The Northwestern University program as pioneered by Winifred Ward and continued by Rita Criste has been influenced in its development by the fact that the Evanston, Illinois, public schools have had for thirty-five years special classes in creative dramatics taught by specialists trained at Northwestern. In the West the immediate motivation for the inclusion of a training program in creative dramatics at the University of Washington in 1947 was a community program pioneered by the Seattle Junior League with the assistance of Junior Programs, Public Schools, Park Board, Art Museum, City Council, and the Council of Social Agencies.

When the demand for classes exceeded the supply of leaders, creative dramatics was added to the curriculum of the School of Drama, with the university assuming responsibility for the children's groups inaugurated by the Junior League in housing projects, Seattle Art Museum, libraries, etc. Having inherited the program from the community, the university has kept in mind always its community source and its own responsibility as a state-wide institution in training leaders on and off campus, in Seattle and throughout the state, cooperating in the process with community organizations and institutions in developing programs. So in classrooms, after-school and Saturday programs, in Sunday schools, in museums, libraries, and social institutions, leaders are sharing informal playmaking with children and youth. [2]

Once a part of the university curriculum, creative dramatics captured the attention of the Education Department, the Recreation Department, the School of Nursing, the School of Social Work, and others as well as students of drama. When Ruth Lease, the Junior League pioneer, and others interested UNESCO in the program, that organization recommended informal drama for the children of Europe. Students from Europe, North Africa, Asia, Hawaii, and the Philippines began to put in an appearance. So the instructor in this particular program, and similarly in programs across the country, finds herself facing a group of students of varied backgrounds, interests, and potentials.

Some Questions and Answers

Faced with such a varied group of students, the instructor wonders: where will these future leaders use their skill . . . in the classroom . . . on the playground . . . in an institution . . . a church program . . . in the home. . . . The answer would seem to include all these situations.

With whom will the student leader eventually share creative dramatics? Obviously with children of all ages from four years through high school years. Some will become involved in community programs, offering both creative dramatics and children's theatre productions; others will finally teach creative dramatics and other drama subjects on the college level.

So, what will be taught? . . . Creative dramatics *per se* as an art complete in itself as dynamic as the human dramatic instinct that is its source, or as a means of bringing to life such school subjects as history and literature? . . . as an approach to formal drama? . . . or a means of unlocking inarticulate children, stepping lightly always not to confuse the art with psychodrama or sociodrama?

What is to be done with the student who wants to major in the field, or the education or recreation major taking one quarter's work as a requirement? What is to be done with the education major who wants to go beyond the beginning course? How can the student be prepared to understand that the joyous, spontaneous quality of the art belies its very complexity and difficulties and leads to an eagerness to achieve right now what only comes after long preparation and experience?

How can the training program cope with the student who has had done for him what creative dramatics does for so many children—"allowing the imprisoned glory to escape" as Browning says—and the student who mistakes this enthusiastic release for an aptitude and an ability to go out and practice on others?

How can creative dramatics training best cope with the student who sees in this art an answer to all the ills of the world or like the blind men with the elephant becomes enthusiastic over but one aspect of the whole: the cultural, the therapeutic, the tool for learning, the means of making democracy live, the answer to delinquency?

How can the training do justice to that rare individual with unique background, experience, basic personality, or gift that makes him a natural in the art of creative dramatics and children's theatre? He must have some frame of reference wherein to practice his art and to grow wise in the experience and art of working with human beings.

All these human personalities with their varying interests, backgrounds, abilities, aspirations, and limitations face the one entrusted with the training of the creative dramatics leader. What kind of program will meet the multiple demands?

Philosophy of the Art of Creative Dramatics

First of all it would seem that the teacher must understand that the urge to create is universal and the desire to dramatize is a basic human instinct. Moreover, to whatever use creative dramatics will be put, in whatsoever situation or by whom, it is first and foremost an art unique to man, and "that every work of art is complete in itself and free of its material is the beginning of any understanding of that art."[3]

This feeling for and understanding of drama as an art comes through experiencing it as an art. Hence any course for students who would be leaders must involve doing, first as a player under a leader who is a living example of the art he practices—a leader who knows and loves and serves that art well with others whom he knows and loves.[4] Second, training should involve seeing that same leader and others in action with children—the better to know the art and the better to know children of all ages.

This firsthand experience can be enriched by reading text and supplementary materials; by exploring children's literature to become acquainted with, to analyze, and to know stories and poems that will appeal and satisfy as well as dramatize. It also involves reading that will broaden and deepen one's knowledge of people and arts related to drama, for the creative process has its universal qualities and ways. A beginning course involves lectures and discussion and whenever possible observation of formal children's theatre productions. Knowledge of drama and children will be greatly enhanced as one sits among children in an audience.

After the Beginning

Ideally after this first quarter of doing, talking, listening, watching, reading, experiencing, and thinking in close association with a practicing, ever growing artist teacher, the student should try his wings as a leader, with his own classmates as the players. The classes should be small enough to allow each student the opportunity to take over several times: (1) to guide an early type of session involving rhythm, movement, pantomime, or a simple dramatic play situation; (2) to motivate, present, and guide the playing of a story. Thus not only does the student leader have the chance to gain experience and receive evaluation of his leadership by the group and the instructors, but each member of the class is continually experiencing in action a variety of good material suitable for a wide age range. This training requires analysis of material to be used (how and why), and a written evaluation following each leadership experience. Conferences outside of class with individual students and the instructor complete the critique. Finally, further reading and continued observation of children in action round out this second phase of training.

Practice Teaching with Children

In a third quarter comes the student leader's "baptism of fire." He begins to work with children. Groups are organized in many locales within community organizations. In Seattle the long list of such groups welcoming practice leaders include preschools, Scout and Camp Fire troops, church groups, social institutions, etc. In other instances laboratory schools connected with departments of education provide the children. The student with the counsel of the instructor selects the situation and the age group closest to the situation in which he hopes to work professionally.

The student meets with his own group of children for an hour each week, each session preceded by a well-thought-out lesson plan and followed by a detailed evaluation. Twice during the quarter the instructor observes the student in action and follows up the observation with a critique conference. No other observers are allowed, therefore the group is the student's own and the children are free to create with an undivided mind under a single authority.

During this third quarter the student continues to attend class sessions to share and analyze successes and failures with others. He continues his required reading and watching of the children's group under faculty leadership. Throughout the year the student has been assembling a valuable notebook of story and poetry material, class notes, observation reports, lesson plans, and evaluations and impressions of his own childhood experiences and current responses to keep alive within himself that very rare, human quality he is attempting to keep alive, to stimulate, and to channel in the children—their creative energy and awareness.

Follow Up

Following this year's course of training and study, the student is able to take further work under a special Projects In Drama course to concentrate on some special aspect of creative dramatics particular to his personal needs, desires, and aspirations. This might be further practice teaching with children or continued research into story, poetry, or music material. Meantime the serious student is being advised on related courses to take in addition to a solid background in the humanities and the specific requirements of his major field, e. g., drama, education, recreation, social work, etc. A question on the survey mentioned in the introduction to this chapter asked what these courses might be. The response covered courses from storytelling and children's books, dance, psychology, rhythms, music, and children's art, to family relationships, oral interpretation, race relations, even botany. But first was advised a good background in the humanities and a sound knowledge of drama in its many aspects.

In response to the request of many elementary education majors who wanted more than the one required quarter of creative dramatics, the School of Drama at the University of Washington in cooperation with the School of Education established a basic academic field in Creative Dramatics for these majors. In addition to the year's work in creative dramatics and the special projects work, the program includes: two quarters of Introduction to the Theatre, two quarters of Theatre Speech, two quarters of Acting, two quarters of Children's Theatre, and two courses in the technical side of theatre. The result is a total of forty credit hours in drama for the education student in addition to the education requirements.

Students who plan to concentrate on children's theatre and creative dramatics take a full drama major on the undergraduate and graduate level. The further one goes into teaching and the arts, the more one realizes that one's education never ends. Any college training is but the beginning of a never-ending search and accumulation of knowledge and experience. That is the joy and the burden of the artist leader. And in the realm of drama nothing is lost. Who would dream that a simple poem like "Imaginings"[5] wherein we are invited to create a world of our own desire behind a little red door would lead a group of teenagers into the mysteries of creation and the atom? But such was the result when one boy found behind the door a book containing the answers to all the mysteries of the world. What were those mysteries? For each his own mystery, from the awesomeness of space, the perplexity of love, the marvel of universes revolving within universes, to the moment when the Cause of all causes started things causing.

The result was an exciting experience in dance and drama wherein the scientific and the Biblical accounts of the creation were found to contain no contradiction. In the process the leader as well as the youngsters had to "bone up" on atoms and elements and Genesis. Another story dramatization involving King Arthur necessitated an acquaintance with the era of knights and tournaments and fair ladies. When Mount Everest was so much in the news, a leader and a group of nine-to-twelve-year olds had to delve into the skill of mountain climbing to make enjoyable and realistic their own personal make-believe ascent.

A Creative Dramatics Leader

One never knows what a day may bring when imaginations and energies are stirred. So we come to the inevitable question: What type of person is the creative dramatics leader, for the personality of the leader colors the whole picture in this art involving players, leader, space, and an idea from which to create?

Since teaching is an extension of one's own personality, we must allow for individual differences as we do with children and as we must do in acknowledging that there is no one way to train future leaders. However, the leader must know and love and serve drama and people, and children in particular. The leader must know a variety of other things as well, for teaching in general and creative teaching in particular is a sharing of mind with mind and heart with heart. The latter can come only when there is a respect for the leader, the subject, and the process. There must be a feeling of trust in the leader. To trust we must feel secure and wanted and liked. Those we trust are people of integrity who will respect and listen to and appreciate and keep confidential the innermost thoughts and feelings we express and share and put into action. He must be one whose own vibrant, creative, positive spirit sets fire to our own and helps us to express our best selves while understanding our present shortcomings—one who enjoys and keeps up with and channels our human energies.

With the truly great teacher there is that indefinable *plus* quality as though Providence had endowed him with just a little more of everything of life: energy, compassion, humor, imagination, perception, humility, patience, wisdom, taste and judgment, joy and sorrow. He is one whose continual labor of love transforms technique into intuition and spontaneity, one who accepts himself and others as creatures of a God who ". . . created man in his own image and likeness, i.e., made him a creator too, calling him to free spontaneous activity . . . the creature's answer to the great call of its creator," realizing that "man's creative work is the fulfillment of the Creator's secret will."[6]

Summary of an Ideal

This deeper dimension plus knowledge and love and the will to serve an art in company with others would seem to sum up the ideal we seek to strive for in our training of the creative dramatics leader. It is an ideal that will enable our students to spend the time and energy and thought to adapt their practice of the art to wherever they find themselves, be it classroom or church or playground, here or on the northern shores of Africa, with kindergartners or teen-agers. It is an ideal that will keep him learning in the process of doing and empower him to take into account the particular abilities, interests, aspirations, limitations of his players while at the same time seeing beyond the handicapped, the delinquent, the disturbed, the natural, to the human being with his deep urge to create and his instinct to dramatize, and his capacity to do and to grow.

It is the ideal that will make it possible for the teacher to guide with firm kindness into more realistic channels the awakened energies of those who may not be wise enough or strong enough to assume the responsibilities of leadership. And it is the ideal that will motivate and enable us to discover and encourage and endure and enjoy and guide the rare individual who is truly creative and dramatic.

Appendix A:
A Directory of Children's Theatre
and Creative Dramatics

Hazel Brain Dunnington ᴓ

This is an extraction from "A Directory of American Colleges and Universities Offering Training in Children's Theatre and Creative Dramatics," published in May, 1958, under the direction of Agnes Haaga, assisted by Werdna Finley. [1] The 1958 directory is a supplement to the College Curriculum Survey Report published in March, 1954. [2] Members of the original College Curriculum Survey Committee were Richard G. Adams, Jed H. Davis, Jeanne Dawson, Agnes Haaga, Kathryn Kayser, James Popovich, Stanley Raiff, and Mouzon Law, Chairman.

Appendix A includes information from questionnaires sent to Alaska and Hawaii.

Courses already in operation at the University of Hawaii and the enthusiastic tone of the questionnaire responses from this university are promising. On the other hand, absence of offerings in children's drama at the University of Alaska and many other universities throughout the United States presents a challenge, particularly in the light of recommendations which introduce this monograph.

Key

1. An asterisk preceding the name of the institution indicates that the work offered may be taken for graduate credit.

2. The name of the college or university and the city in which it is located are given.

3. Titles of specific courses, titles of courses of which formal or informal children's drama are a part, and, in some cases, directly related courses are listed. Descriptions of Children's Theatre production activities are given.

209

Alabama

Birmingham Southern College, Birmingham. Creative Drama; Theatre for Children; Creative Arts. Two productions each year; four performances.

Huntingdon College, Montgomery. Storytelling and Creative Dramatics. Two productions each year; two performances.

Tuskegee Institute, Tuskegee Institute, Alabama. Expressive Arts (six out of 24 lectures on creative dramatics).

University of Alabama, Tuscaloosa. Theatre for children (summer semester). One summer production.

Alaska

University of Alaska, College (near Fairbanks). Music for children (includes singing games, rhythms, and creative experiences).

Arizona

Arizona State College, Tempe. Creative Dramatics; Children's Theatre. One production each year; three performances.

Arkansas

Arkansas State Teachers College, Conway. Children's Theatre unit in play production course. Creative Dramatics allied with activities course for elementary teachers. One production each year; two performances.

Henderson State Teachers College, Arkadelphia. Dramatic Activities for Youth in Schools (one-fourth creative dramatics).

Southern State College, Magnolia. Children's Literature (six out of 36 lectures on creative dramatics).

University of Arkansas, Fayetteville. Construction and Dramatic Play for Young Children (about one-eighth creative dramatics). Summer workshops and occasional productions.

California

Chico State College, Chico. Creative Dramatics. One production each year; one performance.

Claremont College, Claremont. Speech Techniques in the Elementary and Secondary Classroom (about one-twentieth creative dramatics).

College of the Holy Names, Oakland. Creative Dramatics; Children's Theatre. One production; six performances.

Fresno State College, Fresno. Dramatization in Elementary Education. One production; six performances.

Long Beach State College, Long Beach. Children's Theatre (two units); Speech Arts in the Elementary School (one-fourth creative dramatics).

Los Angeles State College of Applied Arts and Sciences, Los Angeles. Speech and Dramatic Activities in Elementary Schools (about one-fourth creative dramatics).

Mills College, Oakland. Creative Dramatics, Children's Theatre. One production each year; two performances.

*Occidental College, Los Angeles. Creative Dramatics (two courses). One production each year.

*San Francisco State College, San Francisco. Children's Theatre, Projects in the Field of Children's Theatre; Children's Theatre Production; Writing of Plays for Children; Creative Dramatics, Children's Literature and Creative Dramatics. One production each year; six performances. One touring production; fifteen to twenty performances.

*San Jose State College, San Jose. Children's Theatre; Creative Dramatics (two courses). Two productions a year; four performances.

*Stanford University, Stanford. Children's Theatre; Creative Dramatics. Variable number of productions each year.

University of California, Santa Barbara College, Santa Barbara. Dramatics and Music in Early Childhood.

*University of California at Los Angeles, Los Angeles. Children's Theatre (two units); Creative Dramatics (two units). One production each year in conjunction with Los Angeles Junior Programs; number of performances varies.

University of Redlands, Redlands. Drama and Speech for Teachers (one-fourth creative dramatics).

University of Southern California, Los Angeles. Theatre for Children; Creative Speech Activities (one-fifth creative dramatics). One production each year; twelve performances.

Yuba College, Marysville. No courses. One production each year; three performances.

Colorado

Colorado State College of Education, Greely. Children's Theatre (one-third creative dramatics).

*University of Denver, Denver. Children's Theatre, Dramatic Activities in the Schools (two courses, about one-half creative dramatics); Drama Workshop for Children in Creative Dramatics. Offers a major in Children's Theatre. Two productions each year; two performances.

Western State College of Colorado, Gunnison. No courses. One production each year; five performances.

Connecticut

Danbury State Teachers College, Danbury. Creative Dramatics; Dramatics for Children; Poetry for Children; Children's Literature.

Teachers College of Connecticut, New Britain. Language Arts in the Elementary School (some creative dramatics).

Delaware

University of Delaware, Newark. Children's Theatre. One production each year; twenty-one performances (nineteen on tour).

District of Columbia

George Washington University, Washington, D. C. Creative Dramatics and Children's Theatre.

Howard University, Washington, D. C. Educational Dramatics (about one-fourth creative dramatics).

Florida

Stetson University, Deland. Children's Theatre (about one-third creative dramatics).

University of Florida, Gainesville. Recreational Dramatics (about one-third creative dramatics); Acting (one-fifth creative dramatics).

Georgia

University of Georgia, Athens. Creative Dramatics for Children; a second course, Teaching of Speech and Drama, is one-eighth creative dramatics.

Hawaii

University of Hawaii, Honolulu. Creative Dramatics; also an occasional workshop for teachers in the College of Education; Dramatic Production (about one-sixth children's drama). Two to six productions each year; four to eight performances of each.

Idaho

College of Idaho, Caldwell. Creative Dramatics (summer session only). Idaho State College, Pocatello. Creative dramatics. Productions occasionally.

Ricks College, Rexburg. Creative Dramatics; Children's Literature. One production each year; three performances.

Illinois

College of St. Francis, Joliet. Creative Dramatics; Children's Theatre. Three productions each year; two performances of each.

Eastern Illinois State College, Charleston. Creative Dramatics.

Illinois State Normal University, Normal. Children's Drama. Experiencing Books through Speech Activities (one-half creative dramatics).

Knox College, Galesburg. No courses. Three productions each year; two to three performances.

Lake Forest College, Lake Forest. Children's Theatre. Two productions each year; ten to twenty performances each.

Monticello College, Alton. Children's Theatre and Creative Dramatics. One production each year; two performances.

Mundelein College, Chicago. Children's Dramatics (about one-half creative dramatics); Drama in the Secondary Schools. Productions occasionally.

*National College of Education, Evanston. Dramatic Art in the Elementary School (one-third creative dramatics). One production each year; eight to ten performances.

Northern Illinois State Teachers College, DeKalb. Oral Interpretation and Creative Dramatics (one-third creative dramatics).

*Northwestern University, Evanston. Creative Dramatics; Children's Theatre; Interpretation of Children's Literature; Independent Study in Children's Theatre and Creative Dramatics. Three productions each year; six performance of each for primary and preschool age. Three productions each year; four performances of each for primary and preschool age.

Pestalozzi Froebel Teachers College, Chicago. Creative Expression: Dramatic.

Rockford College, Rockford. Teaching of Creative Activities for Children (about one-eighth creative dramatics).

*Southern Illinois University, Carbondale. Children's Theatre, Storytelling and Children's Literature. Three productions each year; five performances each.

*University of Illinois, Urbana. Creative Dramatics for Children; Theatre for the Child Audience. (Both courses now offered only in the summer session.) One production each year; three performances.

Indiana

Butler University, Indianapolis. Course in Children's Literature, Storytelling, and Dramatization (about one-fourth creative dramatics).

Ball State Teachers College, Muncie. Speech for Elementary Teachers (one-fifth creative dramatics).

Earlham College, Richmond. Language Arts in the Elementary School (about one-tenth creative dramatics).

*Indiana State Teachers College, Terre Haute. Children's Theatre; Junior Theatre Problems; Storytelling; Storytelling

and Creative Dramatics; Materials and Background of Children's Literature. Three productions each year; seven performances of each.

Indiana University, Bloomington. Theatre for Children. Two productions each year; five performances for each.

Manchester College, North Manchester. Creative Dramatics.

Marian College, Indianapolis. Speech Arts for Children (about one-half creative dramatics).

Saint Mary-of-the-Woods College, St. Mary-of-the-Woods. Storytelling and Creative Dramatics. One production each year; one performance.

Iowa

Clarke College, Dubuque. Verse Speaking and Creative Dramatics (one-fourth creative dramatics); Play Production Project; Children's Literature. One production each year; four performances.

Cornell College, Mt. Vernon. Dramatic Art Course includes children's theatre and creative dramatics. One production each year; two performances.

*Drake University, Des Moines. Creative Dramatics; Children's Theatre. Five productions each year; two performances of each plus tours.

Iowa State College, Ames. Children's Theatre included in Play Production Course. One production each year; one or two performances.

Iowa State Teachers College, Cedar Falls. Dramatics for Elementary Teachers.

Morningside College, Sioux City. Creative and Formal Dramatics for Children.

Wartburg College, Waverly. No courses. One production each year. Two performances.

Kansas

College of Emporia, Emporia. Children's Theatre Workshop. One production each year; two performances.

*Kansas State Teachers College, Emporia. Children's Theatre; Advanced Children's Theatre; Storytelling.

Marymount College, Salina. Methods of Teaching Dramatic Art (one-tenth creative dramatics).

Saint Mary College, Xavier. Creative Dramatics.

*University of Kansas, Lawrence. Creative Dramatics; Children's Theatre. Two productions each year; five or six performances.

Kentucky

Asbury College, Wilmore. Creative Dramatics.

*Morehead State College, Morehead. Workshop in School Drama (about one-third creative dramatics). One production each year; two performances.

Maine

University of Maine, Orono. Creative Dramatics; Children's Theatre (summer session only).

Maryland

*John Hopkins University, Baltimore. Workshop in School Dramatic Activities; Speech Improvement for Children. Eight to ten productions each year; three to five performances each.

State Teachers College, Fostburg. Methods of Teaching the Elementary School Child the Language Arts, Children's Literature (about one-tenth creative dramatics). Three productions each year.

State Teachers College, Towson. Children's Theatre (one-fourth creative dramatics). One production each year; three performances.

Massachusetts

Boston University, Boston. Creative Dramatics.

Northwestern University, Boston. Creative Arts in Elementary Schools.

Regis College, Weston. Classroom dramatics; three weeks of practice teaching.

*School of Public Relations and Communications, Boston.

Children's Theatre Workshop. Five productions each year; three to six performances of each.

Smith College, Northampton. Oral Interpretation of Children's Literature (one-eighth creative dramatics).

Tufts University, Medford. Children's Theatre (one-third creative dramatics).

Wheelock College, Boston. Productions only.

Michigan

Michigan State Normal College, Ypsilanti. Dramatics for Elementary Grades (about one-fifth creative dramatics).

*Michigan State University, East Lansing. Children's Theatre; Creative Dramatics for Children; Studies in Theatre Practice; Storytelling; Honors Course. Three productions each year; 14-17 performances (trouping); three performances in Toy Shop Theatre.

Northern Michigan College, Marquette. Dramatics for Elementary Schools (about one-fourth creative dramatics).

Wayne University, Detroit. Creative Dramatics.

*Western Michigan College, Kalamazoo. Creative Dramatics; Children's Theatre; Speech for Elementary Grades (about one-third creative dramatics). Three productions each year; two to four performances.

Minnesota

College of St. Benedict, St. Joseph. No courses offered. One production; one performance.

College of St. Catherine, St. Paul. Creative Dramatics for Children.

Macalester College, St. Paul. Speech for Elementary Teachers (about one-eighth creative dramatics). One production each year; eight to eleven performances.

State Teachers College, Bemidji. Creative Dramatics in the School.

State Teachers College, Mankato. Creative Dramatics.

State Teachers College, St. Cloud. Children's Literature (about one-twentieth creative dramatics).

State Teachers College, Winona. Creative Dramatics.

*University of Minnesota, Minneapolis. Children's Theatre:
Creative Dramatics. Two productions each year; thirteen to
fourteen performances.
*University of Minnesota, Duluth. Creative Dramatics. Two
productions each year; two performances.

Mississippi

Mississippi College, Clinton. Children's Theatre.
Mississippi Southern College, Hattiesburg. Children's Thea-
tre. Speech in the Elementary Schools includes one-eighth
creative dramatics.
Mississippi State College for Women, Columbus. No courses.
One production each year; one performance.

Missouri

Central Missouri State College, Warrensburg. No courses.
One production each year; two or three performances.
Northeast Missouri State Teachers College, Kirksville.
Creative Dramatics.
Northwest Missouri State College, Maryville. Creative Dra-
matics.
*St. Louis University, St. Louis. Speech Activities—Ele-
mentary (about one-fourth creative dramatics); Children's
Theatre; Workshop in Creative Dramatics and Children's Plays.
Southwest Missouri State College, Springfield. Speech for
the Classroom (about one-third creative dramatics). One pro-
duction each year; six performances.
University of Kansas City, Kansas City. Children's Thea-
tre; Creative Dramatics; Creative Dramatics in Religious
Education offered through extension. Two productions each
year; fourteen performances.

Montana

Eastern Montana College of Education, Billings. Drama
Activity for Children.
University of Montana, Missoula. Occasional extension
courses in creative dramatics.

Nevada

New Mexico Highlands University, Las Vegas. Dramatics
for Elementary and Secondary Schools.

New Jersey

Douglass College, Rutgers University, New Brunswick.
Creative Dramatics. One production each year; two performances.

New Jersey State Teachers College, Trenton. Speech in the
Elementary School (about one-sixth creative dramatics); Children's Plays (about one-third creative dramatics).

New Mexico

New Mexico A & M College, State College. Children's Theatre. One production each year; two performances.

University of New Mexico, Albuquerque. No courses. One
production each year; six performances.

New York

Adelphi College, Garden City. Children's Theatre Workshop;
Creative Dramatics; Creative Arts in Elementary Education.
Occasional productions.

Alfred University, Alfred. No courses. Summer classes
for children in creative dramatics climaxed by a production.

Columbia University, New York. Creative Dramatics (only
in summer); Children's Theatre. One production each year;
five to seven performances.

Cornell University, Ithaca. Creative Dramatics for Children (offered irregularly in the Child Development and Family
Relations Department). One production every few years; three
to four performances.

Hofstra College, Hempstead, Long Island. Creative Dramatics; Children's Theatre (both included in courses on Theatre Methods).

Hunter College, New York. Children's Theatre (course
includes creative dramatics).

Ithaca College, Ithaca. Children's Theatre (about one-third creative dramatics). One or more productions each year; one or more performances.

Long Island University, Brooklyn. Children's Theatre; Classes in Acting for Children in cooperation with Brooklyn Music School. One production each year; one performance.

Queens College, Flushing. Creative Dramatics.

Skidmore College, Saratoga Springs. Creative Dramatics.

*State University Teachers College, Brockport. Creative Dramatics. Occasional productions; two to eight performances.

State University Teachers College, Buffalo. Creative Dramatics. Speech Activities in the Elementary School (one-eighth creative dramatics). One production each year; two to three performances.

State University Teachers College, Cortland. Children's Theatre. Children's demonstration class in creative dramatics in the Campus School. One production each year; four performances.

State University Teachers College, Fredonia. Teaching Speech in the Elementary School (about one-third creative dramatics).

State University Teachers College, Geneso. Children's Theatre (about one-third creative dramatics).

*State University Teachers College, Oneonta. Children's Theatre; Creative Dramatics; Children and Drama (Literature). Two productions (one a touring show) each year; ten performances of each.

*Syracuse University, Syracuse. Children's Theatre (one-fourth creative dramatics). Two productions each year which tour; four to twelve performances of each.

Vassar College, Poughkeepsie. Children's Theatre offered by Drama Department in cooperation with Child Study Department. Production in public schools and settlement houses.

North Carolina

Winston-Salem Teachers College, Winston-Salem. Educational Dramatics (about one-third creative dramatics).

North Dakota

State Teachers College, Mayville. Creative Speech for Children (about one-twentieth creative dramatics. Temporarily suspended.)

Ohio

*Bowling Green State University, Bowling Green. Graduate Research in Children's Theatre. One production each year; four to eight performances.
Capital University, Columbus. Children's Theatre (one-third creative dramatics).
College of Wooster, Wooster. Children's Theatre. One or two productions each year; two performances.
Denison University, Granville. Children's Theatre (about one-third creative dramatics). Two productions each year; twenty performances (temporarily discontinued).
*Kent State University, Kent. Creative Dramatics. One production each year; four performances.
Lake Erie College, Painsville. Children's Theatre. Creative dramatic groups for children.
University of Toledo, Toledo. Children's Theatre (summer courses). One production; three performances (summer).
Western College, Oxford. Children's Theatre. Four productions each year; five performances on campus; three touring.
Western Reserve University, Cleveland. Creative Dramatics; Children's Theatre (latter in cooperation with the Cleveland Playhouse). Work with children offered in cooperation with Cain Park Creative Playshop and Youth Theatre (summer session only). Six productions each year; six performances.

Oklahoma

Northeastern State College, Tahlequah. Speech for the Elementary Teacher (one-third creative dramatics).
Southwestern State College, Weatherford. Speech for the Elementary Teacher (about one-third creative dramatics).

University of Tulsa, Tulsa. Children's Theatre (about one-third creative dramatics).

Oregon

Eastern Oregon College of Education, La Grande. Workshop courses in Drama for Children, with special emphasis on creative dramatics. Occasional productions.

Lewis and Clark College, Portland. Creative Dramatics.

Northwest Christian College, Eugene. Informal drama in religious education.

Portland State College, Portland. Children's Theatre. Summer Children's Creative Dramatic classes for observation. Six productions each year; one performance.

Southern Oregon College of Education, Ashland. Course emphasizing principles of Children's Theatre and Theatre for the Elementary School. Summer workshop in Children's Drama culminating in a children's play. One production each year; three performances.

University of Oregon, Eugene. Children's Theatre.

Willamette University, Salem. Children's Drama Workshop held Saturdays throughout the school year. Children aged six to sixteen work at pantomime, natural dance, storytelling, improvisation, rehearsal of plays and stagecraft.

Pennsylvania

Allegheny College, Meadville. Children's Theatre; Creative Dramatics. Two to three productions each year; five to eight performances of each.

Pennsylvania State University, University Park. Creative Dramatics; Marionettes and Puppetry (both offered summer). Productions occasionally.

State Teachers College, Bloomsburg. Creative Dramatics and Storytelling.

State Teachers College, Edinboro. Creative Dramatics and Storytelling.

State Teachers College, East Stroudsburg. Creative Dramatics and Storytelling.

State Teachers College, Kutztown. Creative Dramatics and Storytelling.

State Teachers College, Indiana. Creative Dramatics and Storytelling.

State Teachers College, Lock Haven. Creative Dramatics and Storytelling.

State Teachers College, Slippery Rock. Creative Dramatics and Storytelling.

State Teachers College, West Chester. Dramatics in the Elementary Grades. One production each year; three to four performances.

*University of Pittsburgh, Pittsburgh. Children's Dramatic Activities (one-third creative dramatics); Workshop in Creative Activities (one-fourth creative dramatics); Creative Dramatics Workshop.

Westminister College, New Wilmington. Speech Methods in the Elementary School.

Wilkes College, Wilkes-Barre. Children's Literature and Storytelling (one-twentieth dramatics).

South Dakota

General Beadle State Teachers College, Madison. Creative Dramatics; Storytelling; Children's Literature.

Sioux Falls College, Sioux Falls. Some work in creative dramatics in religious drama course.

Yankton College, Yankton. Speech and Dramatic Art Methods for the Elementary School. One production each year; two performances.

Tennessee

*Fisk University, Nashville. Dramatics Education (about one-fourth creative dramatics). One production each year; one performance.

Middle Tennessee State College, Murfreesboro. Children's Drama and Speech (one-tenth creative dramatics).

Tennessee A. and I. State University, Nashville. Creative Dramatics (two courses); Creative Dramatics and Children's

Theatre (one course). Three productions each year; two performances of each.

Texas

Austin College, Sherman. Speech and Dramatic Activities
in the Elementary School (about one-fifth creative dramatics).
Baylor University, Waco. Creative Dramatics; Children's
Theatre; Children's Theatre TV Workshop in summer.
East Texas State College, Commerce. Creative Drama.
Hardin-Simmons University, Abilene. Creative Dramatics
with Children.
Lamar State College of Technology, Beaumont. Creative
Dramatics. One production each year.
Midwestern University, Wichita Falls. Children's Theatre
(about one-third creative dramatics).
North Texas State College, Denton. Auditorium Activities
and Children's Theatre (about one-fourth creative dramatics).
Pan American College, Edinburg. Speech for the Class-
room Teacher (one-fourth creative dramatics).
Southern Methodist University, Dallas. Creative Dramatics
offered occasionally.
Southwest Texas State Teachers College, San Marcos. Crea-
tive Dramatics for Children.
*Southwestern University, Georgetown. Creative Dramatics.
*Stephen F. Austin State College, Nacogdoches. Creative
Dramatics in the Elementary School.
Sul Ross State College, Alpine. Speech for the Elementary
Teacher (one-twentieth creative dramatics).
Texas Christian University, Fort Worth. Children's Theatre
(one-fourth creative dramatics).
Texas College of Arts & Industries, Kingsville. Creative
Dramatics; Service Course in Speech Arts for Teachers (about
one-tenth creative dramatics). One production each year;
three to four performances.
Texas Technological College, Lubbock. Creative Dramatics.
University of Houston, Houston. Children's Theatre.
*University of Texas, Austin. Creative Dramatics; Chil-
dren's Theatre. Productions occasionally.

West Texas State College, Canyon. Workshop in Creative Dramatics.

Utah

Brigham Young University, Salt Lake City. Creative Dramatics: Children's Theatre. Extensive touring program.
University of Utah, Salt Lake City. Children's Theatre; Creative Dramatics (summer only). Four productions each year; seven performances.
Utah State Agriculture College, Logan. Some practice work done by project in elementary schools.

Vermont

Bennington College, Bennington. Theatre for Children (about one-third creative dramatics).
University of Vermont, Burlington. No courses. An occasional production; ten to fifteen performances.

Virginia

Mary Washington College of the University of Virginia, Fredericksburg. Children's Theatre (about one-fourth creative dramatics).
Virginia State College, Petersburg. Educational Dramatics (about one-tenth creative dramatics).

Washington

Central Washington College of Education, Ellensburg. Children's Drama (three-fourth creative dramatics), an additional creative dramatics in the planning stage; Speech in the Elementary School (one-fifth creative dramatics). An occasional children's production; three or so performances.
Eastern Washington College of Education, Cheney. Creative Dramatics (two courses): Children's Theatre.
Pacific Lutheran College, Parkland. Two Children's Theatre productions; three performances.

Seattle Pacific College, Seattle. Creative Dramatics.

Seattle University, Seattle. Children's Drama.

State College of Washington, Pullman. Recreational Dramatics (includes formal and informal drama for children). One production a year; one to three performances.

University of Puget Sound, Tacoma. Children's Dramatics (about one-fourth creative dramatics).

*University of Washington, Seattle. Creative Dramatics (three courses); B. A. available in Creative Dramatics; Basic Academic Field open to Education Majors; Extension Courses throughout State. Children's Theatre (three courses). Four productions each year; fourteen to sixteen performances.

Whitworth College, Spokane. Creative Dramatics for Children.

West Virginia

Fairmont State College, Fairmont. Children's Theatre. One production each year; four performances.

Marshall College, Huntington. Storytelling and Dramatization.

West Virginia University, Morgantown. Creative Dramatics.

Wisconsin

Carroll College, Waukesha. Creative Arts for Children (offered through Education Department).

Stout State College, Menomonie. No courses. One production each year; five performances.

Wisconsin State College, Eau Claire. Creative Dramatics (course not being offered at present).

*Wisconsin State College, Milwaukee. Theatre for Children; Dramatization in Elementary Schools; Speech for Children eight to fourteen years of age (about one-fifth creative dramatics). One production each year; two to three performances.

Wisconsin State College, Plattsville. Storytelling and Choral Speaking (about one-third creative dramatics).

Wisconsin State College, River Falls. Summer Drama Workshop in Children's Theatre; Speech for the Elementary Teacher (about one-fifth creative dramatics). One production each year; one to three performances.

Wisconsin State College, Superior. Creative Dramatics.

Wisconsin State College, Whitewater. Creative Dramatics.

Appendix B:
Composite Course Outlines for Children's Theatre and Creative Dramatics at the College Level

Richard G. Adams ✐

Composite outlines for college courses in children's theatre and creative dramatics could never hope to satisfy the requirements or needs of each institution. They should, however, be useful to the university instructor as a guide to course content. The course outlines on the following pages represent ideas from various well-established curricula.[1] First, a master list of all the outlines was made; then these were reorganized into a master syllabus. After careful pruning and simplifying, the outlines were developed to form a composite picture of course content.

Children's Theatre Beginning Course

The outline for a children's theatre course is designed as a survey course in a specialized area of drama. It presupposes a knowledge on the part of the student of, at least, basic theatre history and principles. It is recommended that students who desire to direct or become involved in children's theatre be required to take essential theatre courses: (1) Elements of direction, (2) Technical production, (3) Children's theatre program. Of course, advance instruction in each area of the total production of a children's play will be devised by the department to strengthen the total curriculum. A student specializing in children's theatre should also take an introductory course in creative dramatics in order to more fully understand children and their relations and attitudes toward drama.

Representative Requirements
I. *Lecture:* Usually with participation and outside observation; frequently in conjunction with a production unit.

II. *Text:* Usually required; either one of the few specific books on children's theatre or a general survey book on theatre or a general survey book on theatre production.

III. *Assignments:* Usually three or more of the following: (1) Prompt book preparation. (2) Ten to thirty script evaluations of dramatic content and production possibilities with card-reports on each. (3) Outside reading in allied or tangent fields. (4) Attendance at local children's theatre performances followed by critical discussions of production elements and audience reactions. (5) Evaluation of radio and television programs for children. (6) Presentation of short scenes in class followed by critiques. (7) Attendance at several rehearsals for a current local children's theatre production followed by discussions with the director. (8) Term paper. (9) Class project in organizing and planning a children's theatre program for a community.

Representative outline of course
  I. *Orientation to Children's Theatre*
    A. Definition, nature, and objectives
    B. History of theatre and relation of children's theatre
    C. Children's theatre today
      1. International and national (types, sponsors, variety of media)
  II. *The Children's Play*
    A. Choosing the play (audience considerations, physical facilities, casting limitations, planning a season's program)
    B. Analyzing the script (classifications, sources, requirements, structure, style, cutting and editing)
  III. *Directing and the Actors*
    A. Preparation for the play (prompt book, planning the setting, planning the action, script notations, dance and song)
    B. Tryouts (children, adults)
    C. Rehearsal techniques (spatial design, empathy and aesthetic distance, style of design)
    D. Movement and business (principles of design and composition, stage areas, movement values, blocking the play)
    E. Acting (basic techniques of movement, motivation, basic body positions, voice and diction, concentration and sincerity, clarity, imagination development)

F. Synchronizing the play (mood, style, rhythm, tempo and build, blend of production elements, harmony, audience consideration)

IV. *Technical Aspects*

A. Theatre building (stage and adjacent areas, auditorium, outside versus inside performances)

B. Design and production (scenery, properties, costumes, lighting, make-up, sound)

V. *Organization and Management*

A. Organizing (sponsorship, personnel)

B. Financing (source of income, expenses and budget, box-office procedures)

C. Public relations (publicity, including press, posters, and promotional programs; education and community liaison; house management and audience control)

Creative Dramatics Beginning Course

The outline for a creative dramatics course should serve as a guide to the first of three courses required for a creative dramatics major. The following two courses should emphasize more individual guidance by students with classmates and with children. Students majoring in creative dramatics should be well grounded in theatre background and should be required to take courses in introduction to the theatre, dramatic literature, storytelling, and children's theatre. The outline presented here emphasizes participation, discussion, and evaluation.

Representative Requirements

I. *Lecture:* Usually with participation by students in creative dramatics and with observation of children's classes.

II. *Text:* Usually required; either one of several excellent standard books on creative dramatics and assigned articles or chapters from recent publications.

III. *Assignments:* Usually two or more of the following: (1) Observation of weekly demonstrations with children by the instructor or other approved leader; written and oral reports of observations including analyses of group, dramatic content of literature, and guidance techniques. (2) Regular weekly assigned readings in children's literature with card-reports of analyses of dramatic content and appeal to age-levels. (3) Laboratory project in guiding groups of children or members of class in beginning creative dramatics experiences. (4) Weekly storytelling assignments and oral evaluations of potential values and use. (5) Term reports on outside readings in the field. (6) Term paper on philosophy and dynamics of creative dramatics for children.

Representative outline of course
   I. *Introduction to Creative Dramatics*
     A. Definition, nature, and philosophy
     B. History of theatre with emphasis on the relation of theatre with children to the main streams of dramatic art
     C. Definitions and interpretation of related terms
     D. Objectives and purposes of creative dramatics
     E. Values of creative dramatics for children, teacher or leader, and for community and country
     F. Application of educational principles to creative drama
     G. Requirements of creative dramatics leader
   II. *Drama as an Art*
     A. In the school curriculum (language arts and literature, social studies, integrated studies, choral reading)
   III. *Introduction to Basic Guidance Techniques*
     A. Discussion of nature, needs, interests, and attitudes of each age level (preschool, lower elementary, upper elementary, junior high school)
     B. Discussion and participation in creative rhythms (ensemble movement and pantomimes; individual movement and pantomimes; exploring music materials)
     C. Discussion and participation in dramatic play (motivation techniques; organization of ideas, creative guidance techniques)
   IV. *Introduction to Creative Guidance Techniques in Story Dramatization*
     A. Analysis of dramatic elements and story construction (selecting, preparing, motivating, and presenting story)
     B. Analysis of creative guidance techniques (building the story with characterization, scenes, plot, interaction, and dialogue)
     C. Analysis of evaluation techniques (evaluation of charac-

terization and basic dramatic elements, imagination in interpretation, cooperation, sincerity in style and expression)

D. Analysis of guidance techniques in creating a play from
entire story

V. *Organization of Physical Aspects of Creative Dramatics
Class*

A. Discussion of space, optimum size of class, length of
sessions, number of sessions, adult observers, public relations, and parent education

Appendix C:
Twenty-Five Recommended Three-Act Plays for Children's Theatre

Rita Criste ❧

Theatre should assist children to interpret past, present, and future life; there should be historical plays of the past, plays to make children imaginatively aware of present surroundings, and uninhibited, challenging plays of the future. If present practices, principles, theories, and criteria are outmoded, playwrights must free themselves and seek a breadth of vision, a new vitalizing approach to an ever-changing world.

To recommend plays from the presently available supply of published ones is only a temporary step toward providing a source of inspiring and entertaining theatre experiences for children. With this in mind, the following twenty-five plays, intelligently directed and artistically staged, can bridge the gap until more really great plays, worthy of the tremendous responsibility inherent in them, are created. [1]

The Adventures of Tom Sawyer
Dramatized by Charlotte Chorpenning; Coach House Press. *Cast:* five women, nine men, five boys, one girl; *four sets* (one interior, one exterior). The familiar episodes—the whitewashing, the graveyard, the island, and the funeral—are all dramatically brought to life from Mark Twain's novel.

Beauty and the Beast
Dramatized by Nora MacAlvay; Coach House Press. *Cast:* six women, three men; *one set* (interior, with huge mirror and curtains for varied effects). Elaborate devices are used to augment and enrich this familiar fairy tale.

The Blue Bird
By Maurice Maeterlinck; Samuel French. *Cast:* an indefinite number depending upon the choice of scenes used; *five sets* (one

interior, four exterior). An elaborate and beautiful play in
which Tyltyl and Mytyl search for the Blue Bird, the symbol
of happiness. The story emphasizes the philosophy that complete happiness is an ideal; it can never be held even if attained
for a little while. A wise selection of scenes is preferable to
the production of the whole play.

Buffalo Bill

By Aurand Harris; Children's Theatre Press. *Cast:* two
women, fifteen men, settlers and Indians; numerous scenes,
with alternate entr'actes. Historical saga, told in dramatic
action and dance mime. Young Bill Cody risks his life in helping to make the West a place where all might live together in
peace.

Cinderella

Dramatized by Charlotte Chorpenning; Children's Theatre
Press. *Cast:* six women, four men, *two sets* (one interior,
one exterior). The beauty and humor of this ageless story are
reinforced by the introduction of frequent dancing and music.

The Cricket on the Hearth

Dramatized by Marian Jonson; Coach House Press. *Cast:*
two women, five men, boys; *one set.* A sensitive play based
on the Charles Dickens' story emphasizes the philosophy that
truth is seen through the eyes of love.

The Emperor's New Clothes

Dramatized by Charlotte Chorpenning; Samuel French. *Cast:*
indefinite number of characters; *two sets* (one interior, one
exterior). An excellent play from the Hans Christian Andersen
tale of the vain emperor, based on the idea that his subjects
fear to tell the truth about what they see.

Hans Brinker and the Silver Skates

Dramatized by Charlotte Chorpenning; Children's Theatre
Press. *Cast:* three women, five men, eleven children; *four
sets* (two interior, two exterior). All the important episodes
from the famous story of the Holland canals by Mary Mapes
Dodge are retold in highly dramatic form.

Huckleberry Finn

Dramatized by Corinne Rickert and Frank Whiting; Children's
Theatre Press. *Cast:* five women, nine men, four children;
four sets (one interior, three exterior). An effective version
of Mark Twain's story. The episodes are held together through
the intermission by Huck's own narration.

Jack and the Beanstalk

Dramatized by Charlotte Chorpenning; Children's Theatre
Press. *Cast:* one boy, two women, three men, four or five
villagers, one cow; *four sets* (one interior, three exterior).
The magic, beauty, humor, and suspense in the dramatization
of this popular fairy tale are well worth the effort necessary
to solve the difficult production problems.

King Midas and the Golden Touch

Dramatized by Charlotte Chorpenning; Children's Theatre
Press. *Cast:* two women, two men, four children; *one set.* The
Goddess of Wishes, Cybele, grants King Midas his Golden Touch
which leads him, through grief, to discover an eternal truth.

The Land of the Dragon

By Madge Miller; Children's Theatre Press. *Cast:* five
women, three men, one small dragon, extras; *one set* (a completely empty stage with appropriate stage properties provided
by a Property Man according to the ancient Chinese manner,
to create the illusion of thirteen scenes). A delightful, stylized
Chinese play with humor and fantasy. It would add variety to
a season of plays.

Little Red Ridinghood or Grandmother Slyboots

Dramatized by Charlotte Chorpenning; Children's Theatre
Press. *Cast:* one little girl, two women, two men, two wolves;
three sets (one interior, two exterior). In this delightfully
unusual version, a young Wolf thinks he is smarter than man,
but since he cannot control his wolf nature, Grandmother outwits him and saves Red Ridinghood.

Mary Poppins

Dramatized by Sara Spencer; Manuscript—Children's Theatre

Press. *Cast:* four men, three women, two children, one bear, one lion, one penguin; *four sets.* A modern day fanciful comedy from the book by P. L. Travers. Mary Poppins, a nursemaid, assumes a matter-of-fact attitude while performing the most wonderful magic. (Not available at present writing.)

Mr. Popper's Penguins
Dramatized by Rosemary Musil; Manuscript—293 W. Fremont St., Elmhurst, Illinois. *Cast:* two women, four men, two children, twelve penguins; *two sets.* An amusing modern comedy based on the book by Richard and Florence Atwater. The Popper family falls heir to two penguins and ends up with a whole troop of them. The problem of feeding and training them for a vaudeville act provides unusual and humorous situations.

The Plain Princess
By Aurand Harris and Phyllis McGinley; Children's Theatre Press. *Cast:* five girls, one boy, two women, three men, courtiers; *two sets* (interior). A present-day fairy tale in which a bit of magic and good, hard sense change a plain princess into one whose "mouth turns up, nose turns down and eyes sparkle like candles on a birthday cake."

Peter Pan
By James M. Barrie; Samuel French. *Cast:* two women, nine children, pirates, mermaids (if this scene is not omitted, as it often is because of the length of the play); *four sets* (one interior, three interior). A play in which fantasy and reality combine to reveal, in unforgetable language and situations, what childhood means to children.

Rama and the Tigers
Dramatized by Charlotte Chorpenning; Coach House Press. *Cast:* one woman, one man, one boy, five monkeys, four tigers; *two sets* (exterior). Originally entitled "Little Black Sambo," Mrs. Chorpenning's revision of her play with Hindu names, costumes, and makeup maintains the beauty and charm of the Hindu story by Helen Bannerman.

Rumpelstiltskin
Dramatized by Charlotte Chorpenning; Children's Theatre Press. *Cast:* five women, five men, one dwarf, courtiers; *two sets* (one interior, one exterior). The underlying philosophy, greed can never master this world, gives great depth to the characters and plot of this favorite fairy tale.

The Sandalwood Box
Dramatized by Geraldine Brain Siks; Children's Theatre Press. *Cast:* three women, nine men, three children; *three sets* (exterior). A play of Oriental mystery, based on the "Legend of the Moor's Legacy," from *The Alhambra* by Washington Irving. Peregil, a water carrier, receives a sandalwood box from a dying Moor and discovers that it tells of a treasure available only to him who lives by the Rule of Brotherhood.

The Snow Queen and the Goblin
Dramatized by Martha Bennett King; Coach House Press. *Cast:* two women, three men, one boy, one girl, extras; *two sets* (one interior, one exterior). Based on Andersen's story in which the Snow Queen sends the Goblin to steal two earth children in an attempt to find happiness. The settings offer excellent opportunities for beautiful staging.

Snow White and the Seven Dwarfs
Dramatized by Jessie Braham White; Samuel French. *Cast:* indefinite number of characters; *four sets* (three interior, one exterior). The skillful delineation of characters, the imaginative dialogue, and the choice bits of humor make this an excellent dramatization of one of the best fairy tales.

Toad of Toad Hall
Dramatized by A. A. Milne; Samuel French. *Cast:* three women, two girls, seventeen boys, animal characters; *nine sets* (three interior, six exterior). Milne has maintained the charm and fine human qualities of the animals found in the great classic, *The Wind in the Willows*, by Kenneth Grahame.

Treasure Island
Dramatized by Dorothy Drew; Children's Theatre Press.

Cast: one woman, thirteen men, one boy; *three sets* (one interior, two exterior). A skillful adaptation from Stevenson's great adventure story. The Admiral Benbow Inn, the ship, and the stockade on Treasure Island provide the settings for most of the thrilling episodes.

Young Ben

By Faye Parker; Coach House Press. *Cast:* two women, four men, one boy, one girl, extras; *one set* (interior-exterior). An exciting play of young Ben Franklin's fight for freedom. A dual setting of his brother's printing shop and the wharf provides a flexible setting in which Ben outwits the British by printing the words that arouse the colonists to action.

Notes

Chapter 1

1. *Population Estimates: Current Population Report* (United States Bureau of the Census, Series P-25, No. 194, Dept. of Commerce, (Washington, D. C., 1959). Population estimate of children from 5 to 17 years of age in Continental United States is 40,164,000.

2. International Report on Theatre for Youth in Twenty-Seven Countries, (Washington, D. C.: UNESCO, International Theatre Institute, 1955). Unpublished. See also Geraldine B. Siks, "Theatre for Youth: An International Report," *Educational Theatre Journal,* VII (December, 1955), 306-14.

3. Lyof N. Tolstoi, *What Is Art?* (New York: Thomas Y. Crowell and Co., 1899), p. 57.

4. *Ibid.,* p. 183.

5. Leon Chancerel, delegate from France, spoke at the First International Conference on Theatre and Youth, International Theatre Institute, UNESCO House, Paris, France, April, 1952.

6. Sir Herbert Read, "Art and Life: Adventures of the Mind 36," *The Saturday Evening Post,* CCXXXII (September 26, 1959), 35, 103-6.

7. Maxwell Anderson, "The Basis of Artistic Creation in Literature," in *The Bases of Artistic Creation,* essays by Maxwell Anderson *et al.* (New Brunswick: N. J., Rutgers University Press, 1942), p. 18.

8. Mr. Eisenhower named a Commission on National Goals in February, 1960, to report to him a consensus of aims for the United States during the next decade. Commission members included Erwin D. Canham, editor of the *Christian Science Monitor* and president of the U. S. Chamber of Commerce; Colgate W. Darden, Jr., former governor of Virginia; Commission Vice Chairman Frank Pace, Jr., chairman of General Dynamics Corp.; Dr. Henry M. Wriston, Commission chairman, president emeritus of Brown University; General Alfred M. Gruenther, president of the American Red Cross; William P. Bundy, executive secretary of the Commission; Dr. James R. Killian, Jr., chairman of the Massachusetts Institute of Technology; Crawford H. Greenewalt, president of E. I. du Pont de Nemours and Co.; Dr. James B. Conant, former president of Harvard University; Dr. Clark Kerr, president of the University of California; and A. F. L.-C. I. O. President George Meany.

9. William Miller, "Provocative Goals For a Hard Decade," *Life*, Vol. 49, No. 24 (December 12, 1960) 108-16.

10. *Ibid.*, p. 113.

Chapter 2

1. Burton Stevenson (ed.), *The Home Book of Quotations* (8th ed.; New York: Dodd Mead and Co., 1956), p. 28.

2. This concept and the two following questions were proposed by the director of the Children's Theatre Conference for the work of a committee on definitions, ninth annual meeting, Adelphi College, Garden City, New York, 1953. The committee consisted of the following members: Isabel Burger; Kenneth L. Graham; Mouzon Law; Dorothy Schwartz; Sara Spencer; Winifred Ward; and Ann Viola, Chairman.

3. Jay Judkins (ed.), *National Associations of the United States* (Washington, D.C.: U.S. Dept. of Commerce, 1949), p. 538.

4. *Encyclopedia of American Associations* (2nd ed.; Detroit, Michigan: Gale Research Co., 1959), p. 249.

5. Judkins, *National Associations of the United States*, p. 431.

6. *Ibid.*, p. 540.

7. *Encyclopedia of American Associations*, p. 282.

8. *American Educational Theatre Association Brochure* (Columbia, Missouri: Artcraft Press, n.d.), p. 2.

9. Judkins, *National Associations of the United States*, p. 545.

10. Yearbook of International Organizations (7th ed.; Brussels, Belgium: Union of International Associations, 1958), p. 58.

11. Judkins, *National Associations of the United States*, p. 551.

12. *Ibid.*, p. 551.

Chapter 3

1. Campton Bell, Children's Theatre Growing Up (AETA meeting, December 30, 1958), official files.

2. Mouzon Law, "A Directory of American Colleges and Universities Offering Curricular Programs in Children's Theatre," *Educational Theatre Journal*, VI, (March, 1954), 40-46.

3. George L. Lewis, "Children's Theatre and Creative Dramatics: A Bibliography," *Educational Theatre Journal*, VII (May, 1955), 139-46.

4. Campton Bell, University of Denver, was editor and publisher of *Newsletter* from 1951 to 1954.

5. Information in minutes of CTC Governing Board meetings: August 25 to August 29, 1958.

Chapter 4

1. Information in Junior Programs, Inc., files; possessed by Dorothy McFadden; shown to the author, September 10, 1956.

2. Mimeographed Report, College Curriculum Survey Committee, CTC, 1953; cf. also Appendix A.

Chapter 5

1. Geraldine Brain Siks, *Marco Polo* (Anchorage, Ky.: The Children's Theatre Press, 1941).

2. Charlotte B. Chorpenning, *Twenty-One Years with Children's Theatre* (Anchorage, Ky.: The Children's Theatre Press, 1954).

3. Alice Minnie Herts, *The Children's Educational Theatre* (New York: Harper and Brothers, 1911), p. 1.

4. Jane Addams, *The Spirit of Youth and the City Streets* (New York: The Macmillan Co., 1909), p. 75.

5. G. Stanley Hall in Foreword to *The Dramatic Instinct in Education* by Elnora Whitman Curtis (New York: Houghton Mifflin Co., 1914), p. xi.

6. Lauretta Bender and Reginald S. Laurie, "The Effect of Comic Books on the Ideology of Children," *The American Journal of Orthopsychiatry,* XI (July, 1941), 540.

7. *A Handbook for Children's Theatres* (New York: The Association of the Junior Leagues of America, Inc., 1942), p. 5.

8. *Ibid.*

9. Louis P. Thorpe, *Child Psychology and Development* (New York: The Ronald Press, 1946), p. 553.

10. *Ibid.*

11. Winifred Ward, *Theatre for Children* (3rd ed. rev.; Anchorage, Ky.: 1958), pp. 76-77.

12. Hallie Flanagan, *Arena* (New York: Duell, Sloan and Pearce, 1940), p. 299.

Chapter 6

1. Geraldine B. Siks, "Theatre for Youth: An International Report," *Educational Theatre Journal,* VII (December, 1955), 306-14.

2. Freida Reed, "Why I Like Working in Children's Plays," *Players Magazine,* XXIX (February, 1953), 20-21.

3. See Appendix A.

4. Information in an unpublished paper by Edwin R. Schoell for Western Speech Association, Salt Lake City, Utah, Nov. 28, 1958.

5. Caroline E. Fisher and Hazel G. Robertson, *Children and the Theatre* (rev. ed.; Stanford, Calif.: Stanford University Press, 1950), p. 52.

6. Frank M. Whiting, *An Introduction to the Theatre* (New York: Harper and Brothers, 1954), p. 228.

7. Recommended in Seattle Junior Programs, Inc. (eds.), *Children's Theatre Manual* (Anchorage, Ky.: The Children's Theatre Press, 1951), pp. 10-12.

8. Nancy Stamey, "A Theatre is Born," *Players Magazine,* XXXII (October, 1955), 17.

9. Winifred Ward, *Theatre for Children* (3rd ed. rev.; Anchorage, Ky.: The Children's Theatre Press, 1958), p. 56. cf. also

Ward's statement of common practices in organization, pp. 53-54.

10. Jean Ogden, "A Theatre for Children," *Recreation,* XXXVII (February, 1944), 623.

11. Fisher and Robertson, *Children and the Theatre,* cite an increase between 1942 and 1945 from 292,000 to nearly 369,000.

12. The current season is furnished by Children's Theatre of the West; Lasseli Marionettes; Tree House Children's Theatre; Denver Junior League, University of Denver; West Denver High; Denver Civic Theatre.

13. Yakima, Washington, Jr. Programs, Inc., charges (for three plays) $1.25 or fifty cents per play. Lynchburg, Virginia, charges only ten cents with a free ticket for every child certified as unable to pay. Adults pay fifty cents.

14. Lynchburg, Virginia, Children's Theatre.

15. Fisher and Robertson, *Children and the Theatre,* p. 146.

16. The school system in Salt Lake City makes it possible for plays by the University of Utah to be presented at several high schools, after their university showings.

17. L. R. Kremer, "Trends in High School Children's Theatre," *Dramatics,* XXIX (May, 1958), 22-23.

18. *Ibid.*

19. Tufts University, Medford, Mass., produces in arena style.

20. For a representative program see Robert Kase, "Delaware Children's Theatre on Tour," *Players Magazine,* XXVI (April, 1950), 163.

21. Joseph Golden, "Off We Go!" *Players Magazine,* XXXVI (May, 1956), 178-79. An account that describes Elmira College's having maintained, simultaneously, on state tours, three companies with three plays.

22. W. N. Viola, "Clare Tree Major," *Dramatics,* XXIII (December, 1951), 16; see also Ward, *Theatre for Children,* p. 25.

23. Cf. *New York Times,* April 4, 1956, Magazine Section, for article on Rockefeller Productions.

24. Fisher and Robertson, *Children and the Theatre,* p. 51.

25. Figures by Edwin Schoell, unpublished paper for Western Speech Association, Salt Lake City, Nov. 28, 1958.

26. Information in a letter to the author from Sara Spencer, Editor, The Children's Theatre Press, August 13, 1958.

27. Information in a letter to the author from William Talbot of Samuel French, Inc., May 12, 1958.

28. *Children's Theatre Manual,* Seattle Junior Programs, Inc., p. 39.

29. Edwin Schoell, p. 9.

30. Sara Spencer, "Children's Theatre, Past and Present," *Educational Theatre Journal,* VII (March, 1955), 46.

Chapter 7

1. Monograph drawn from interviews with delegates at annual educational, theatre, and speech meetings; correspondence with educational theatre workers; review of files, *Educational Theatre Journal,* and *The Speech Teacher.*

2. Winifred Ward, *Theatre for Children* (3rd ed. rev. ; Anchorage, Ky. : The Children's Theatre Press, 1958), p. 1.

3. Ann Viola, "Drama with and for Children: An Interpretation of Terms," *Educational Theatre Journal,* VIII (May, 1956), 139-42.

4. Cf. lists of certification requirements from state departments of education.

5. Ann Viola, "Drama with and for Children. "

6. Caroline E. Fisher and Hazel G. Robertson, *Children and the Theatre* (rev. ed. ; Stanford, Calif. : Stanford University Press, 1950), Ch. 4.

Chapter 8

1. Dorothy Gordon, *All Children Listen* (New York City: George W. Stewart, Publisher, Inc. , 1942), pp. 51-57.

2. *Ibid.,* pp. 62-67.

3. National Association of Broadcasters, *The NAB Code for Radio* (Washington, D. C. : National Association of Broadcasters, 1939).

4. Howard Rowland, I. Keith Tyler, and Norman Woelfel, *Criteria for Children's Radio Programs* (Washington, D. C. : Federal Radio Education Committee, 1942).

5. Herta Herzog, *Survey of Research on Children's Radio Listening* (New York: Office of Radio Research, Columbia University, 1941).

6. Dorothy Lewis, *Broadcasting to the Youth of America* (Washington, D. C. : National Association of Broadcasters, 1940).

7. "Children's Programs: Work Study Group," *Education on the Air, 1943 Yearbook of the Institute for Education by Radio,* ed. Josephine H. MacLatchy (Columbus, Ohio: Ohio State University, 1943), pp. 231-42.

8. *Ibid.*

9. Association of Junior Leagues of America, Inc. , Waldorf Astoria, New York 22, N. Y.

10. Patricia Green Swenson, Manager, KBPS, Educational Station, Portland, Ore. , where recordings of this series are still in use.

11. Salt Lake City Junior League, Inc. , Salt Lake City, Utah.

12. Dorothy Lewis, *Broadcasting to the Youth of America.*

13. Gloria Chandler Recordings, Inc. , 320 Aurora, Seattle 9, Wash. (Four series of thirteen recordings each available.)

14. Broadcasting and Film Commission, National Council, Churches of Christ in the U. S. A. , 220 Fifth Ave. , New York 1, N. Y.

15. National Association of Broadcasters, *The NAB Television Code*, (Washington, D. C.: National Association of Broadcasters, 1959).

16. *Television for Children* (Boston: Boston University, Foundation for Character Education, 1955).

17. Broadcasting and Film Commission, National Council, Churches of Christ in the U. S. A.

18. "The Giant That Is Television," *TV Guide*, VII (February 14, 1959), 23.

19. "Preface to Books—How Television Encourages Children to Read," *TV Guide*, VII (March 7, 1959), 24-26.

20. Josette Frank, *Your Children's Reading Today* (New York: Doubleday, Doran and Co., 1954), pp. 257-96. With a section on "The Noisy Arts: Pictures and Voices."

Chapter 9

1. Information in a letter to the authors from Joseph Reddy, February 9, 1959.

2. Henri Storck, *The Entertainment Film for Juvenile Audiences* (Paris, France: UNESCO Publications, 1930), p. 154.

Chapter 10

1. Paul McPharlin, *The Puppet Theatre in America, A History 1524 to Now* (New York: Harper and Brothers, 1949), p. 320.

2. *Ibid.*, pp. 327-28.

3. *Ibid.*, pp. 334-39.

4. Sarg discovered the secrets of puppetry by lying on the floor in the dark in London theatres and peering up into the puppet bridge to watch the manipulators.

5. McPharlin, *The Puppet Theatre in America*, pp. 342-43.

6. *Ibid.*, p. 332. The term *puppeteer* was coined by Ellen Von Volkenburg. Not knowing how to refer to the puppet manipulators she "thought if you could say 'muleteer' you could say 'puppeteer'."

7. *Ibid.*, p. 340.

8. Winifred Mills and Louise Dunn, *Marionettes, Masks and Shadows* (Garden City, N. Y.: Doubleday, Doran and Co., 1927).

9. Helen Haiman Joseph, *A Book of Marionettes* (New York: B. W. Huebsch and Co., 1927.)

10. Information in a June 15, 1959, letter to the author from Madeline Leonardo, Children's Theatre Assistant, The American Association of Junior Leagues, Inc.

11. Budd L. Gambee, Puppet Film List (Master's thesis, Ball State University, 1957).

12. *Ibid.*

13. Marjorie Batchelder, *The Puppet Theatre Handbook* (New York: Harper and Brothers, 1947). This book contains the most concise material available on writing and producing the puppet play.

Chapter 11

1. This section is based on information received from: Hazel Aamodt, MacPhail School of Music, Minneapolis, Minn. ; Mary R. Braithwaite, Otto Junior High School, Lansing, Mich. ; Ann Flagg, Karamu House, Cleveland, Ohio; Gilbert Hartwig, Mississippi Southern College, Hattiesburg, Miss. ; L. R. Kramer, Sioux Falls (South Dakota) High School; Nora MacAlvay, Dunes Arts Foundation, Michigan City, Ind. ; Gil Oden, Detroit Institute of Arts, Detroit, Mich. ; Faye Parker, Pittsburgh Children's Theatre, Pittsburgh, Pa. ; Frances Schram, Briggs Management, New York; Sally Six, University of Kansas, Lawrence, Kan. ; Ann Viola, Community Children's Theatre, Kansas City, Mo. ; Mary Jane Watkins, Michigan State University, East Lansing, Mich. ; Muriel M. Wilkinson, Wyandotte (Michigan) Public Schools.

2. *A Handbook for Children's Theatre* (New York: The Association of Junior Leagues of America, Inc. , 1942), p. 28.

3. Winifred Ward, *Theatre for Children* (3rd ed. rev. ; Anchorage, Ky. : The Children's Theatre Press, 1958), p. 94; see also *A Handbook for Children's Theatre*, pp. 22-26.

4. *Tenth Anniversary Brochure* (Kansas City, Mo. ; Community Children's Theatre, 1957); see also Echo Ellick and Emmy Gifford, "Omaha Junior Theatre Builds Toward a High Point," *Brochure*, 1957, p. 3.

5. Louise C. Horton (ed.), *Handbook for Children's Theatre Directors* (Cincinnati, Ohio: National Thespian Society, 1949), p. 7.

6. This section has been drawn from: Jed H. Davis, The Art of Scenic Design and Staging for Children's Theatre (Ph. D. dissertation, University of Minnesota, 1958).

7. "Operating Code of the Children's Theatre Conference, " *Educational Theatre Journal*, IX (December, 1958), 351.

8. Some of the terminology employed for these functions is from Mordecai Gorelik, "The Scenic Imagination, " *Theatre Arts*, XL, No. 4 (April, 1956), 77; also from Robert Edmond Jones, *The Dramatic Imagination* (New York: Duell, Sloan and Pearce, 1941), p. 26.

9. Bonnie E. Mellinger, *Children's Interests in Pictures* "Contributions to Education, " No. 516 (New York: Bureau of Publications, Teachers' College, Columbia University, 1932), p. 30; see also Betty Lark-Horovitz, "On Art Appreciation of Children, " Journal of Educational Research, XXXI (October, 1937), 128-29.

10. This section is based on an unpublished paper by James Crider, Assistant Professor of Drama, University of Washington.

11. This section is by Mary Jane Larson Watkins, Instructor in Speech, Michigan State University.

12. Kenneth L. Graham, An Introductory Study of Evaluation of Plays for Children's Theatre in the United States (Ph. D. dissertation, University of Utah, 1947), pp. 199-201.

13. H. D. Albright, *Working Up A Part* (Boston: Houghton Mifflin Co., 1947), p. 124.

14. Barnard Hewitt, *The Art and Craft of Play Production* (Chicago: J. B. Lippincott Co., 1940), p. 220.

15. *Ibid.*, pp. 228-29.

16. Charles McGaw, *Acting Is Believing* (New York: Reinhart and Co., 1955), pp. 89-90.

Chapter 12

1. Winifred Ward, *Theatre for Children* (3rd ed. rev.; Anchorage, Ky.: The Children's Theatre Press, 1958), p. 76.

2. "Report of the First International Conference on Theatre and Youth," United States National Commission for UNESCO, 1952. Unpublished.

3. Charlotte Barrows Chorpenning (b. 1875, d. 1955) was for twenty-one years director of children's productions, Goodman Memorial Theatre, Chicago, Illinois.

4. Information in a letter to the author from Charlotte Barrows Chorpenning, February 2, 1953.

5. Information in an October 2, 1956, letter to the author from Edward Borgers, author of *The Strange Case of Mother Goose*.

6. Information in a November 10, 1953, letter to the author from Donald Weissman, University of Texas.

7. Maxwell Anderson, "The Basis of Artistic Creation in Literature," in *The Bases of Artistic Creation,* essays by Maxwell Anderson *et al.* (New Brunswick, New Jersey: Rutgers University Press, 1942), p. 18.

8. Information in an address by Burdette Fitzgerald, "Anything is Good Enough for Children," CTC annual meeting, East Lansing, Mich., August, 1954.

9. The Children's Theatre Press, Anchorage, Ky.; The Coach House Press, Chicago, Ill.; Samuel French, New York.

10. Birmingham Jr. Programs, Birmingham, Ala.; Denver Jr. Entertainment, Denver, Colo.; Seattle Jr. Programs, Seattle, Wash.; The YMHA Children's Theatre, New York; The Jewish Theatre for Children, New York.

11. Motto of the now-defunct Junior Programs, Inc., New York.

12. Information in an address by Virginia Lee Comer at CTC annual meeting, Bloomington, Ind., August, 1947.

Chapter 13

1. Constantin Stanislavski, *An Actor Prepares* (New York: Theatre Arts Books, 1952), pp. 174-75.

2. University of Minnesota, Minneapolis, Minn.

3. For excellent discussions on the importance of inner motivation see: Stanislavski, *An Actor Prepares*, Chaps. III, IV.

Chapter 14

1. Andrew P. Hollis, *The Contribution of the Oswego Normal School to Educational Progress in the United States* (Boston: D. C. Heath and Co., 1898).

2. John Merrill, "The Value, Place, and Use of the Dramatic Instinct in the Education of Young People," in *Francis W. Parker School Studies in Education*, I (1912).

3. John Dewey, "Educational Principles," *The Elementary School* (June, 1900) p. 143.

4. Evelyn Dewey, *New Schools for Old* (New York: E. P. Dutton and Co., 1919), p. 300.

5. So solid was the growth of the auditorium phase in the Gary system that by 1954 sixty-six teachers (all holding degrees in speech and drama) were employed to guide children in creative speech and dramatic activities.

6. In all the research undertaken in this area, no use of the term "creative dramatics" connoting this method of teaching dramatics was encountered prior to this time. Although Miss Ward disclaims credit for inventing the term, it can be reasonably assumed that she originated it.

7. Winifred Ward, *Stories to Dramatize* (Anchorage, Ky.: The Children's Theatre Press, 1952).

8. Mouzon Law, "A Directory of American Colleges and Universities Offering Curricular Programs in Children's Theatre," *Educational Theatre Journal*, VI (March, 1954), 40-46.

Chapter 15

1. Geraldine B. Siks, *Creative Dramatics: An Art for Children* (New York: Harper and Brothers, 1958), p. 57.

2. Ruth Sawyer, *The Way of the Storyteller* (New York: The Viking Press, 1945), p. 117.

3. Winifred Ward, *Playmaking with Children* (2nd ed.; New York: Appleton-Century-Crofts, 1957), p. 7.

4. *Ibid.*, p. 6.

5. Siks, *Creative Dramatics*, p. 23.

6. Isabel B. Burger, *Creative Play Acting* (New York: The Ronald Press, 1950), p. 4.

7. As a result of a seven-year study, Viktor Lowenfeld and his associates in the Art Education Dept., Pennsylvania State University, have determined eight criteria of creativity which significantly differentiate creative from less or noncreative persons. The eight criteria are: *sensitivity to problems, fluency of ideas, flexibility, originality, redefinition and the ability to rearrange, analysis or the ability to abstract, synthesis and closure, coherence of organization.* At the same time, J. P. Guilford and his staff at the University of Southern California were making a study for the same pur-

pose, except that they were primarily concerned with creativity as it applies to science. It is significant that, although this study was completely independent from Dr. Lowenfeld's the findings were almost exactly the same. The first four criteria were recorded in the same terms.

8. Siks, *Creative Dramatics,* p. 37.

9. *Ibid.,* p. 24.

10. Ward, *Playmaking with Children,* p. 3.

11. *Ibid.,* p. 4.

12. Viktor Lowenfeld, *Creative and Mental Growth* (3rd ed. rev. ; New York: The Macmillan Co. , 1952), p. 2.

13. Peter Slade, *Child Drama* (London, University of London Press, Ltd. , 1954), p. 106.

14. Siks, *Creative Dramatics,* p. 27.

15. Hughes Mearns, *Creative Power* (2nd ed. rev.; New York: Dover Publications, Inc. , 1958), p. 92.

16. Siks, *Creative Dramatics,* p. 37.

Chapter 16

1. Rita Criste, Assistant Professor of Speech, Northwestern University, and Supervisor of Dramatics, Evanston Public Schools, District 65.

2. Carleton Washburne, *A Living Philosophy of Education* (New York: The John Day Co. , 1940), p. 175-90.

3. Marcella Bellmar, Barbereux School, Evanston, Ill.

4. Lawrence K. Frank, *Understanding Children's Play* (New York: Columbia University Press, 1952), p. viii.

5. Evanston, Illinois.

6. Barbara Geismer and Antoinette Suter (eds.), *Very Young Verses* (Boston: Houghton Mifflin Co. , 1945).

7. Geraldine B. Siks, *Creative Dramatics: An Art for Children* (New York: Harper and Brothers, 1958), p. 75.

8. Esther Livingston, Hale Cook School.

9. Jean Mills, Foster Schools, Evanston, Illinois.

10. Nancy Cantrell Fritz, Campus School, University of Wisconsin, Milwaukee, Wisconsin.

11. Winifred Ward, *Stories to Dramatize* (Anchorage, Kentucky, 1952), p. 86.

12. Virginia Wilhoit.

13. Jean Collins.

14. Esther Livingston.

15. Livingston.

16. Florence Gorman.

17. Reba Mirsky, *The Seven Grandmothers* (Chicago: Wilcox and Follett Publishing Co. , 1955).

Chapter 17

1. *The Education of Exceptional Children* (Forty-Ninth Yearbook, Part II, Chicago: National Society for the Study of Education, 1950), p. 3.

2. *Ibid.*, p. 6.

3. M. E. Frampton and Eleva D. Gall, *Special Education for the Exceptional Child* (Boston: Porter Sargent, 1955), I, xxvi.

4. Harry J. Baker, *Introduction to Exceptional Children* (New York: The Macmillan Co., 1953), p. 11.

5. Directory for Exceptional Children, *Educational and Training Facilities* (3rd ed. ; Boston: Porter Sargent, 1958).

6. *College and University Programs for the Preparation of Teachers of Exceptional Children* (U. S. Dept. of Health, Education, and Welfare. Bulletin No. 13, Washington, D. C. , 1954).

7. See Appendix A.

Chapter 18

1. Marvin P. Halverson is Executive Director of the Department of Worship and Arts, National Council of Churches of Christ in America.

2. Information obtained by the author in an interview with Mr. Halverson, November 10, 1958.

3. Robert E. Seaver is Director of Religious Drama, Union Theological Seminary, New York.

4. Information quoted in a panel discussion, CTC regional meeting, Columbia Teachers' College, New York, May 4, 1957.

5. Information in a November 19, 1958, letter to the author from Rev. Francis W. Voelcker, Director of Evaluation, National Council of the Protestant Episcopal Church.

6. Hulda Niebuhr, *Ventures in Dramatics* (New York: Charles Scribner's Sons, 1935). *Passim.*

7. Nancy Cole is wife of Dr. George D. Cole, Minister of Education, Congregational Church, New Canaan, Connecticut.

8. Polly Bond, "Puppets in the Pulpit," *The Living Church*, (June, 1958), MXXXVI, 12.

9. Moana B. Bennett, Drama Director for MIA, supplied these figures.

10. Samuel J. Citron, "Socio-Drama in Teaching Bible or Humash," *Jewish Education Committee Bulletin* (New York: March, 1954). Reprint.

11. Mrs. George Anderson (Methodist) has since 1953 been teaching creative dramatics in religious drama summer workshops for National Council of Churches of Christ; since 1954 she has been offering workshops at various Protestant churches located in Joliet, Ill. ; Des Moines, Iowa; Dayton, Ohio; Lake Junalaska, N. C.

12. Mrs. William E. Brobston (Episcopalian), has been teaching in creative dramatics workshops in Birmingham, Ala., since January, 1958; in July, 1958, she taught a workshop in creative dramatics for the Presbyterian Church at Montreat, N. C.

13. William H. Cleveland, Jr. (Quaker) has conducted creative dramatics workshops for religious education groups in the Philadelphia area.

14. Miss Ella B. Magee (Methodist), former Dean of the Council of Churches Leadership School, Seattle, Wash., began in 1956 to organize interdenominational teacher-training facilities, with trained creative dramatics teachers coming from the drama department of the University of Washington.

15. Agnes Haaga, "A Directory of American Colleges and Universities Offering Training in Children's Theatre and Creative Dramatics," *Educational Theatre Journal*, X (May, 1958), 150-63.

16. Information in a November 2, 1958, letter from Harold Ehrensperger to the author.

17. Winifred Ward, *Creative Dramatics* (New York: Appleton-Century-Crofts, Inc., 1930).

18. Isabel B. Burger, *Creative Play Acting* (New York: The Ronald Press, 1950).

19. See Bibliography.

20. *Children's Religion* (XVIII: Boston: The Pilgrim Press, September, 1957).

21. Information in a questionnaire to the author from William H. Cleveland, Jr., The George School, Pa., October 10, 1958.

22. Plato, *The Republic*.

Chapter 19

1. This figure was arrived at as a reasonable compromise. A "trend projection" of figures from our questionnaire resulted in a higher figure. Robert L. Rowland, *Statistics on Public Institutions for Delinquent Children: 1956* (U. S. Children's Bureau Statistical Series, No. 48, Washington, D. C.: U. S. Dept. of Health, Education, and Welfare, 1954), lists the following figures: Approximately 33,000 children were living in public training schools for delinquent children on the last day of 1956. This was 18 per cent more than in 1953. About 72,000 children had been served by public training schools during the year, i. e., that many children had been in training schools at some time or other during the year. The average (median) age of the children was close to sixteen years. Seventy-five per cent were boys; sixty-seven per cent were white. Fifteen per cent of the children admitted to the training schools during 1956 had been there before at some time or other and were returned because of aftercare (parole) violation or commitment of a new offense. On the average, children

released from institutions have been there for 9. 5 months; boys, 8. 6 months; girls, 12. 2 months. One half of the institutions had capacities of over 150 children (the maximum size generally recommended); 4 out of 10, over 200. About three out of ten institutions were housing more children than their rated capacity. There were almost twice as many institutions in 1956 as in 1953 with an occupancy rate of over 100 per cent.

2. J. Paget-Fredericks, "Imaginings," quoted by Winifred Ward, *Playmaking with Children* (2nd ed. ; New York: Appleton-Century-Crofts, Inc. , 1957), p. 46.

3. Arnold Gesell is author and child specialist, research consultant, Gesell Institute of Child Development.

Chapter 20

1. Monograph drawn from personal interviews, correspondence with community theatre leaders, and reports of annual CTC meetings.

2. Nancy Taft Smuck was Program Consultant for the Nursery Schools of Seattle Public Schools from 1943 to 1945.

3. Agnes Haaga in Foreword to Geraldine Brain Siks, *Creative Dramatics: An Art for Children* (New York: Harper and Brothers, 1958), p. xii.

4. *Ibid.*

5. Bam Whitebrook, "Half Fare," *Puget Soundings, Seattle Junior League Association,* (May, 1950). p. 9.

6. Alice Myers Winther, "Littlest Ones Play-Act What Stories Mean," *Christian Science Monitor,* June 27, 1956, p. 13.

7. *Ibid.*

8. Information in a January 27, 1958, letter to the author from Nora McAlvay.

9. Information in a November 12, 1957, letter to the author from Dorothy Miller.

10. Information in a March 20, 1958, letter to the author from Isabel Burger.

11. See Appendix A.

12. Information in a January 27, 1958, letter to the author from Martha Brush.

13. Information in a September 4, 1959, letter to the author from Grace Stanistreet.

14. Seattle Creative Activities Center (unpublished mimeographed report, Seattle, Wash. , May, 1959) p. 1).

15. Information in a September 20, 1958, letter to the author from Betty Joe Kelsey.

16. Information in an August 29, 1959, letter to the author from Helen Brown.

17. National Creative Arts Symposium; an associated meeting of

the National Conference of the Association for Supervision and Curriculum Development, Seattle, Washington, March, 1958.

18. Information in an August 17, 1959, letter to the author from Robert Isenberg, Assistant Director of Rural Service, NEA.

19. Howard Hanson, "The Arts in an Age of Science," *NEA Journal,* XLVII, (February, 1958), 73.

Chapter 21

1. Winifred Ward, *Playmaking with Children* (2nd ed. ; New York: Appleton-Century-Crofts, 1957, p. 12.

2. Geraldine Brain Siks, *Creative Dramatics: An Art for Children* (New York: Harper and Bros. , 1958), pp. 92-93.

3. Marie Dienesch, "Jeu Dramatique et Theatre-Scolaire," *World Theatre Magazine,* II (Brussels, Belgium: World Theatre Institute, 1953), 30.

4. Charlotte B. Chorpenning, *Twenty-One Years with Children's Theatre,* (Anchorage, Ky. : The Children's Theatre Press, 1954), p. 26.

5. Information in a September 6, 1958, letter to the author from Mary Fluhrer Nighswander, Director Children's Theatre, Davenport, Iowa.

6. *Child Drama Questionnaire,* CTC Survey, 1958.

7. Information in an October 4, 1956, report to the author from Constance Welsh, former Branch Director, Children's Theatre Association, Baltimore, Maryland.

8. Information in a letter to the author from Winifred Ward and Rita Criste, November 9, 1958.

9. Information in a December 2, 1958, letter to the author from Ella Heimbrodt, Director, Children's Theatre, Western Springs, Ill.

10. Information in an October 19, 1958, letter to the author from Patt Merrick, Director, Tell-a-Tale Theatre, Arlington County Public Schools, Arlington, Va.

11. John De Puglio is Managing Director, Children's Theatre Association, Baltimore, Md.

12. Information in a November 20, 1958, letter to the author from Dan Lipschutz, Associate Director, Children's Theatre, Stockholm, Sweden.

13. Information in a November 8, 1957, report to the author from Mrs. Robert Potts, President, Board of Directors, Children's Theatre Association, Baltimore, Md.

14. Information in a December 4, 1958, letter to the author from Burdette Fitzgerald of University of California.

15. Ward, *Playmaking with Children.*

16. Geraldine B. Siks, *Creative Dramatics,* p. 75.

17. Information from excerpts in personal letters to the author from teachers and directors who have completed training courses in creative dramatics.

Chapter 22

1. *Recreation and Park Yearbook,* National Recreation Association, 1956, p. 40.
2. The Performing Arts in Public and Private Recreation Programs, National Recreation Association, 1960. Unpublished.
3. Nancy Eichsteadt, "Dramatics on the Playground, " Recreation, (April, 1960), pp. 176-78.
4. *Recreation Program,* The Athletic Institute (Chicago, 1955), V, 79.

Chapter 23

1. Agnes Haaga, "A Directory of American Colleges and Universities Offering Training in Children's Theatre and Creative Dramatics," *Educational Theatre Journal,* X (May, 1958), 150-63.
2. Examples of such programs include Seattle PTA Community Program; Seattle Creative Activities Programs; Olympia Jr. Programs' Creative Dramatics Program; Yakima Jr. Programs' Creative Dramatics Program.
3. Stark Young, *The Theatre* (New York: Hill and Wang, 1954), p. 17.
4. If approached as an art, creative dramatics because of its very nature—communal and communicative—fulfills the needs of body, soul, and mind.
5. J. Paget-Fredericks, "Imaginings, " quoted by Winifred Ward, *Playmaking with Children* (2nd ed. : New York: Appleton-Century-Crofts, Inc. , 1957), p. 46.
6. Dorothy L. Sayers, *The Mind of the Maker* (Living Age Ed. ; New York: Meridian Books, 1956), p. 67. Citing Berdyaer, *The Destiny of Man.*

Appendix A

1. Agnes Haaga, "A Directory of American Colleges and Universities Offering Training in Children's Theatre and Creative Dramatics," *Educational Theatre Journal,* X (May, 1958), 150-63.
2. Mouzon Law, "A Directory of American Colleges and Universities Offering Curricular Programs in Children's Theatre, " *Educational Theatre Journal,* VI (March, 1954), 40-46.

Appendix B

1. Monograph drawn from college course outlines from Birmingham-Southern College, Birmingham, Ala. ; Michigan State University,

East Lansing, Mich.; Northwestern University, Evanston, Ill.: University of Denver, Denver, Colo.; University of Minnesota, Minneapolis, Minn.; University of Pittsburgh, Pittsburgh, Pa.; University of Texas, Austin, Texas; University of Washington, Seattle, Wash.; University of California, Los Angeles, Calif.

Appendix C
   1. Publishers of plays in this recommended list include: Association of Junior Leagues, New York; Coach House Press, 53 W. Jackson Blvd., Chicago 4; Children's Theatre Press, Anchorage, Ky.; Dramatic Publishing Company, Chicago, Ill.; Charles Scribner's Sons, New York; Henry Holt, New York; Little Brown and Company, Boston; Samuel French, New York.

Bibliography

Paul Kozelka ✒

This is a selective list of the best books, periodicals, bibliographies, and reports available in the field of children's drama. It includes all references cited in this study and additional selected references. The bibliography is classified into five sections to correspond with the divisions of the study: Children's Theatre, Radio and Television, Puppetry, Creative Dramatics, and bibliographies and reports.

CHILDREN'S THEATRE

Addams, Jane. *The Spirit of Youth and the City Streets*. New York: The Macmillan Company, 1909.

Adix, Vern. *Theatre Scenecraft*. Anchorage, Kentucky: The Children's Theatre Press, 1956.

Albright, H.D. *Working Up a Part*. Boston: Houghton Mifflin Company, 1947.

Albright, H.D., William P. Halstead, and Lee Mitchell. *Principles of Theatre Art*. New York: Houghton Mifflin Company, 1955.

Allen, John. Going to the Theatre. London: Phoenix House Ltd., 1949.

Anderson, John. "Psychological Aspects of Child Audiences," *Educational Theatre Journal*, II (December, 1950), 285-92.

Anderson, Maxwell. "The Basis of Artistic Creation in Literature" *(The Bases of Artistic Creation,* essays by Maxwell Anderson *et al.).* New Brunswick, New Jersey: Rutgers University Press, 1942.

Arnheim, Rudolf. *Art and Visual Perception*. Berkeley: University of California Press, 1954.

Association of Junior Leagues of America, Inc. (ed.). *A Handbook for Children's Theatre*. New York, 1942.

Bannister, Robert Lyle. Maurice Maeterlinck's The Blue Bird, A Project in Lyric Theatre. Master's thesis, University of Denver, 1947.

Barton, Lucy. *Historic Costume for the Stage*. Boston: Walter Baker and Company, 1935.

Bement, Merlin. The Designs for Two Children's Theatre Touring Plays. Master's thesis, Michigan State University, 1956.

Bender, Lauretta, and Reginald S. Laurie. "The Effect of Comic

Books on the Ideology of Children," *The American Journal of Orthopsychiatry,* XI (July, 1941), 540.

Best, Mrs. A. Starr. "The Drama League at 21," Drama, XXI (May, 1931).

Braithwaite, Mary. A Study of American Local Legends for Children's Theatre. Master's thesis, Michigan State University, 1956.

Burris-Meyer, Harold, and Edward C. Cole. *Scenery for the Theatre.* Boston: Little, Brown and Company, 1951.

Butterworth, Bette. "Theatre in the Round We Go," *Recreation,* XLVII (June, 1954), 342-43.

Chandler, M. Corrine. Organization and Conduct of Drama for Children. Master's thesis, University of Oklahoma, 1932.

Children's Theatre . . . That Captures Its Audience. Chicago: The Coach House Press, 1958.

Chorpenning, Charlotte. "Adults in Plays for Children," *Educational Theatre Journal,* III (May, 1951), 115-19.

Chorpenning, Charlotte. *Twenty-One Years with Children's Theatre.* Anchorage, Kentucky: The Children's Theatre Press, 1955.

Ciaccio, Mary Eleanor. *Prologue to Production.* New York: Association of Junior Leagues of America, Inc., 1951.

Comer, Virginia. "A Children's Theatre Takes to the Road," *Recreation,* XXXIV (September, 1940).

————. "The White House Conference and Educational Theatre," *Educational Theatre Journal,* III (October, 1951), 218-23.

Cornberg, Sol, and Emanuel Gebauer. *A Stage Crew Handbook.* New York: Harper and Brothers. 1951.

Corson, Richard. *Stage Make-up.* Rev. ed. New York: F.S. Crofts, 1947.

Currie, Helen Workman. A Psychological Approach to the Production of Children's Plays. Master's thesis, University of Michigan, 1947.

Curtis, Elnora Whitman. *The Dramatic Instinct in Education.* With a Foreword by G. Stanley Hall. New York: Houghton Mifflin Company, 1914.

Davis, Jed Jr. The Art of Scenic Design and Staging for Children's Theatre. Ph.D. dissertation, University of Minnesota, 1958. Microfilmed.

Davis, Jed H., and Mary Jane Larson Watkins, *Children's Theatre,* New York: Harper and Brothers, 1960.

Devine, George. "Theatre for Children: Art That is Different," *World Theatre,* II (1952), 9-21.

Dolman, John. *The Art of Play Production.* New York: Harper and Brothers, 1946.

Fisher, Caroline, and Hazel Robertson. *Children and the Theatre.* Rev. ed. Stanford, California: Stanford University Press, 1950.

Flanagan, Hallie. *Arena.* New York: Duell, Sloan and Pearce Company, 1940.

Friederich, Willard J. and John J. Frazer. *Scenery Design for the Amateur Stage*. New York: The Macmillan Company, 1950.

Fry, Emma Sheridan. *Educational Dramatics*. New York: Moffat, Yard and Company, 1913.

Gassner, John. *Producing the Play*. New York: The Dryden Press, 1953.

Golden, Joseph. "Off We Go!" *Players Magazine*, XXXII (May, 1956), 178-79.

Gorelik, Mordecai. "The Scenic Imagination,"*Theatre Arts*, XL (April, 1956), 77.

Graham, Kenneth L. An Introductory Study of the Evaluation of Plays for Children's Theatre in the United States. Ph. D. dissertation, University of Utah, 1947.

Gustafson, Alrik. "Children's Theatre in Sweden," *Educational Theatre Journal*, III (March, 1951), 40-44.

Hake, Herbert V. *Here's How*. Evanston, Illinois: Row, Peterson and Company, 1947.

Healy, Daty. *Dress the Show*. Evanston, Illinois: Row, Peterson and Company, 1948.

Herts, Alice M. *The Children's Educational Theatre*. New York: Harper and Brothers, 1911.

Hewitt, Barnard. *The Art and Craft of Play Production*. Chicago: J. B. Lippincott Company, 1940.

Horton, Louise (ed.). *Handbook for Children's Theatre Direction*. Cincinnati: National Thespian Society, 1949.

Hughes, Glenn. *A History of the American Theatre*. New York: Samuel French Company, 1951.

Jones, Charles. An Evaluation of the Educational Significance of the Children's Theatre of Evanston. Ph. D. dissertation, Northwestern University, 1953.

Jones, Robert Edmond. *The Dramatic Imagination*. New York: Theatre Arts Books, 1956.

Jones, Wyatt. "The Junior League Story," *Town and Country*, CX (August, 1956), 52-53.

Kase, C. Robert. *Children's Theatre Comes of Age*. New York: Samuel French Company. 1956.

-----. "Delaware Children's Theatre on Tour," *Players Magazine*, XXVI (April, 1950), 163.

Kramer, E. Dorothy. Children's Theatre in Arena Style. Master's thesis, University of Denver, 1950.

Kremer, Lester R. Children's Theatre as Produced by High Schools. Master's thesis, University of South Dakota, 1956.

-----. "Trends in High School Children's Theatre," *Dramatics*, XXIX (May, 1958), 22-23.

Lark-Horovitz, Betty. "On Art Appreciation of Children," *Journal of Educational Research*, XXXI (October, 1937), 128-29.

Lewis, George L. A Stage Crew Handbook for Children's Theatre Directors. Ph.D. dissertation, University of Denver, 1954.

Lobdell, Robert. "Planning a Show Wagon," *Recreation*, XLVIII (January, 1955), 32-33.

McGaw, Charles. *Acting Is Believing*. New York: Reinhart and Company, 1955.

Mackay, Constance D'Arcy. *Children's Theatres and Plays*. New York: Appleton-Century-Crofts, 1927.

-----. *How to Produce Children's Plays*. New York: Henry Holt and Company, 1915.

-----. "The School Theatres of New York City," *Players Magazine*, XXI (May, 1945), 26.

McCaslin, Nellie. A History of Children's Theatre in the United States. Ph.D. dissertation, New York University, 1957. Microfilmed.

McFadden, Dorothy. "Europe Challenges American Parents," *National Parent-Teacher Magazine*, XXI (June, 1937), 10-11.

Meek, Beryl. The Establishment of a Children's Theatre in a Teacher Training Institute. Ph.D. dissertation, New York University, 1942.

Meier, Norman Charles. "Studies in the Psychology of Art," *Psychological Monographs* (University of Iowa Studies in Psychology), XLV (1933), iii-184.

Mellinger, Bonnie E. *Children's Interest in Pictures*. ("Contributions to Education," No. 516) New York: Columbia University, Teachers' College, Bureau of Publications, 1932, p. 30.

Morton, Evelyn Anice. A Study of the Art of Make-up for Children's Theatre. Master's thesis, Baylor University, 1953.

Murphy, O.P., Sister Honora. An Analysis of the Theory and Directorial Practice of Five Well-known Children's Theatre Directors. Master's thesis, Catholic University, 1953.

Nelms, Henning. *Play Production*. New York: Barnes and Noble, 1956.

Ogden, Jean. "A Theatre for Children," *Recreation*, XXXVII (February, 1944), 623.

Patenburg, Sister Rosaleen. A Critical Analysis of Four Successful Plays for Children's Theatre. Master's thesis, Catholic University, 1956.

Pethybridge, David C. *Directed Drama*. London: University of London Press Ltd., 1954.

Philippi, Herbert. *Stagecraft and Scene Design*. Boston: Houghton Mifflin Company, 1953.

Schwartz, Dorothy Thames. A History of the Children's Theatre Conference, 1944-55. Master's thesis, University of Alabama, 1956.

Seattle Junior Programs, Inc. (eds.). *Children's Theatre Manual*. Anchorage, Kentucky: The Children's Theatre Press, 1951.

Selden, Samuel, and Hunton D. Sellman. *Stage Scenery and Lighting*. 3rd ed. New York: Appleton-Century-Crofts, 1951.

Shohet, Max. "Scrapbook of WPA Children's Theatre," New York: Theatre Collection of the New York Public Library, n. d.

Siks, Geraldine. *Marco Polo*. Anchorage, Kentucky: The Children's Theatre Press, 1941.

Spencer, Sara. "Children's Theatre in England," *Educational Theatre Journal*, III (December, 1951), 329-34.

−−−−−. "Children's Theatre, Past and Present," *Educational Theatre Journal*, VII (March, 1955), 44-46.

Stamey, Nancy. "A Children's Theatre Is Born," *Players Magazine*, XXXII (October, 1955), 17.

Stanislavski, Constantin. *An Actor Prepares*. New York: Theatre Arts Books, 1952.

Strawbridge, Edwin. "Do Your Play for, Not to, the Children," *Recreation*, XLVII (October, 1954), 484-86.

Storck, Henri. *The Entertainment Film for Juvenile Audiences*. Paris: UNESCO Publications, 1930.

Stroh, Mary Jane. A Developmental Approach to the Production of Children's Plays Through the Experimental Production of *Little Red Riding Hood*. Master's thesis, Ohio State University, 1950.

Thorpe, Louis P. *Child Psychology and Development*. New York: The Ronald Press, 1946.

Viola, W. N. "Clare Tree Major," *Dramatics*, XI (December, 1939), 11.

Walton, Cecile. *The Children's Theatre Book*. London: Adam and Charles Black, Ltd. , 1949.

Ward, Winifred. *Theatre for Children*. 3rd ed. rev. Anchorage, Kentucky: The Children's Theatre Press, 1958.

Watkins, Mary Jane Larson. The Writing and Production of a Children's Play Based Upon Thackeray's *The Rose and the Ring*. Master's thesis, Michigan State University, 1955.

Wilson, Margery. "Children's Theatre in the Round," *Educational Theatre Journal*, II (May, 1950), 104-7.

Whiting, Frank. *An Introduction to the Theatre*. New York: Harper and Brothers, 1954.

Wright, Laura. The Organization and Administration of Children's Theater in the Upper Midwest. Master's thesis, Marquette University, 1947.

"Youth and the Theatre," *World Theatre*, II (1952). Entire Issue.

RADIO AND TELEVISION

Eisenberg, Azriel L. *Children and Radio Programs*. New York: Columbia University Press, 1936.

Frank, Josette. *What Books for Children*. With a section on Children's Radio Programs. New York: Doubleday Doran and Company, 1941, pp. 131-47.

—————. *Your Children's Reading Today.* With a section on "The Noisy Arts: Pictures and Voices." New York: Doubleday, Doran and Company, 1954, pp. 257-96.

"The Giant That Is Television," *TV Guide* (Philadelphia), VII:7 (February 14, 1959).

Gordon, Dorothy. *All Children Listen.* New York: George W. Stewart Publisher, Inc., 1942.

Gruenberg, Sidonie M. *Radio and Children.* New York: Radio Institute of the Audible Arts, 1935.

Herzog, Herta. *Survey of Research on Children's Radio Listening.* New York: Columbia University; Office of Radio Research, 1941.

Jersild, Arthur T. "Writing Script for Children." *(Education on the Air, Yearbooks of the Institute for Education by Radio, 1930-44.* ed. by Josephine H. MacLatchey.) Columbus, Ohio: Ohio State University, 1945.

Lewis, Dorothy. *Broadcasting to the Youth of America.* Washington, D. C.: National Association of Broadcasters, 1940.

—————. *Radio Patterns for Children's Programs.* New York: National Association of Broadcasters, 1943.

Mead, Margaret. "How Violence Affects Your Child," *TV Guide* (Philadelphia), VII:12 (March 21, 1959).

The NAB Code for Radio. Washington, D. C.: National Association of Broadcasters, 1939.

The NAB Television Code (5th ed.). Washington, D. C.: National Association of Broadcasters, 1959.

Olson, Joe (ed.). *Education on the Air.* With sections on "What Our Children See" and "What Is Television Doing to Our Children." Columbus, Ohio: Ohio State University, 1950, pp. 170-85.

Pedell, Katherine. "Are Children's Programs Through?" *TV Guide* (Philadelphia) VI:12 (January 19, 1958).

"Preface to Books—How Television Encourages Children to Read," *TV Guide* (Philadelphia), VII:10 (March 7, 1959).

Rowland, Howard, Tyler, Keith I., and Woelfel, Norman. *Criteria For Children's Radio Programs.* Washington, D. C.: Federal Radio Education Committee, 1942.

Television for Children. Boston: Boston University, Foundation for Character Education, 1955.

Tyler, I. Keith, and Nancy Marion Dashu (eds.). *Education on the Air, 1946 Yearbook.* Columbus, Ohio: Ohio State University, 1947.

Waller, Judith C. *Radio, the Fifth Estate.* With a section on "Children's Programs." New York: Houghton Mifflin Company, 1946, pp. 237-49.

PUPPETRY

Batchelder, Marjorie. *The Puppet Theatre Handbook.* New York: Harper and Brothers, 1947.

Batchelder, Marjorie, and Virginia Lee Comer. *Puppets and Plays: A Creative Approach.* New York: Harper and Brothers, 1956.

Beaton, Mabel, and Les Beaton. *Marionettes: A Hobby for Everyone.* New York: Thomas Y. Crowell, 1948.

Bond, Polly. "Puppets in the Pulpit," *The Living Church,* MXXXVI (June, 1958), 12.

Gambee, Budd L. Puppet Film List. Master's thesis, Muncie, Indiana: Ball State Teachers College, 1957.

Joseph, Helen Haiman. *A Book of Marionettes.* New York: B.W. Huebsch and Co., 1927.

McPharlin, Paul. *The Puppet Theatre in America: A History 1524 to Now.* New York: Harper and Brothers, 1949.

Mills, Winifred, and Louise Dunn. *Marionettes, Masks, and Shadows.* Garden City, New York: Doubleday, Doran and Co., 1927.

CREATIVE DRAMATICS

Andrews, Gladys. *Creative Rhythmic Movement for Children.* Englewood, New Jersey: Prentice-Hall, Inc., 1954.

Baker, Harry J. *Introduction to Exceptional Children.* New York: The Macmillan Company, 1953.

Blank, Earl William. The Effectiveness of Creative Dramatics in Developing Voice, Vocabulary, and Personality in the Primary Grades. Ph.D. dissertation, University of Denver, 1953.

Bond, Polly, "Puppets in the Pulpit," *The Living Church,* MXXXVI (June, 1958), 12.

Bowen, Frances C. "Educational Theatre," *The Johns Hopkins Magazine,* IV (January, 1953).

Brown, Helen. The Account of an Experiment Showing the Effects of a Year's Work in Creative Dramatics. Master's thesis, Northwestern University, 1936.

Burger, Isabel. *Creative Play Acting.* New York: The Ronald Press, 1950.

Chambers, Robert E. Creative Dramatics: Learning or Play? A Study of Three Informal Educational Situations. Master's thesis, Ohio State University, 1956.

Children's Religion, XVIII (Boston: The Pilgrim Press, September, 1957).

Citron, Samuel J. "Socio-Drama in Teaching Bible or Humash." New *York Jewish Education Committee Bulletin,* March, 1954.

Cole, Natalie. *The Arts in the Classroom.* New York: The John Day Company, 1942.

D'Amico, Victor E. "Theatre as a Teaching Tool," *Theatre Arts,* XXVIII (July, 1944), 406-9.

Dewey, Evelyn. *New Schools for Old.* New York: E. P. Dutton and Company, 1919.

Dewey, John. "Educational Principles," *The Elementary School* (June, 1900), p. 143.

Dienesch, Marie. "Jeu Dramatique et Theatre-Scolarie," *World Theatre Magazine*, II (1953), 30.

The Education of Exceptional Children. (Forty-Ninth Yearbook, Part II, Chicago: National Society for the Study of Education, 1950).

Eichmann, G. S. "Drama in Juvenile Delinquency Prevention," *Recreation*, XXXVII (January, 1944), 563-74.

Fitzgerald, Burdette S. *Let's Act the Story*. San Francisco: Fearon Publishers, 1957.

Frampton, M. E., and Eleva D. Gall. *Special Education for the Exceptional Child* (Boston: Porter Sargent Publisher, 1955), I.

Gaffney, John P., Jr. "Creative Dramatics for Hard-of-Hearing Children," *Volta Review*, LIV (October, 1952), 321-26.

Geismer, Barbara, and Antoinette Suter (eds.). *Very Young Verses*. Boston: Houghton Mifflin Company, 1945.

Gillies, Emily P. "Crosses and Knives," *Childhood Education*, XXII (May, 1946), 382-87.

Goodall, Grace M. "Drama in the Parks," *Recreation*, XLV (March, 1952), 545-47.

Guilford, J. P. "Can Creativity Be Developed?" *Art Education*, XI (June, 1958), 3-7.

Haaga, Agnes. "Creative Dramatics in the Recreation Program," *Recreation*, XLV, 77-80.

–––––. "Creative Dramatics: An Excellent Try-Out Method," *Dramatics*, XXVI (March, 1955), 6-7.

–––––. "I Teach Creative Dramatics," *Dramatics*, XXII (May, 1951), 6-7.

–––––. "Objectives and Standards for Children's Theatre," *Players Magazine*, XXX (December, 1952).

Haaga, Agnes, and Patricia A. Randles. *Supplementary Materials for Use in Creative Dramatics with Younger Children*. Seattle: University of Washington Press, 1952.

Hanson, Howard. "The Arts in an Age of Science," *NEA Journal*, XLVII (February, 1958), 73.

Hartley, Ruth E., Lawrence K. Frank, and Robert M. Goldenson. *Understanding Children's Play*. New York: Columbia University Press, 1952.

Hill, Wilhemina, Helen K. Mackintosh, and Arne Randall. *How Children Can be Creative*. (U.S. Dept. of Health, Education, and Welfare Bulletin, No. 12, Washington, D.C.: Government Printing Office, 1954).

Hollis, Andrew P. *The Contribution of the Oswego Normal School to Educational Progress in the United States*. Boston: D.C. Heath and Company, 1898.

Jersild, Arthur. *Child Psychology*. Englewood, New Jersey: Prentice-Hall, Inc., 1947.

Knapp, Katherine. "Guiding Creative Experiences in the Primary Grades," *Social Education*, XV (January, 1951), 24-25.

Lease, Ruth, and Geraldine Brain Siks. *Creative Dramatics in Home, School, and Community*. New York: Harper and Brothers, 1952.

Lowenfeld, Viktor. *Creative and Mental Growth*. 3rd ed. rev. New York: The Macmillan Company, 1952.

-----. "Current Research on Creativity," *NEA Journal*, XLVII (November, 1958), 538-40.

McIntyre, Barbara. The Effects of a Program of Creative Activities Upon the Articulation Skills of Adolescent and Pre-Adolescent Children with Speech Disorders. Ph. D. dissertation, University of Pittsburgh, 1957.

Mearns, Hughes. *Creative Power*. 2nd rev. ed. New York: Dover Publications Inc., 1958.

-----. *Creative Youth*. New York: Doubleday, Doran and Company, 1928.

Merrill, John. "The Value, Place, and Use of the Dramatic Instinct in the Education of Young People," *Frances W. Parker School Studies in Education*, I (1912).

Mirsky, Reba. *The Seven Grandmothers*. Chicago: Wilcox and Follett Publishing Company, 1955.

Niebuhr, Hulda. *Ventures in Dramatics*. New York: Charles Scribner's Sons, 1935.

Ogilvie, Mardel. *Speech in the Elementary School*. New York: McGraw-Hill Book Company, 1954.

Pierini, Patricia Maries. Application of Creative Dramatics to Speech Therapy. Master's thesis, Stanford University, 1956.

Plato, *The Republic*.

Popovich, James E. A Study of Significant Contributions to the Development of Creative Dramatics in American Education. Ph. D. Dissertation, Northwestern University, 1955.

Rassmussen, Carrie. *Speech Methods in the Elementary School*. New York: The Roland Press, 1949.

Rogers, Dorothy. "Teaching Children to Think Creatively," *Peabody Journal of Education*, XXIX (March, 1952), 268-73.

Sawyer, Ruth. *The Way of the Storyteller*. New York: The Viking Press, 1945.

Seeling, Martha. "Creative Experience for Young Children," *Education*, LXXV (February, 1955), 355-60.

Siks, Geraldine Brain. *Creative Dramatics: An Art for Children*. New York: Harper and Brothers, 1958.

-----. "Theatre Magic," *The Instructor*, LXVIII (June, 1959), 21.

Slade, Peter. *Creative Drama.* London: University of London Press, Ltd. , 1954.

Stanistreet, Grace M. "Pantomime is Easy," *Recreation,* XXXVIII (May, 1944).

Strickland, Ruth G. *The Language Arts in the Elementary School.* Boston: D. C. Heath and Company, 1957.

Ward, Winifred. *Creative Dramatics.* New York: Appleton-Century-Crofts, 1930.

––––––. "Creative Dramatics in the Elementary School," *Quarterly Journal of Speech,* XXVIII (December, 1942), 445-49.

––––––. "Let's Pretend," *Junior League Magazine,* LX (February, 1953).

––––––. *Playmaking with Children.* 2nd ed. New York: Appleton-Century-Crofts, 1957).

––––––. *Stories to Dramatize.* Anchorage, Kentucky: The Children's Theatre Press, 1952.

Washburne, Carleton. *A Living Philosophy of Education.* New York: The John Day Company, 1940.

Whitebrook, Bam. "Half Fare," *Puget Soundings,* Seattle Junior League Association (May, 1950), p. 9.

Willcox, Helen L. *Bible Study Through Educational Dramatics.* Nashville, Tennessee: Abingdon Press, 1924.

Winther, Alice Myers. "Littlest Ones Play-Act What Stories Mean," *Christian Science Monitor* (June, 1956), p. 13.

Woods, Margaret S. "Creative Dramatics in Your Community," *The Seattle Grade Teacher,* XXXII (March, 1951).

––––––. "Dramatic Arts Within the Reach of Every Child in the Nation," *The Washington Parent Teacher,* IX (November, 1957).

––––––. A Survey of Effective Practices in Creative Dramatics in the Classroom. Master's thesis, University of Washington, 1955.

Young, Stark. *The Theatre.* New York: Hill and Wang, 1954.

BIBLIOGRAPHIES AND REPORTS

Barnhard, Clarence L. (ed.). *The American College Dictionary.* Text ed. New York: Harper and Brothers, 1957.

Briggs, Elizabeth D. *Subject Index to Children's Plays.* Chicago: American Library Association, 1940.

Children's Theatre Conference Committee. "Children's Theatre," *Theatre Arts,* XXXIII (September, 1949), 50-60.

College and University Programs for the Preparation of Teachers of Exceptional Children. (U. S. Dept. of Health, Education, and Welfare Bulletin, No. 13, Washington, D. C.: 1954.)

Directory for Exceptional Children, Educational and Training Facilities. 3rd ed. Boston: Porter Sargent Publisher, 1958.

Encyclopedia of American Associations. 2nd ed. Detroit, Michigan: Gale Research Company, 1959.

Ervine, Jean. "Bibliography of Dramatics in the Elementary School," *The Speech Teacher,* III (December, 1954).

Garrison, Geraldine. "Bibliography of Puppetry for the Elementary School," *The Speech Teacher,* III (September, 1954).

Griffin, Alice. "Theatre USA-Children's Theatre," *Theatre Arts,* XXXVIII (May, 1954), 82-86.

———. *Ibid.,* XLI (May, 1957), 65-66.

———. *Ibid.,* XLII (May, 1958), 92-93.

Guimaud, Jead, (ed.). *International Bibliography, Theatre and Youth.* Paris: UNESCO, International Theatre Institute, n.d., II.

Haaga, Agnes. "A Directory of American Colleges and Universities Offering Training in Children's Theatre and Creative Dramatics," *Educational Theatre Journal,* X (May, 1958), 150-63.

Judkins, Jay (ed.). *National Associations of the United States.* Washington, D.C.: U.S. Dept. of Commerce, 1949.

Law, Mouzon. "A Directory of American Colleges and Universities Offering Curricular Programs in Children's Theatre," *Educational Theatre Journal,* VI (March, 1954), 40-46.

Lewis, George L. "Children's Theatre and Creative Dramatics: A Bibliography," *Educational Theatre Journal,* VIII (May, 1955), 338-45.

Melnitz, William W. (ed.). *Theatre Arts Publications in the United States,* 1947-52. American Educational Theatre Monograph No. 1, 1959.

"Operating Code of the Children's Theatre Conference," *Educational Theatre Journal,* IX (December, 1958), 351.

Possemiers, Jean (ed.). *International Bibliography, Theatre and Youth.* Paris: UNESCO, International Theatre Institute, n.d., I.

Rowland, Robert L. *Statistics on Public Institutions for Delinquent Children.* (U.S. Children's Bureau Statistical Series, No. 48, Washington, D.C.: U.S. Dept. of Health, Education, and Welfare, 1954).

Seattle Creative Activities Center. Mimeographed Report, Seattle, Washington, May, 1959).

Siks, Geraldine Brain. "Theatre for Youth: An International Report," *Educational Theatre Journal,* VII (December, 1955), 306-14.

Stevenson, Burton (ed.). *The Home Book of Quotations,* 8th ed. New York: Dodd, Mead and Company, 1956.

Tenth Anniversary Brochure. Kansas City, Missouri: Community Children's Theatre, 1957.

Viola, A. "Drama with and for Children: An Interpretation of Terms," *Educational Theatre Journal,* VIII (May, 1956), 139-42.

Yearbook of International Organizations. 7th ed. Brussels, Belgium: Union of International Associations, 1958.

Index

Acting: in children's theatre, 48, 93-95; as based on playscript, 94; and sincerity of approach, 94; approval of presentational style in, 95; creative dramatics approach to, 186-87

Action: must dominate dialogue, 41; and "exercise spots," 43

Actors: professionals in children's theatre as, 40; attitude toward children, 43, 94; children as, 45, 49; casting of, 88; adults as, 93; responsibilities of, 93, 95; empathy, 186

Adventure: importance of, 87, 100

Aesthetics: values in children's theatre, 27; appreciation of, 30; need for, 43; in television, 70; in puppetry, 81; and responsibility of actor, 94

Age of children: participation in children's drama governed by, 10, 49; and selection of plays, 41; as factor in audience response, 87

American Association of University Women: 11; and Children's Film Library Committee, 72; as sponsor of children's theatre, 83

American Childhood Education Association International; 11

American Educational Theatre Association: children's drama study conducted by, 5; CTC as division of, 15

American National Theatre and Academy, 11, 24

Anderson, Maxwell, 6, 31, 101

Arts: disciplines of, 4; need for in children's theatre, 41, 95; in communication, 70; in puppetry, 81; community participation in, 181; workshops for, 182; in recreation, 192, 194, 196; in creative arts programs, 195

Association of Junior Leagues of America: 11; and CTC, 15; and dramatic activities, 23; community service by, 34-35; and volunteer service in children's theatre, 35-37; as source for scripts 42; in radio, 57, 61; in puppetry, 77; as sponsors of children's theatre, 83; Junior League of Seattle's participation in creative dramatics program, 177

Attention of children: held by rhythm pattern, 89

Audience: entertainment of, 41; problem of mixed ages, 41; comfort of, 42, 43, 85; impression on, 46; management of, 85; as factor in determining style of play, 90; response of, 95

Authors: need for, 43; practices of, 101; need of firmer standards, 103

Awards: Zeta Phi Eta-Winifred Ward, 19, 52; Monte Meacham, 19; George Foster Peabody Citation, 61, 62, 65; at the Institute for Education by Radio, 61

Baker, Harry J., director of the Psychological Clinic, Detroit schools, 153

Ballet: *See* Edwin Strawbridge
Barrie, James, 98, 101. *See also*
    Classics for children
Behavior patterns: theatre as a
    means of teaching, 29; and
    Yasha Frank, 29
Burger, Isabel B., 125, 165, 185-
    91, 193
Business management, 84

Camp Fire Girls: trained as rec-
    reation leaders, 180
Casting of play: empathic quality
    stressed, 88; and creative dra-
    matics, 185-88
Characters, evil: costuming for,
    93; as repudiation of evil, 130
Child audience: reaction of, 7;
    training of, 30; appeal to, 40;
    development of critical faculty
    in, 67-68; transportation prob-
    lems of, 85, 86; need for action
    of, 88; as most rewarding au-
    dience, 97; building appreciation
    for theatre art in, 190-91
Child psychology: need for under-
    standing of, 43; and children's
    drama specialists, 191
Children: population of in U.S.,
    4; natures of, 5; participation in
    children's theatre, 50; inability
    to abstract, 95; creative dra-
    matics for mentally retarded,
    155; "buddy" system for, 156;
    institutional, 169-75; delinquent,
    170
Children's drama: international
    report on, 4; educational en-
    deavor in, 4; philosophy of, 5;
    defined, 8; programs in colleges
    and universities for, 199-200
Children's Educational Theatre:
    founding of, 21, 25
Children's needs: for aesthetic
    satisfaction, 27, 30; for psycho-
    logical satisfaction, 28, 41; for
    humor, 41; for critical viewing
    and listening, 67-68; for commu-
    nication, 70

Children's theatre: need for col-
    lege training programs, 5; de-
    fined, 8; correlated with creative
    dramatics, 10; historical devel-
    opment of, 22-26; Chicago Civic
    Theatre, 22; Goodman Theatre
    of Chicago, 23; trends in, 25;
    values of, 27; at Northwestern
    University, 33; adult productions
    for, 33-44; and community thea-
    tres, 37, 50-51; play selection
    for, 41-42, 86-88; challenge of,
    45-46; evaluation of, 85; direct-
    ing for, 88-90; production of, 90-
    92; costuming for, 92-93; acting
    in, 93-95; publicizing of, 95-97;
    directing of, 104-12; need for
    standards in, 110; as adjunct to
    creative dramatics, 185-91; of
    Evanston, Ill., 185; National
    Recreation Association survey of,
    193
Children's Theatre Conference:
    interpretation of terms by, 8-11,
    17, 53; defined, 13; membership
    of, 13; development of, 14-20;
    annual conference of, 15; news-
    letters of, 16, 17, 20; regional
    organization of, 16; theatre pro-
    jects of, 16; college curriculum
    survey by, 18, 198; founded, 24;
    summer theatre and workshops
    of, 24; magazines sponsored by,
    25; popular plays listed by, 41;
    "New Scripts Room" of, 42; and
    puppetry, 80; and manuscripts,
    87, 102; and creative dramatics,
    151; and correctional institutions,
    170; list of credit or noncredit
    workshops available from, 180;
    need for closer liaison with rec-
    reational programs, 196
Children's Theatre Foundation, 19
Children's Theatre Press, 24, 42
Coach House Press, 17, 42
Classics for children: *Blue Bird,*
    26, 42, 43, 66; *Peter Pan,* 26;
    Snow White, 26; *Treasure Island,*
    26; *Cinderella,* 66; *Sara Crewe,*

66; *Johnny Tremaine,* 66, 67;
Little Women, 67, 72; *David
Copperfield,* 72; *Heidi,* 72; *Alice
in Wonderland,* 76. *See also*
Films, Television
Classroom teacher: as director,
45, 47; importance of training,
48, 50, 52; and children's drama,
52; radio and television evaluated by, 67-68; creative dramatics used by, 133, 137
Cleveland Playhouse, 77
Clubs: Council of Jewish Women,
34; Young Hebrew Association,
40; Boy Scouts, 51; Girl Scouts,
51, 61; YMCA, 51; YWCA, 51;
Child Study Association and
Josette Frank, 67; PTA as sponsor of children's theatre, 83;
Rotary Club as sponsor of children's theatre, 83
College curriculum survey, 198
Color: in designing production, 91;
in lighting, 91, 92; in costumes,
91, 92, 93; nonconventional harmony in, 93
Communication: as aesthetic ex-
perience, 27; as art in televi-
sion, 70; in education, 120; de-
veloping skill in, 130
Committees: international, for-
mation of, 17; CTC College Cur-
riculum Survey, 18; selected bib-
liography of plays, 18; Radio
Council on Children's Programs,
57; Federal Radio Education
Committee of the U.S. Dept. of
Education, 57; Foundation for
Character Education, 64; Child
Study Association, 67; Children's
Film Library Committee, 72;
Catholic Legion of Decency, 73;
Jewish Education Committee, 163
Community and civic groups:
Youngstown, Ohio, Civic Chil-
dren's Theatre, 52; Nashville,
Tenn., Children's Theatre, 52;
Detroit Institute of Arts, 81;
groups sponsoring children's

theatre, 83; exploration of resources for productions, 86; Mott
Foundation program in Flint,
Mich., 138; in creative dramatics, 176-84
Community service groups, 34;
Junior Entertainment, Inc., of
Denver, 36; educational institutions, 37; training of leaders, 180
Conferences: congress of parents
and teachers, 20; summer theatre and workshops, 24. *See* Children's Theatre Conference
Costuming, 16; and James Crider,
92; visual aspects of, 92; respect
for playwright's integrity in, 92;
nonconventional color harmony
in, 93; of evil characters, 93;
standard construction in, 93
Creative dramatics: defined, 8,
124, 129, 200; in dramatic play,
9; uses in formal play, 10; history of, 115-23; college development in, 122, 123; values of, 124-
31; therapeutic treatment by
means of, 128, 171-74; drama
appreciation developed by, 131;
in schools, 133-51; specialists
in, 137-39; techniques of, 145,
146; basic principles of, 149, 150;
for exceptional children, 152-58;
in speech clinic, 155; in religious
education, 159-67; in correctional institutions, 171-75; and
Dr. Harlan McNutt, 172; in community programs, 176-84; in
children's theatre, 185-91; in
tryouts, 187-88; in recreation,
192-97; leader in, 199-202; philosophy of, 201, 202
Creative plays, 9
Creativity: in personality, 3;
stimulation of, 3, 4, 134; in expression, 4; nurtured by drama,
6; developed by plays, 9; first
evidence in classrooms, 116;
development of, 124-28; opportunity for created by playmaking,
125; fluency of ideas stressed by,

126; stimulates awareness, 126; and flexibility of thought, 127, 134; need for, 182

Criste, Rita, 186, 187, 199. *See* Appendix

Dance: in creative play, 9; in creative arts program, 195

Democracy: fostered by participation in arts, 181

Designing: for children's theatre, 90-93; visual elements of, 90; style of, 90

Dewey, John, 118, 119, 123

Dialogue: creation of, 10; improvised by children, 10

Director: teacher in school as, 38; responsibility in casting, 88; training and childhood environment of, 104; basic requirements for, 105, 106; psychology important for, 107; general education imperative for, 107, 108; major weaknesses of, 108; courses on stage direction valuable to, 109-11

Discipline: as requirement of creative arts, 8; problems in, 180

Drama League of America, 22

Dramatic instinct, 5; value in childhood education, 117, 132

Dramatic play: for young children, 9; for older children, 9; in kindergarten, 134

Education in creative dramatics: to develop sense awareness, 134; for appreciation of literature, 135, 141; for interest in social studies, 135; for oral communication, 135

Educators: question use of drama, 4; membership in CTC, 13; participate in radio and television, 69; sponsor children's theatre, 83; contribute to creative dramatics development, 115; mentioned and described, 115-23; Winifred Ward's belief in crea-

tive dramatics in education expressed, 132

Educational Theatre Journal, 25

Ego: as satisfied by entertainment, 28; of institutional children, as strengthened by creative dramatics, 194

Eisenhower, Dwight E.: report of his commission on national goals, 7

Elementary school: practices in children's theatre, 46, 49, 50

Emotional stability: development of, 128

Empathy: in children's drama, 7; as criterion for entertainment, 41; paramount in casting for children's theatre, 88; building and control of, 94; in children's theatre, 186

Entertainment: in drama, 6; defined, 27, 28; as criterion for children's plays, 41; importance in children's theatre of, 100. *See also* Communication

Exceptional children: definition of, 152; creed for given by Dr. Leonard Mayo, 152; creative dramatics programs for, 154-58

Fantasy: as entertainment for children, 41. *See also* Classics

Federal Theatre: *See* American National Theatre and Academy

Festivals: summer play festival, 51; International Doll and Puppet Festival, 80; evidence of National Recreation Association Survey, 193. *See* Puppetry

Films: Western films in television, 68; cartoon comedies, 68; Disney films, 68, 71; films and the classics, 71; and Hollywood, 71-74; Children's Film Library Committee and film selections, 72; UNESCO survey of films, 73; need for children's cinema, 74; as creative dramatics aid, 151

Formal drama: building appreci-

ation for, 10; improvisation of
scenes, 10
Gesell, Dr. Arnold, 175
Gifted children: in children's theatre plays, 49, 50; in creative
dramatics, 157; need for disciplined freedom, 157. *See* Exceptional children
Girl Scouts, 34, 57, 61, 180

Haaga, Agnes, 139, 171, 192, 193,
198-207
Handicaps, physical, and creative
dramatics, 156
Herts, Alice Minnie, and Children's Educational Theatre, 21-
22

Junior high schools, 46, 47, 49,
50, 51; use of creative dramatics,
137, 148
Junior Programs, Inc.: and Dorothy McFadden, 23; founding of,
23; in touring plays, 24, 38; as
service groups, 35; list of, 37;
in radio, 60; in films, 73; in
creative dramatics, 199

Kindergarten: dramatic play in,
133; creative rhythmic movement in, 133-35; free, imaginative play in, 140
"Kukla, Fran and Ollie," 79; Burr
Tillstrom, 79, 80

Leaders: training programs for,
194, 198, 207; aims and abilities
of, 201; deeper dimensions of,
206
Learning: by entertaining, 100; by
object lesson, 116; by graphic
means, 117; by dramatics, 117-
19
Libraries: children's films in, 72;
and children's theatre publicity, 96; use of stimulated by
creative dramatics, 178-79
Lighting, 91, 92
Literature: relation to illusion,

94; taught through drama, 117;
dramatization of, 132

Magazines: *Players,* 23; *Recrea-
tion,* 23 *Educational Theatre
Journal,* 25 *Children's Theatre
Newsletter,* 25
Major, Clare Tree: founding of
theatre by, 23; repertories organized by, 40; plays written by, 40
Meacham, Monte: award named
for, 19; as founder of Children's
World Theatre, 26
Music: for creative play, 9; Rïse
Stevens, 55; Rogers and Hammerstein's *Cinderella,* 66;
C. B. S., 66; Music Clubs' part
in film programs, 72; Detroit
Symphony Orchestra, 81; Debussy's *La Boîte à Joujoux,*
81; inclusion in creative arts
recreational program of, 195

National Congress of Parents and
Teachers: 11; 12; participation
in children's film library committee, 72; as sponsors of children's theatre, 83; as speakers
for publicity, 96
National Recreation Association:
drama committee organized by,
192; workshop in creative dramatics of, 193, 196; liaison with
CTC, 193; emphasis on creative
arts, 194; appraisal of cultural
trend, 194
Newsletter of CTC: approvement
of, 15; development of, 17; mentioned, 20, 25

Palo Alto Children's Theatre, 50,
60, 63, 129
Pantomime in creative dramatics,
142, 194
Parents: in evaluating television
programs, 67, 68; publicity appeals to, 96; programs for, 179
Parker, Col. Francis, 116, 117,
118, 123

Pestalozzi, John Henry: 116, 117, 118, 123

Philosophy: of children's drama, defined, 5-7; of living, helped by creative dramatics, 130. *See also* Siks, 3-7

Plays: action in, 41; entertainment in, 41; realistic, 41; selection of, 41, 84, 86, 88; classical, 41, 87; fantasy in, 41, 87; historical, 41, 87; demand for, 43, 98; Madam de Genlis, 45; unworthy scripts, 48, 52; romantic, 87

Playwrights: total works of art provided by, 87; need for in children's theatre, 88, 98; Thornton Wilder, 98; James Thurber, 98; Charlotte Chorpenning, 99; attitude toward child audiences, 99

Playwriting: in U.S., 98

Playwriting contests: as stimulation for scripts, 42, 53, 87

Play producers: adults as, 33; general principles and methods of, 34, 41; in service groups, 35; school productions by, 38, 39; in educational institutions, 39; in high school trouping systems, 39; in professional-commercial groups, 40; in private studios, 40; in touring groups, 40; criterions listed by, 41; rewards of, 82; and business management, 84, 85

Platoon schools: and William Wirt, 138

Practice teaching, 203, 204

Presses: as publishers of children's plays, 17, 42

Producing children's theatre: organization and management of, 82-86; sponsoring organizations, 83-85; directing, 88-89; designing and technical considerations of, 90-93; styles of, 91; acting in, 93-95; limitations of, 101

Productions: number of, 43; rhythmic pattern in, 89; standards necessary for, 90; visual elements of, 90

Psychologists: panel of CTC conducted by, 15; needs of children explained by, 28. *See* Harry J. Baker, 153

Public schools: speech departments in, 38; children's theatre in, 38, 45; and school theatre subsidy, 39; and children's theatre during school hours, 39; high school touring systems in, 39; and school theatre practices, 46; inadequacies of children's theatre in, 47; casting children in plays in, 49; evidence of creativity in, 116; creative dramatics in Evanston, Ill., Winnetka, Ill., Gary, Ind., Akron, Ohio, 137-38

Publications: CTC Newsletter, 15; *Players Magazine*, 23, 38; *Recreation*, 23; *Educational Theatre Journal*, 25; *Dramatics, A Manual of Elementary Instruction*, 116; *Playmaking and Plays*, 118; *Progressive Education*, 119; *Creative Dramatics*, 121; *Playmaking with Children*, 122; *Creative Play Acting*, 165; *Children's Religion*, 166; need for creative dramatics handbook in recreation, 196

Publicity: distinguishing factors in, 95, 96; and sensibilities of community, 96; timing of, 96; and cooperation of community groups, 96; and public schools, 96

Puppetry: "Kukla, Fran and Ollie," 65; origins of, 75; Gordon Craig, 75; Tony Sarg, 76; Igor Stravinsky, 76; and *Oedipus*, 76; William Patten, 76; Ellen Van Volkenburg, 76; Helen Haiman Joseph, 77; Walter Wilkinson, 77; Burr Tillstrom, 77; history of, 77; Marjorie Batchelder McPharlin, 80; need for scripts in, 80; mentioned, 17

Radio: NBC, 55; Women's National Radio Committee, 56; code and criteria of, 56, 57; Radio Council on Children's Programs, 57; Federal Radio Education Committee of U.S. Dept. of Education, 57; American Broadcasting Company, 58; Grace Johnson, 58; Institution for Education by Radio, 58; Herta Herzog, 58; and National Council of Churches of Christ, 60, 61; and public schools, 67, 68

Recreation: athletic coaches as directors of, 48; summer theatre programs in, 51, 57; Trailer Theatre in, 51; need for trained leaders of creative drama in, 53, 194, 196; development of, 192-97; creative and fine arts in, 194, 195

Religious drama: joint religious radio committee of the National Council of Churches of Christ, 61; and Bible stories, 65; explanations of terms, 159-60; early use of creative dramatics by Hulda Niebuhr, 160; taught through creative dramatics, 161, 162; and puppet shows, 162; and Mutual Improvement Association Roadshow, 163; and Jewish Education Committee of New York, 163; and McCormick Theological Seminary, 165; and Union Theological Seminary, 165; and University of Kansas City, 165; and Northwest Christian College, 165; and Boston University School of Theology, 165

Rhythmic movement: director's problems with, 88, 89; used in kindergarten and primary grades, 134; included in creative arts recreational programs, 195

Rhythm pattern, 89

Royalties, 42

Samuel French, Inc.: as source for children's plays, 17, 42

Sawyer, Ruth, 125

Schools of acting: as reported by Drama League, 22, 23; King-Coit School, 23

School administrator, active help needed for producing, 85

Seattle, Washington, 37, 51, 61, 73, 177, 178

Seattle Creative Activities Center, 181

Settlements, social: interest in children's dramatics, 22; listed, 22

Shank, Helen C.: leadership in child welfare and social fields, 169, 170, 171; and Maple Lane School, 169-71

Sheldon, Edward, 116, 117, 123. See also John Henry Pestalozzi

Siks, Geraldine B., 3-7, 125, 126, 127, 128, 130, 139, 185, 190

Social studies: research in, 9; use of in creative dramatics, 145-47

Social workers: use of creative dramatics as relief of tension, 173. See also Helen C. Shank

Speech: and children's theatre, 38; and importance to creative dramatics development, 117-20; used in therapy, 155

Spencer, Sara, 24, 98-103. See also Children's Theatre Press

Story dramatization, 9

Story materials: primary children's use of, 135; integrated with African study, 147; in junior high school, 148-49; requirements for creative dramatics, 149

Storytelling: in recreation programs, 193; in creative dramatics leader training, 204

Strawbridge, Edwin, 40

Studebaker, John, 57, 58. See Radio

Styles: of children's theatre production, 91; and representational

vs. naturalistic approach, 94;
presentational, approved in a
acting, 95
Symbols: their significance for institutional child, 173

Teachers: training in children's
drama, 5, 52
Teamwork: in playmaking, 10;
preferable to favoritism, 111
Technicians need for, 43
Television: "Kukla, Fran and
Ollie," 63; and "Ding Dong
School," 64; Ruth Prins, 64;
"Wunda Wunda," 64; "Mr. I.
Magination," 65; "Captain
Kangaroo," 65; Children's Thea-
tre Series, 66; "Omnibus," 66;
Shirley Temple Series, 67; and
public schools, 68; scripts
needed by, 68; educational
trends in, 69; and chamber theatre, 69; and video tape, 70; for
children's theatre publicity, 96.
See also Radio
Theatre board (community children's): needed in expanding program, 84
Touring: increase in, 25; of educational groups, 39; annual
scheduling of, 40; of Children's
World Theatre, 40; of Grace
Price Productions, 40; of Merry
Wanderers Theatre, 40; of National Children's Theatre, 40;
of Rockefeller Productions, 40;
of puppet theatres, 78
Tryouts: mood set by music in,
10; creative dramatics as preparation for, 185; music as motivation for, 188; as motivation
for characters, 188
Twain, Mark, 29, 98

UNESCO: defined, 12; theatre resource specialists for, 122, 200;
survey of children's films by,
173

Universities and colleges: training
programs in children's drama,
5, 52, 191; recreational training in, 196; Northwestern University, CTC organizational
meeting, 14; program of dramatic activities, 23; University
of Tulsa, 23; Emerson College,
23; University of Denver, 36;
University of Utah, 36; University of Washington, 36, 60, 80,
179, 199, 203-4; University of
Los Angeles, 37, 80; series of
children's plays in, 42; puppetry
training in, 80; influence on
creative dramatics trend, 139;
National College of Education,
140; Rockford College, 146;
Adelphi College, 181

Viola, Ann and Albert: use of creative dramatics in children's
worship by, 161
Voelcker, Francis W., and religious drama, 160

Ward, Winifred, 14, 19, 26, 52,
121; work at Northwestern University by, 107; *Playmaking with
Children*, 122; as theatre resource specialist, 122; contributions in the Evanston schools of,
123, 125, 128, 130, 132-51, 165,
176; as director of "The Children's Theatre of Evanston,"
185, 186, 187, 190, 193, 199; as
theatre resource person for
UNESCO, 200
Wert, William, 116, 118, 119;
educational methods of, 120
Workshops, annual; as part of
CTC, 16; and University of Minnesota, 16; as partial solutions
to problem of untrained leaders,
136; in national recreation congresses, 193; needed in creative
dramatics in recreation programs, 196

Young Men's Christian Association, 12, 51

Young Men's Hebrew Association, 12; and Rockefeller Productions, 40

Young Women's Christian Association, 12, 51

Contributors

RICHARD G. ADAMS *is former Assistant Professor of Theatre, University of California, Los Angeles, California.*

ISABEL B. BURGER *is founder and Administrative Coordinator of Children's Theatre Association, Inc., Baltimore, Maryland.*

GLORIA CHANDLER *is Director of Public Service and Education, King Broadcasting Company, Seattle, Washington, and Producer of* "Books Bring Adventure," "Televenture Tales," *and* "Wunda Wunda."

RITA CRISTE *is Assistant Professor, School of Speech, Northwestern University, and Director of the Children's Theatre of Evanston, Illinois.*

JED H. DAVIS *is Assistant Professor of Speech, Michigan State University, East Lansing, Michigan.*

MRS. ROBERT C. FINLEY *is Editor, Children's Theatre Conference Newsletter.*

BURDETTE FITZGERALD *is Associate Professor and* ERNEST ROSE *is Assistant Professor in Theatre Arts at the University of California at Los Angeles.*

EMILY GILLIES *is Consultant in Creative Dramatics, National Council of the Protestant Episcopal Church.*

KENNETH L. GRAHAM *is Professor of Speech and Theatre Arts, University of Minnesota.*

AGNES HAAGA *is Associate Professor of Drama and Director of Creative Dramatics, University of Washington.*

DOROTHY KESTER *is Coordinator of Speech Education, Public Schools, Akron, Ohio.*

PAUL KOZELKA *is Professor of Speech and Theatre, Teachers' College, Columbia University, New York City.*

GEORGE LATSHAW *is Director-Producer of George Latshaw Puppets, Cleveland, Ohio.*

NELLIE McCASLIN *is Director of Dramatic Arts, Mills College of Education, New York City.*

BARBARA M. McINTYRE *is Assistant Professor of Speech, University of Pittsburgh, and chairman of Recreation Committee, National Association for Retarded Children.*

ALBERT O. MITCHELL *is Professor of Speech and Dramatic Arts and Director of Youtheatre, Brigham Young University.*

VIRGINIA MUSSELMAN *is Program Service Director, National Recreation Association.*

JAMES E. POPOVICH *is Associate Professor of Speech, University of Georgia.*

DOROTHY THAMES SCHWARTZ *is Child Drama Consultant, Loveman's, Birmingham, Alabama; she conducts workshops and seminars throughout the state of Alabama, under the auspices of Loveman's.*

SARA SPENCER *is Editor of The Children's Theatre Press, Anchorage, Kentucky.*

ANN VIOLA *is Lecturer in Creative Dramatics, University of Kansas City, Kansas City, Missouri.*

WINIFRED WARD *is former Supervisor of Dramatics in the Elementary schools of Evanston, Illinois, and Assistant Professor, School of Speech, Northwestern University.*

FRANK M. WHITING *is Professor of Speech and Theatre Arts and Director of the University Theatre, University of Minnesota.*

MARGARET S. WOODS *is Lecturer in Education, Seattle Pacific College, Seattle, Washington.*

ELEANOR CHASE YORK *is Instructor in Field Services at Western Michigan University, Kalamazoo, Michigan.*